Troubleshooting

The WordPerfect 6 for Windows Interface

WordPerfect has several ways of presenting information on the screen. You can specify one as your default, or you can change the editing screen dynamically as you need.

For general editing and data entry, the best choice for most users is Draft mode with the button bar, power bar, status bar, and scroll bars enabled. This is the default configuration, as shown in Figure 1.

You can add or subtract these on-screen features with the View menu from the main menu bar. Use **View** **P**age, for example, to enable Page view, which shows you a near WYSIWYG (What-You-See-Is-What-You-Get) display. The check mark beside the Draft menu choice should disappear and a check mark should appear beside the Page selection from the View menu.

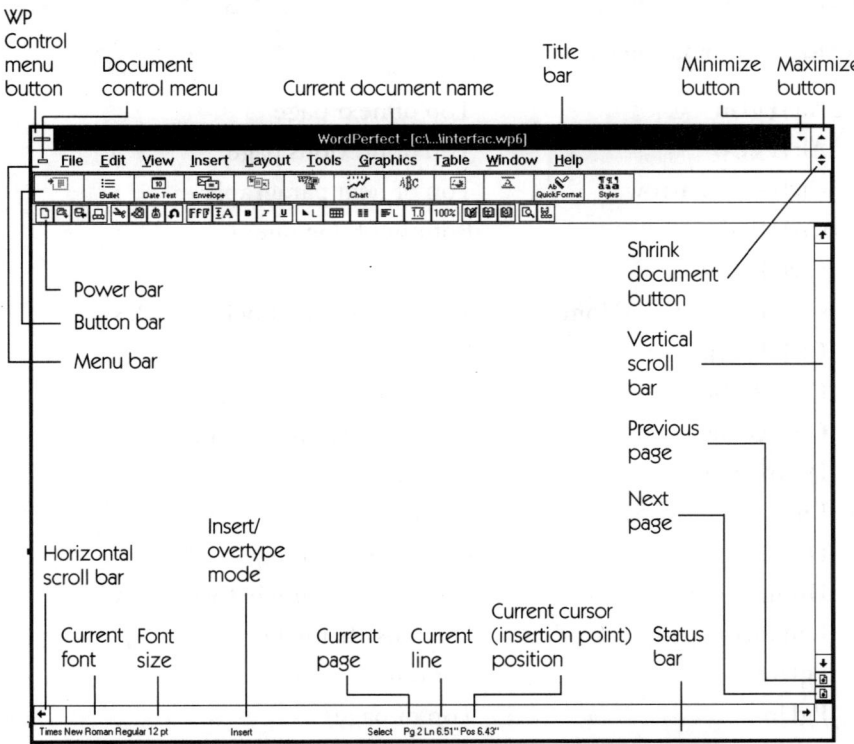

Figure 1 **Default WP6WIN screen with button bar, power bar, status bar and scroll bars enabled. Main screen components are labeled.**

TIP

You can also toggle between Draft and Page view from the keyboard. Use **Ctrl+F5** to choose Draft view. Use **Alt+F5** to choose Page view. Use **Alt+Shift+F5** to hide all bars.

The two-page view, also selectable from this menu, gives you two document pages, side by side. This view is helpful when you want to see the transitions between pages or how facing pages will appear when printed. If you are using a high-resolution screen mode, you probably won't be able to enter and edit text in this mode.

If your tastes run more toward a clean, uncluttered screen, use **View Hide Bars**. This removes all of the on-screen bars, including the title bar, menu bar, and scroll bars. You can return to the configuration shown in Figure 1 by pressing **Escape** from the Hide Bars view.

Figures 2 and 3 show the WordPerfect 6 for Windows screens with the various buttons and sections labeled for your reference. Many people prefer using the keyboard instead of the mouse. See Tables 1–3 for keyboard shortcuts and hints.

Table 1	The Navigation Keys
Key Combination	**Effect**
Alt+PgDn	Top of next page
Alt+PgUp	Top of previous page
Ctrl+Down arrow	Top of next paragraph
Ctrl+End	Bottom of document
Ctrl+Home	Top of document
Ctrl+Home, Ctrl+Home	Top of document before codes
Ctrl+Left arrow	Previous word
Ctrl+Right arrow	Next word
Ctrl+Up arrow	Top of previous paragraph
Down arrow	Next line
End	End of line
Home	Beginning of line
Home Home	Beginning of line before codes
Left arrow	Previous character
PgDn	Bottom of page
PgUp	Top of page
Right arrow	Next character
Up arrow	Previous line

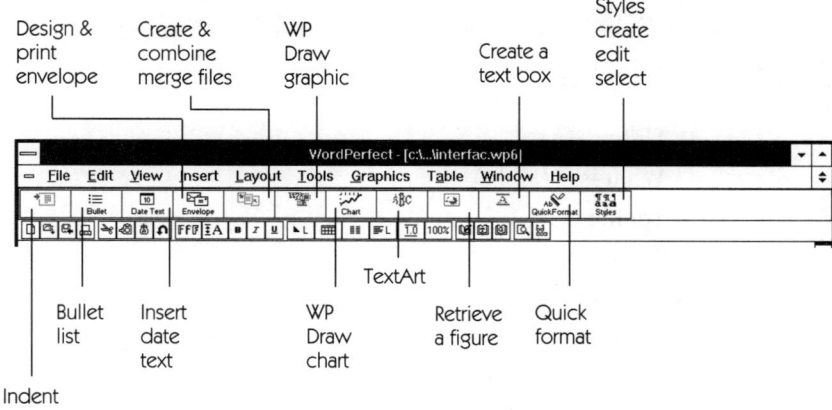

Figure 2   WP6WIN Screen with button bar labeled.

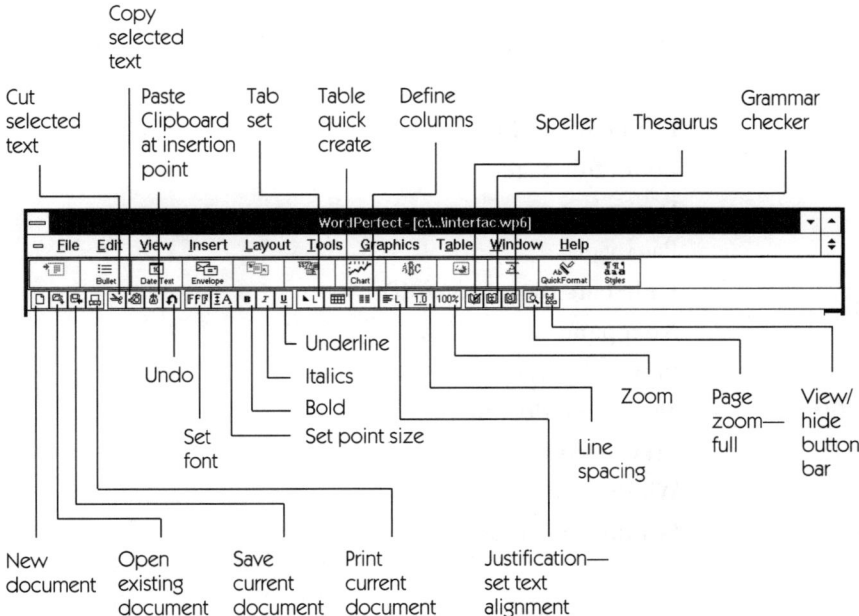

Figure 3   WP6WIN Screen with power bar labeled.

Table 2   The Function Keys

Key	Function
F1	Help
Shift+F1	What is... (Help)
Ctrl+F1	Speller
Alt+F1	Thesaurus
Alt+Shift+F1	Grammatik
F2	Find text
Shift+F2	Find next text (down)
Ctrl+F2	Find and replace text
Alt+F2	Find next text (up)
F3	Save As...
Shift+F3	Save
Ctrl+F3	Redisplay
Ctrl+Shift+F3	Show paragraph marks/spaces
Alt+F3	Reveal codes (toggle off/on)
Alt+Shift+F3	Toggle ruler bar on/off
F4	Open...
Shift+F4	New document
Ctrl+F4	Close current file
Alt+F4	Exit WordPerfect
F5	Print current file
Shift+F5	Zoom full page
Ctrl+F5	Draft view
Alt+F5	Page view
Alt+Shift+F5	Hide bars (toggle on/off)
F6	Next pane
Shift+F6	Previous pane
Ctrl+F6	Next open document
Ctrl+Shift+F6	Previous open document
Alt+F6	Window next
Alt+Shift+F6	Window previous

Table 2   (continued)

Key	Function
F7	Paragraph indent
Shift+F7	Center line
Ctrl+F7	Paragraph hanging indent
Ctrl+Shift+F7	Paragraph double indent
Alt+F7	Line flush right
Alt+Shift+F7	Tab decimal
F8	Select
Shift+F8	Select cell
Ctrl+F8	Margins
Alt+F8	Styles
F9	Font
Shift+F9	Merge
Ctrl+F9	Generate list
Alt+F9	Sort
Shift+F10	Repeat...
Ctrl+F10	Record macro
Alt+F10	Play macro
Alt+Shift+F10	Feature bar
F11	Figure
Shift+F11	Edit box
Ctrl+F11	Horizontal line
Ctrl+Shift+F11	Vertical line
Alt+F11	Text box
F12	Table create
Shift+F12	Table lines/fill
Ctrl+F12	Table format
Alt+F12	Table number type
Alt+Shift+F12	Calculate document

Table 3	Command Shortcut Keys
Key	Function
Ctrl+=	Table sum
Ctrl+,	Decrease column width (table)
Ctrl+Shift+,	Decrease column width (table)
Ctrl+.	Increase column width (table)
Ctrl+Shift+.	Increase column width (table)
Ctrl+/	Ignore hyphenation
Ctrl+-	Hyphen character
Crtl+Shift+-	Soft hyphen
Ctrl+A	Abbreviations expand
Ctrl+B	Bold
Ctrl+Shift+B	Bullet insert
Ctrl+C	Copy
Ctrl+D	Date text
Ctrl+Shift+D	Date code
Ctrl+E	Center justification
Ctrl+Enter	Force page break
Ctrl+F	Font
Ctrl+G	Goto page
Ctrl+H	Outline body text
Ctrl+I	Italics
Ctrl+J	Full justification
Ctrl+K	Case toggle
Ctrl+L	Left justification
Ctrl+N	New document
Ctrl+O	Open existing document
Ctrl+Shift+O	Outline define
Ctrl+P	Quick print
Ctrl+Shift+P	Formatted page number
Ctrl+Q	Goto bookmark (Quickmark)
Ctrl+Shift+Q	Quickmark set

Table 3	(continued)
Key	**Function**
Ctrl+R	Right justification
Ctrl+S	Save current file
Ctrl+Shift+S	Save all open files
Ctrl+T	Template open (use)
Ctrl+U	Underline
Ctrl+V	Paste
Ctrl+W	WordPerfect characters
Ctrl+X	Cut
Ctrl+Z	Undo
Ctrl+Shift+Z	Undelete

WORDPERFECT® 6 FOR WINDOWS™ SOLUTIONS

Tom Badgett
Corey Sandler

John Wiley & Sons, Inc.

New York • Chichester • Brisbane • Toronto • Singapore

Publisher: Katherine Schowalter
Editor: Tim Ryan
Associate Managing Editor: Jacqueline A. Martin
Editorial Production: Impressions

WordPerfect is a registered trademark of WordPerfect Corporation. Windows is a trademark of Microsoft Corp. Designations used by companies to distinguish their products are often claimed as trademarks. In all instances where John Wiley & Sons, Inc. is aware of a claim, the product names appear in initial capital or all capital letters. Readers, however, should contact the appropriate companies for more complete information regarding trademarks and registration.

This text is printed on acid-free paper.

Library of Congress Cataloging-in-Publication Data:
Badgett, Tom.
    WordPerfect 6 for Windows solutions / by Tom Badgett and Corey Sandler.
       p.   cm.
    Includes index.
    ISBN 0-471-30329-1 (paper)
    1. WordPerfect for Windows (Computer file)   2. Word processing.
I. Sandler, Corey, 1950- . II. Title.
Z52.5.W655B53   1994
652.5'536—dc20   93-48317
                                          CIP

Printed in the United States of America
10 9 8 7 6 5 4 3 2 1

In recognition of the unprocessed words in all of us.

Introduction

This Solutions book is a complete reference to WordPerfect 6 for Windows and is written so that you can find quick, complete answers to your questions and problems. Start by looking up your question in the Troubleshooting Guide at the front of the book. The shortcut keys listed next to your question are there in case you only need a quick reminder. If you have a more complicated problem or are trying something for the first time, turn to the page listed in the Troubleshooting Guide for a detailed solution.

On each page you'll find a "task" devoted to answering your specific question, so you won't have to read a lot of extra text that doesn't apply. The Solutions Series is designed to answer your questions quickly so you can get on with your work. Each task has a brief introduction, a list of Assumptions and Exceptions that tells you how to set up your computer and software to make sure you will complete the task successfully, and clear, concise steps that get right to the point. In case there is a glitch, the What To Do If section tells you how to fix it.

The Solutions Series doesn't just tell you the mechanics of using WordPerfect 6 for Windows; it also gives you tips on savvy things to do with the software, such as how to locate your data quickly, how to produce reports with a minimum of fuss, and how to customize WordPerfect 6 for Windows so it works the way you want it to.

WordPerfect 6 for Windows Solutions is full of the answers you need to keep your business going.

Conventions

The Solutions series uses these conventions to make instructions clear:

Keys that you should press are written in bold. "Press **3**" means press the **3** key on the keyboard.

Key combinations are written with a "+" sign. "Press **Ctrl+S**" means press and hold the **Ctrl** key, then press the **s** key. Notice that we show the alphabetic key that is part of this sequence as a captial letter, but you don't need to press the Shift key as part of this procedure.

WordPerfect menu choices are written with certain letters in boldface, indicating that you can use the Alt key in combination with the bolded character to choose the specified menu instead of selecting it with the mouse. For example, if we say, "Open the **F**ile menu," this indicates you can click on **F**ile on the menu bar, or you can press **Alt** to activate the menu bar, then press **F** to select **F**ile.

We use the same technique for submenu choices, and these may not be the first letter in the word. If we tell you "Use **E**dit Select," for example, that means you can use the mouse to choose Sel**e**ct from the **E**dit menu, or you can press **Alt**, then **E** and **E** again to do the same thing.

Contents

Chapter
1

Using Editing Commands

BASIC
DOCUMENT
SKILLS

Creating a Document

When you first start WordPerfect, a blank document is loaded and you are ready to start typing. The document is configured according to whatever defaults (preferences) you have established for new documents. After you have typed one document, or loaded one or more documents for editing, however, you must create a new document to start over with a new file.

Assumptions

- You want to start over with a fresh file, creating a new document instead of opening an existing document for editing.

Exceptions

- None.

Steps

- Use **File New.**
  OR
- Press **Ctrl+N.**
  OR
- Click on the new document icon on the power bar.

What To Do If

- If the new document formatting isn't what you expected, use the techniques described in Chapter 2 for formatting a document.

See Also

- Opening an Existing Document, p. 36.

Using Editing Commands

Typing Over Existing Text

2

By default in WordPerfect when you enter new text, any existing information is bumped ahead of the cursor so that new text is inserted behind existing text. You can change this default by turning on Typeover mode.

Assumptions

- WordPerfect is in the default Insert text mode.
- The insertion point is at the location on the screen where you want to enter new text.

Exceptions

- If *Typeover* appears on the status line, the program is already in Typeover mode and you don't need to change anything to type over existing text.

Steps

1. Press **Ins** to turn on Typeover mode (turn off Insert mode).
2. Type the new text you want to replace existing text.
3. Press **Ins** again to return to Insert mode.

What To Do If

- If you typed too far, erasing text you meant to keep, position the insertion point where you want the original text to appear, press **Ins** to turn on Insert mode, and type the original text.

> **TIP**
> The Ins (or Insert) key serves as a toggle, switching between Typeover and Insert modes. The word Insert on the status line indicates new text will bump existing text to the right; the word Typeover on the status line indicates that new text will replace existing information.

- If you change your mind about the text you just entered, simply press **Ctrl+Z** (or use **E**dit **U**ndo) to replace the original text. Do not turn off Typeover mode until after you have replaced the original text.

See Also

- Deleting Text, below.

Deleting Text

In addition to typing over existing text to delete it (see Typing Over Existing Text, p. 3), you can use a number of other Word-Perfect features to remove text.

Assumptions

- None.

Exceptions

- Remember that Del and Backspace are repeating keys. When you hold them down, they send repeated instructions to WordPerfect until you release the key.
- With most delete operations, the text you erase is not placed on the Clipboard. That means you can't copy it back from the Clipboard to place it somewhere else.

Steps

- Select the text you want to delete and press **Del.**

  OR

- Place the insertion point to the right of the last character you want to delete and press **Backspace** repeatedly until all of the text you want to remove is erased.

  OR

> **TIP**
> You can quickly delete a block of text—a sentence, a paragraph, or a page of information—with the **E**dit Select command. Place the insertion point within the text you want to delete. Choose the type of text you want to delete and press **Del** when WordPerfect selects the block.

- Place the insertion point to the left of the first character you want to delete and press **Del** repeatedly until all of the text you want to remove is erased.

What To Do If

- If you accidently remove too much text, press **Ctrl+Z** (Undo) to replace the text you just erased.
- If you want to restore previous deletions, press **Ctrl+Shift+Z** (Undelete), click on **Previous (Alt+P)** or **Next (Alt+N)** until the text you want to restore appears, then click on **Restore.**

See Also

- Block Operations, p. 64.

Using Undelete   4

No matter how careful you are, there will be times when you will delete text or other data you didn't intend to. WordPerfect provides the Undelete command to correct these mistakes.

Assumptions

- You have deleted text or other data by mistake. You may want to restore this information to a location different from where it originated.

Exceptions

- The Undelete buffer stores only the three most recent deletions. On the fourth deletion, the first information you deleted is lost.

Steps

1. Position the insertion point where you want the restored text to appear.

TIP

If you are restoring text that includes formatting codes, turn on Reveal Codes **(Alt+F3)** before using Undelete.

2. Use **E**dit U**n**delete (**Ctrl+Shift+Z**) to display the Undelete dialog.

3. Click on **N**ext or **P**revious until the text you want to restore is displayed.

4. Click on **R**estore to replace the text.

What To Do If

- If you restore the wrong data, press **Ctrl+Z** (**E**dit **U**ndo) to remove it, then use Undelete again to restore the proper information.

See Also

- Using Undo, below.
- Deleting Text, p. 4.

Deleting Text, p. 4.

5 Using Undo

In addition to Undelete, WordPerfect offers an Undo command. They work slightly differently, but both will help greatly in creating and editing your documents.

Assumptions

- You have deleted some information by mistake and you want to restore it to its original location.

Exceptions

- Undo remembers only the most recent operation. It can be a delete function or typing, but you can't use Undo to restore previous operations.

- Many operations can be reversed with Undo, but not everything. These can't be reversed: selecting a block of text, erasing a file, saving a file, printing, changing any setup options, the Goto feature, and switching between windows.

_____ **Steps**

- Press **Ctrl+Z** or use **E**dit **U**ndo to reverse the most recent change.

_____ **What To Do If**

- If you decide you don't want to reverse the last change, you can use Undo again (Undo Undo) to put things back the way they were.

_____ **See Also**

- Using Undelete, p. 5.
- Deleting Text, p. 4.

Storing a Document   6

When you first enter information into a new WordPerfect document, whatever you type is stored in temporary memory, electronic RAM that remembers only as long as the computer is turned on. One of the first things you want to do as you create a new document is to store your work to disk. Not only does this protect against a power outage or other RAM memory loss, but it also gives your new document a name so you can store new versions or additions easily, and you can recall the document at a later time to edit.

_____ **Assumptions**

- You have created a new document that has not yet been saved. Therefore, the document doesn't have a name.

Exceptions

- When you name a WordPerfect file, you are limited to an eight-character filename with no spaces. WordPerfect filenames carry the same restrictions as any DOS filename.

- WordPerfect automatically adds the three-digit file extension .WPD. You can override this default by simply including the extension letters you want to use as part of the filename when you create the file.

Steps

1. Use **F**ile Save **A**s... (**F3**) to display the Save As dialog, shown in Figure 1.1.

   Select a disk drive in the Drives: field of this dialog if you want to store the document on a drive other than the current one. You can click in this field and enter a drive specification from the keyboard, or you can click on the down arrow to the right of this field to step through the drives available on your system.

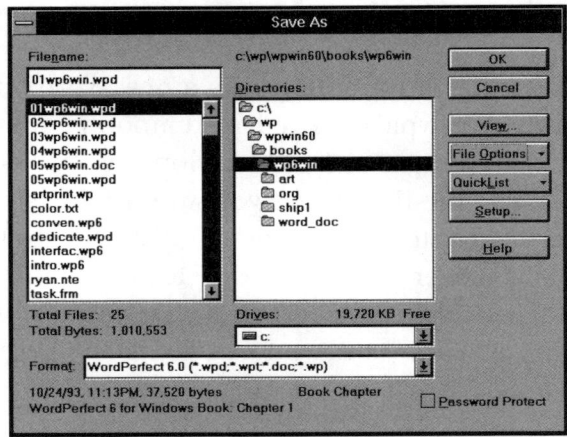

Figure 1.1   File Save As... dialog.

TIP

WordPerfect automatically saves files in WordPerfect 6 format. However, you can use the Save As... option to convert the WordPerfect file to another format. Simply click on the down arrow beside the Format: field to display available formats. Select one before you click on OK to save the file. WordPerfect will save the file in the specified format. It is a good idea to store non-WordPerfect files under separate filenames. That way you have a WordPerfect copy in reserve. And, by choosing filenames carefully, you can tell by looking at a file which format it is in.

2. Specify a directory to hold the file in the Directories: window if you want to store the file in a directory other than the current one. The current directory is listed at the top of this dialog, just under the title bar.

3. Enter a filename in the File**n**ame: field of this dialog. Use up to eight characters for the main name and up to three characters for the extension (after the period).

4. Click on **OK** to save the file and return to the editing window.

_____ **What To Do If**

If you get an error message when you click on OK, check to make sure you have not exceeded the eight-character filename limit. Also check disk space to make sure you have enough room to save the file.

_____ **See Also**

• Opening an Existing Document, p. 36.

> **TIP**
> If you work with a large number of documents it is a good idea to store some summary information with each file. Use **File Document Summary...** to display the Document Summary dialog before saving each document. The more information you enter here, the more options you have for directory displays and file searches (see Chapter 3).

Working with More Than One Document at a Time   **7**

In WordPerfect you can work with up to nine open documents at a time. This lets you switch among documents to get information, copy data from one document to another, or simply work on multiple jobs in parallel.

_____ **Assumptions**

• WordPerfect is running and one document file is open.

Exceptions

- None.

Steps

1. Use **File Open** (or **File New**) to open a second document.
   Repeat step one up to seven more times until as many as nine documents are open.

2. Use **Window Tile** or **Window Cascade** to display all open documents on the screen simultaneously. Figure 1.2 shows a sample screen with several documents in Tile format; Figure 1.3 shows the same documents in Cascade format.

3. Click anywhere in a document to make it current. Click on the Maximize button (at the upper right corner of the document screen) to enlarge the document, if you want it bigger. See Table 1.1 for shortcut keys used in switching among documents.

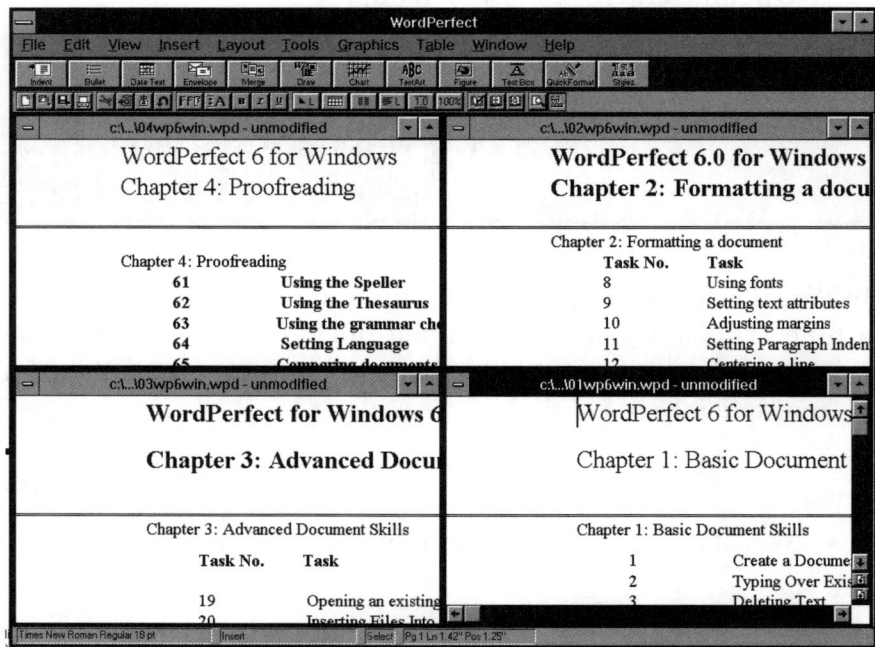

Figure 1.2   Multiple documents in Tile format.

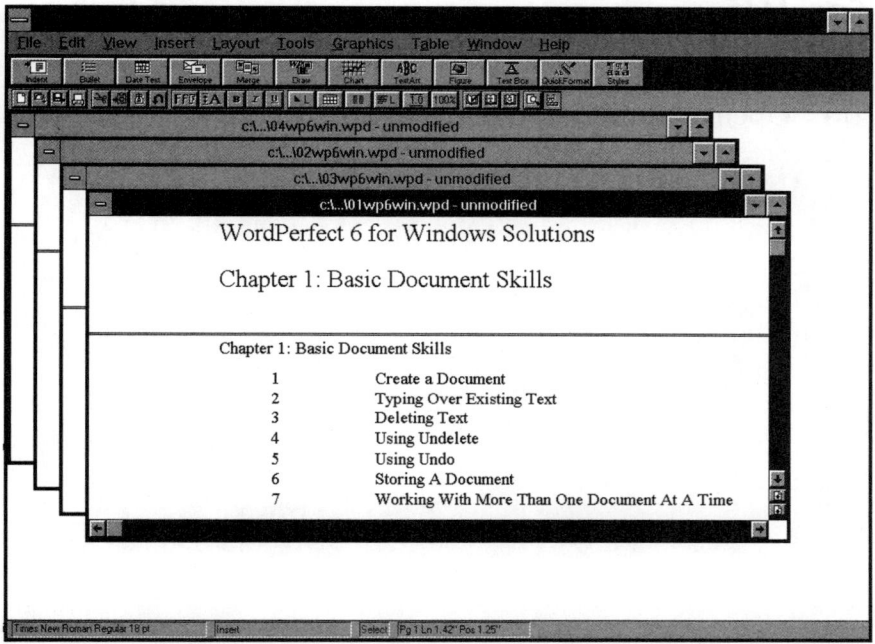

Figure 1.3   Multiple documents in Cascade format.

Table 1.1	Shortcut Keys for Switching Among Full-Screen Documents
Action	**Shortcut Key**
Previous document	Ctrl+Shift+F6
Next document	Ctrl+F6
Previous window	Alt+Shift+F6
Next window	Alt+F6
Previous pane	Shift+F6
Next pane	F6

What To Do If

- If the File Open and File New options are grayed out so you can't access them, it means you already have nine documents open at once. To open another document you must first close one of the open documents to make room for it.

See Also

- Creating a Document, p. 2.
- Opening an Existing Document, p. 36.

Chapter
2

Using Special Characters and Symbols

FORMATTING
A DOCUMENT

WordPerfect 6 for Windows starts with many document defaults preset. That's why you can start the program and begin typing a new document immediately. What you get is a document formatted according to the predefined design criteria provided by WordPerfect.

Fortunately, however, WordPerfect 6 for Windows includes a number of tools to help you design your own document formats. We will show you how to use several of these formatting tools in this chapter.

8 ▼ Using Fonts

Today's word processors support an almost unbelievable range of typefaces that you can use to enhance the appearance of any document. And you can change the size of the characters plus set other attributes to specify fonts that make your documents appear more professional. A *font* is a collection of all of the characters and symbols available for a particular typeface and style.

Assumptions

- The insertion point is at the point in your document where you want a new font to be activated, or you have selected a block of text for which you want to specify a font.

Exceptions

- Some printers don't support a full range of fonts. If the font you want is not available during this procedure, try making a different printer current.

Steps

1. Use **Layout Font (F9)** to display the Font dialog, shown in Figure 2.1.

TIP

When designing any document, choose a typeface appropriate to the application and the target audience. A face that complements a greeting card, for example, will probably not increase the credibility of a business letter or a technical publication.

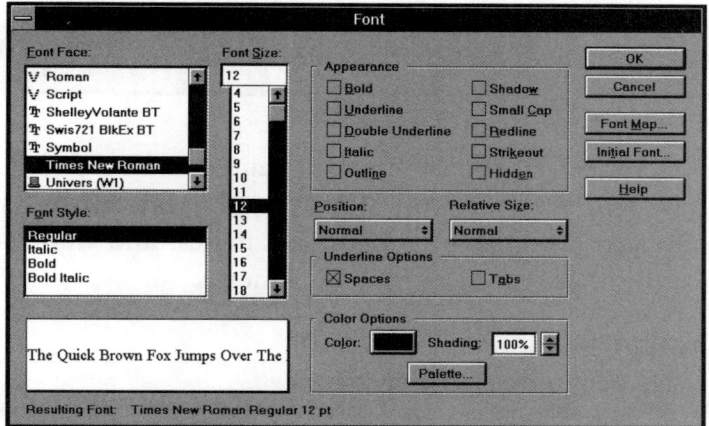

Figure 2.1   Layout Font... Font dialog.

2. Select the font you want to use from the Font Face: window of this dialog.

3. Use the Font Size: window of this dialog to specify the size of the next characters you enter or of the characters included in the block you marked before displaying the Font dialog.

4. Change other attributes as desired (see complete instructions in setting Text Attributes).

5. Click on **OK** to accept the settings you have specified.

What To Do If

• If the fonts don't appear as you expected, use Reveal Codes **(Alt+F3)** to see where the font on and off codes appear. You may have misplaced the codes, causing the fonts to be placed in the wrong location.

See Also

• Setting Text Attributes, p. 16.

TIP

If you only want to specify the typeface or the character size, you can use the pull-down menus from the power bar. Use **Layout Font (F9)** to display the full Font dialog and choose other character attributes.

Setting Text Attributes

Specifying fonts is only part of the document formatting features offered by WordPerfect 6 for Windows. You can also set special character attributes, such as boldface, italics, and underline to enhance the appearance of your documents.

Assumptions

- You have previously specified the font you want to use for existing or new text.
- The insertion point is positioned where you want the character attribute to begin, or you have previously selected a block of text to which you want to give a certain attribute.

Exceptions

- None.

> **TIP**
> Many character attributes can be set with shortcut keys. Bold = Ctrl+B. Underline = Ctrl+U. Italics = Ctrl+I.

Steps

1. Select **Layout** and choose **Font** or press **F9** to display the Font dialog (see Figure 2.1).
2. Choose from among the text attributes available on this dialog: Boldface, Underline, Italics, Outline, Shadow, Small Cap, Double Underline, Redline, Strikeout, Superscript, Subscript.

What To Do If

- If you change your mind about the character attributes you set, reissue the same command to turn off the attribute. The selections are toggles. The first time you select them they turn on; the second time they turn off.

See Also

- Using Fonts, p. 14.

Adjusting Margins   10

The default WordPerfect page margins are one inch all around: top, bottom, left, and right. This produces a well-proportioned page that is appropriate for many applications. There are times when you need to reduce margins to help fit information on a page, or make margins wider to emphasize text. The procedures presented in this section will help you do either one.

Assumptions

- The insertion point is located where you want the margin change to occur.

Exceptions

- Most laser printers can't work with margins any smaller than 0.3 inches. If you try to set a margin less than this with a laser printer selected as the active printer, WordPerfect will present an error message. Simply increase the margin width.

- Unlike some word processors, WordPerfect supports multiple margin settings within a document and even on a single page. You must place the insertion point where you want new margin settings to begin.

Steps

1. Use **L**ayout **M**argins... (**Ctrl+F8**) to display the Margins dialog. The Left Margin: field is highlighted; the sample page at the right of this dialog shows you how the current page appears. This sample changes as you change the current margin settings.

2. To change the left margin, either type the margin width from the keyboard or click on the up or down arrows to the right of this field.

3. Step to the next margin field by pressing **Tab,** or use the mouse to highlight the field you want to change.

4. Type in the additional changes, or use the up and down arrow keys beside the additional fields to select new values.

5. Click on **OK** to enable the changes.

What To Do If

• If the margin setting is not what you expected, use Reveal Codes (**Alt+F3**) to locate where the margin change code is located. You can erase this code, then conduct the margin change process again.

See Also

• Using Reveal Codes, p. 146.

• Setting Paragraph Indent, below.

11 ▾ Setting Paragraph Indent

Use margin settings when you want to change the overall appearance of a document. When you want to emphasize a block of text, such as a lengthy quote, for example, use WordPerfect's indent features. The indent feature is paragraph-oriented.

Assumptions

• The insertion point is positioned where you want the indent to begin.

Exceptions

• Use these procedures for paragraph indenting. For margin changes over a larger portion of the document, use **L**ayout **M**argins (described on p. 17).

• To create bulleted lists or hanging indents, use the procedures described under Paragraph—Hanging Indents, p. 76.

Steps

1. Use **L**ayout **P**aragraph **I**ndent **(F7)** to indent the entire current paragraph one tab space from the left. See Figure 2.2.

2. Use **L**ayout **P**aragraph **D**ouble Indent **(Ctrl+Shift+F7)** to indent the entire paragraph one tab space from the left and from the right. See Figure 2.3.

TIP

You can issue Indent and Double Indent commands more than once to increase the left and right margins more than a single tab space.

Introduction

    On a casual evening stroll, a man walks out of the light into the darkness of a moonless night. This is an educated man, yet as he walks, a fearful sensation creeps over him, a sensation that is all too familiar.

He knows there is nothing in the night, as he goes deeper into the darkness. His innermost fears begin to overwhelm him. He talks to himself, saying, "There is nothing here to be afraid of." Yet the back of his neck begins to crawl, goose bumps raise on his arms, and his skin begins to prickle. His heart pounds harder in his chest. An alarming urgency clutches him as he closes the distance to the light.

In the safety of the light, he feels foolish. His intelligence tells him there was nothing there, yet some genetic memory warned him of perhaps another time when there was evil in the night.

Figure 2.2   Sample document with paragraph indent.

Introduction

    On a casual evening stroll, a man walks out of the light into the darkness of a moonless night. This is an educated man, yet as he walks, a fearful sensation creeps over him, a sensation that is all too familiar.

He knows there is nothing in the night, as he goes deeper into the darkness. His innermost fears begin to overwhelm him. He talks to himself, saying, "There is nothing here to be afraid of." Yet the back of his neck begins to crawl, goose bumps raise on his arms, and his skin begins to prickle. His heart pounds harder in his chest. An alarming urgency clutches him as he closes the distance to the light.

In the safety of the light, he feels foolish. His intelligence tells him there was nothing there, yet some genetic memory warned him of perhaps another time when there was evil in the night.

Figure 2.3   Sample document with paragraph double indent.

What To Do If

- Although this is a paragraph-oriented command, WordPerfect begins the indent where the insertion point rests when the command is issued. The entire paragraph from the insertion point to the end will be indented, but any text ahead of the insertion point will not be indented. If the results are not what you expected, press Backspace to erase the code, move the insertion point, and issue the command again.

See Also

- Adjusting Margins, p. 17.
- Paragraph—Hanging Indents, p. 76.

12 Centering a Line

WordPerfect supports a couple of methods for centering information. When you want to center data on a single line, use the Line command described here. For more general settings, use the Justification command.

Assumptions

- The insertion point is positioned where you want the Center command to take effect. This should be at the beginning of a line.

Exceptions

- This is a line-oriented command, yet WordPerfect begins centering at the insertion point location. To center an entire line, make sure the insertion point is positioned at the beginning of the line.

- Even in a line-wrapped paragraph, this procedure centers only a single line.

_____ **Steps**

This is a one-step procedure. Do one of the following:

- Use **L**ayout **L**ine **C**enter (**Shift+F7**) to center information on an existing line.

- Use **L**ayout **L**ine **C**enter (**Shift+F7**) on a blank line, then type the text you want centered. Press **Enter** to move to the next line and set the centered text.

_____ **What To Do If**

- If the line doesn't seem to change, you probably have a margin-font size combination that fills the line. Decrease margins, reduce the size of the font on that line, or remove some information from that line for centering to be enabled.

- If the information on the line appears to be centered around a point in the middle of the line, you positioned the insertion point somewhere other than at the beginning of the line when the Center command was issued. Use **Backspace** or **Del** to remove the Center command (use Reveal Codes if necessary to locate the code), reposition the insertion point, and issue the Center command again.

_____ **See Also**

- Setting Flush Right Text, p. 22.
- Setting Document Justification, p. 25.

TIP

You can actually create more than one center point on a line as long as you separate the codes by one or more tabs. However, use care in placing the centering code because WordPerfect will overwrite existing text as it adheres to the Center command.

TIP

To remove the centering on a block of text, select the text and press **Ctrl+L** (for Left Justification).

Setting Flush Right Text

The Flush Right command forces text to line up along the right margin. If you insert this code before you enter text, the insertion point remains fixed at the right margin and text moves from right to left as it is entered.

Text set to Flush Right is useful in emphasizing text, in positioning page titles or numbers, and sometimes in lists. Because WordPerfect will set text flush right beginning at the location of the insertion point, you can split a line, setting some text on the line flush left, some flush right. Like the Line Center procedure described on p. 20, setting text flush right is a line-oriented command.

Assumptions

- The insertion point is positioned where you want the Flush Right command to take effect.

Exceptions

- If you try to align an existing line of text flush right that doesn't end in a hard return, you may experience difficulties in aligning the text.

Steps

This is a one-step procedure. Do one of the following:
- Use **L**ayout **L**ine **F**lush **R**ight **(Alt+F7)** to set all text on the current line after the insertion point flush right.
- Use **L**ayout Line **F**lush **R**ight **(Alt+F7)** at the beginning of a blank line to have all text you enter after that set flush right.

TIP
To right-align more than one line of text, you can select a block of text, then issue the **L**ayout Line **F**lush **R**ight command **(Alt+F7)** to set all of the marked lines flush right. For more than a few lines, use the Layout Justification command instead.

What To Do If

- If the flush right text starts at the wrong place, simply use **Backspace** or **Del** to remove the misplaced flush right code (use Reveal Codes if necessary to locate the code), reposition the insertion point, and issue the command again.

See Also

- Centering a Line, p. 20.
- Setting Document Justification, p. 25.

Setting Other Line Codes | 14

WordPerfect lets you specify a number of line-oriented features in addition to centering and flush right. For example, you can specify a hard tab when you want a permanent tab that won't change when general tab settings are changed. Suppose you need a few decimal tabs in a document to line a short list of numbers, but you don't want to change that tab location to decimal for the rest of the document. Use this feature to insert a hard decimal tab.

Use the Other Codes dialog to insert a hard space between two words so they will stay together on the same line instead of wrapping to the next line if one of the words falls at the end of the line.

To insert a dash to separate a compound word such as re-sort or co-op, use the Special Codes dialog and choose Hyphen Character. This dash tells WordPerfect that the two parts of this word should stay together and not be hyphenated.

The Insert Special Codes dialog includes four main areas: Hard Tab Codes, Hard Tab Codes with Dot Leaders, Hyphenation

Codes, and Other Codes. Most of these codes are used to force WordPerfect to use a particular type of character in a specific situation.

Assumptions

- The insertion point is positioned where you want a special code inserted.

Exceptions

- You can duplicate some of these codes from the keyboard. The special hyphen code is the same as pressing the hyphen key on the keyboard, for example.

Steps

1. Use **L**ayout **L**ine **S**pecial **C**odes... to display the dialog shown in Figure 2.4.

2. Click on the entries you want to toggle on or off. A dot in the button beside the entry indicates it is enabled.

3. Click on **OK** to insert the codes.

What To Do If

- If you accidentally misplace a special code, turn on Reveal Codes (**Alt+F3**), locate the code you want to reset, and use

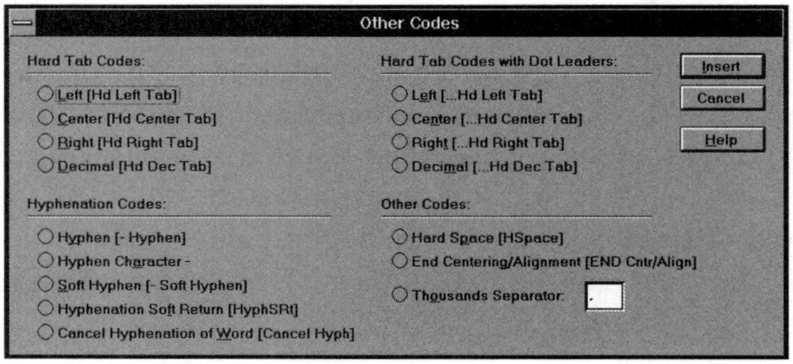

Figure 2.4   Insert Special Codes dialog.

Backspace or **Del** to remove it. Position the insertion point where you want the special code, then conduct these steps again.

_____ **See Also**

- Centering a Line, p. 20.
- Hyphenation, p. 92.
- Setting Document Justification, below.
- Setting Tabs, p. 88.
- Paragraph Formatting, p. 69.

| Setting Document Justification | 15 |

Use line-oriented settings to change orientation on a single line or on a range of a few lines. To change text orientation on a page or throughout a document, use the **L**ayout **J**ustification commands described in this section.

For most document applications you will use standard left justification. But for some reports, memos, newsletters, and other specialty documents, you may want center, right, or full justification.

_____ **Assumptions**

- You want to change text orientation for a broad range of text: a paragraph, a page, or an entire document.
- The insertion point is located where you want the text justification to change.

_____ **Exceptions**

- The Layout Justification commands apply to the entire paragraph that holds the insertion point when the command is issued and also affects the entire rest of the document after the insertion point. To change one line or a few lines, use the Layout Line commands instead.

Steps

1. Use **L**ayout **J**ustification to pull down the Justification menu box.

2. Select Left, Right, Center, Full, or All from this menu.

What To Do If

- If you select the wrong type of justification, simply delete the code you just entered and issue the command again, selecting another justification code. You may need to use Reveal Codes (**Alt+F3**) to display the code so you can delete it.

- If you can't find a code you want to remove, even with Reveal Codes enabled, look at the beginning of the paragraph where you first entered the code. Justification codes usually are placed at the beginning of the current paragraph, even if the insertion point is located elsewhere in the paragraph.

See Also

- Centering a Line, p. 20.
- Setting Flush Right Text, p. 22.

16   Centering Information on a Page

Just as you can center a line of text from left to right, you can center all of the text on a page top to bottom. This also is an easy process. You will want to use this technique when you are preparing fliers, document title pages, or other pages where the information needs to fit in the middle of the page, top to bottom as well as left and right.

Assumptions

- You are preparing a document or a page within a document and the information on one or more pages must appear in the center of the page, top to bottom.

Exceptions

- When you have a large amount of information on a page, it is difficult or impossible to tell when you have centered this information. The data will appear centered when the page is printed.

Steps

1. Use **L**ayout **P**age **C**enter... to display the Center Page(s) dialog.
2. Select Current **P**age or Current and **S**ubsequent pages from this dialog.
3. Click on **OK** to accept the change.

> **TIP**
>
> To view the information as it will appear when printed, use **V**iew **Z**oom... Full **P**age to display the full page of information.

What To Do If

- If you don't get the results you want, it may be that the page is too full of text for proper centering. Try reducing the margin, removing some text from the page you want to center, or entering a hard page break **(Ctrl+Enter).** The hard page reduces the overall information on the page, causing the remainder of the information to center, adding emphasis to it.

See Also

- Centering a Line, p. 20.
- Setting Document Justification, p. 25.

Using Special Characters and Symbols

17 | **Using WordPerfect Characters**

WordPerfect is very strong in supporting special characters and symbols. The easiest and most straightforward way to enter special characters into your documents is with the WP Character feature. WordPerfect supports 15 separate character sets, displayed in the WordPerfect Characters dialog.

Assumptions

- The insertion point is located where you want a WordPerfect character to appear.

Exceptions

- None.

Steps

> **TIP**
> You can move the Characters dialog around the screen if it gets in your way as you work with it. And, you can resize the box. Select the box by clicking anywhere inside, then grab one edge and drag it outward or inward to change the size of the box.

1. Use **Insert Character...** (**Ctrl+W**) to display the WordPerfect Characters dialog shown in Figure 2.5.

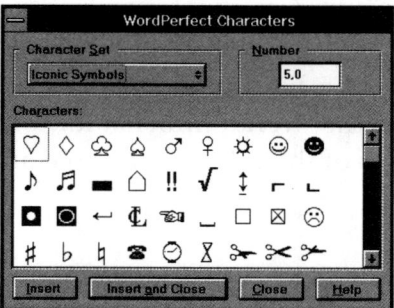

Figure 2.5   WordPerfect Characters dialog.

2. Choose the character set you want to use by clicking on the bar beneath the Character **S**et title in this dialog. The choices are shown in Figure 2.6.

3. Click on the character you want to use inside the Characters: window of this dialog. Use the scroll bars to the right of the dialog to display additional characters.

4. Click on **Insert** to place the selected character in your document at the location of the insertion point. This leaves the WordPerfect Characters dialog on the screen so you can enter another special character if you wish. If you only want to insert a single character, then click on Insert **a**nd Close to insert the selected character and close the dialog box.

What To Do If

- Some characters you find on the Character Map may not display in WordPerfect the same way. If this happens, choose another character, or use the Windows Control Panel Fonts utility to make sure True Type fonts are displayed in your applications (open the Program Manager, select the Control Panel, and double-click on Fonts. Select **T**rue Type... and choose **E**nable True Type Fonts and **S**how Only True Type Fonts in Applications.) This may improve compatibility

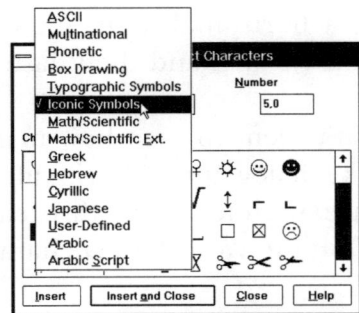

Figure 2.6 **WordPerfect character set choices from WordPerfect Characters dialog.**

between the Character Map and WordPerfect. Unfortunately, you can't use WordPerfect's WP Characters... utility under the Font menu because you can't access additional menu items while inside another menu.

See Also

- Constructing Special Characters with Overstrike, below.

18 Constructing Special Characters with Overstrike

If you don't find the character you want to use as part of the WordPerfect character set, you can try building your own characters and symbols using the overstrike feature of the Font dialog. You can use Overstrike to combine two or more keyboard characters to form a new character. This routine shows some simple intelligence in that when you enter two characters, one after the other, WordPerfect knows what you actually want to print and inserts that character for you.

With Overstrike you can display and print characters that aren't on your keyboard. For example, to produce the é character, you use the e and ′ characters. Combine 0 and / to produce the computer-type slashed zero (Ø). Want to produce European-style characters with a horizontal dash, such as 7 or z? Simply enter 7 and then dash (-) or Z and then dash in the Overstrike dialog box.

WordPerfect doesn't seem to care how many characters you enter in the Overstrike dialog and will print all of them on top of each other. You can experiment with this feature to construct characters that aren't in the WordPerfect character set.

Assumptions

- The insertion point is positioned where you want the special character to appear.

Exceptions

- Use the WordPerfect Character feature for conventional symbols and international characters where possible. The overstrike process is harder to use.

- Not all printers can produce the complex characters you can construct with the Overstrike feature. To find out about your printer, just create the characters you'd like to use, then try to print them.

Steps

1. Use **L**ayout **T**ypesetting **O**verstrike... to display the Overstrike dialog shown in Figure 2.7.

2. Click on the left-facing arrow at the right of the Overstrike: field of this dialog to display the Character Attribute menu shown in Figure 2.8.

3. Choose one of the attributes from this menu to insert the attribute codes into the Overstrike dialog, as shown in Figure 2.9.

4. Place the insertion point between the attribute codes. Do this by pointing between the attribute codes with the mouse and clicking the left mouse button.

5. Type the character combinations you want to construct special characters.

6. Click on **OK** or press **Enter** to insert the resulting character in your document.

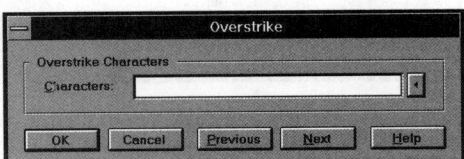

Figure 2.7   Overstrike dialog.

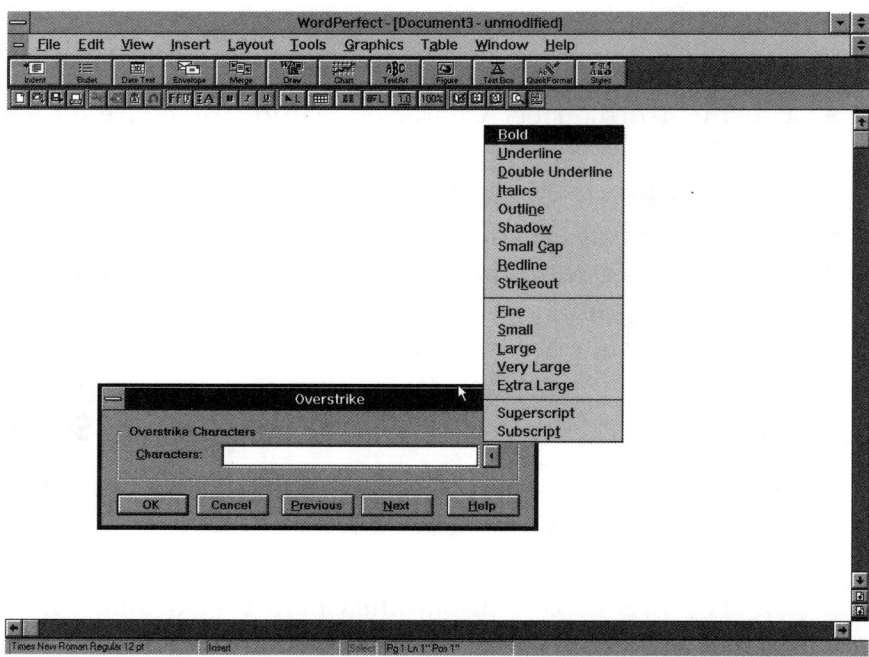

Figure 2.8   Overstrike Character Attribute menu.

What To Do If

- If one of the combined characters you create isn't quite what you wanted, you can edit it easily. Use **L**ayout **T**ypesetting **O**verstrike to display the Overstrike dialog, then click on Next or **P**revious to display the special characters in your document. When the one you want to edit is shown in

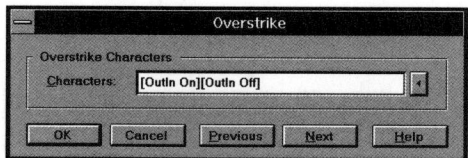

Figure 2.9   Overstrike dialog with character attributes shown.

the dialog box, make any changes you want, then click on **OK** to put the changed character back into the document where it came from.

_____ **See Also**

- Using WordPerfect Characters, p. 28.

Chapter
3

Configuring the Document Summary Dialog

Using the WordPerfect File Manager

Using QuickFinder

Block Operations

Paragraph Formatting

Using Outlining

ADVANCED DOCUMENT SKILLS

The good news about WordPerfect 6 for Windows is that you can realize a lot of benefit from this program by using only the most basic features. As you gain experience and attempt more complicated tasks, however, you can access more and more of what WordPerfect has to offer. In this chapter we'll introduce you to some of the advanced document skills that can help make your WordPerfect documents special.

We'll also show you some of the special features available in WordPerfect's File Manager, accessible when you load or save a document. These are powerful utilities that let you do more work from inside WordPerfect instead of exiting to DOS or to Windows.

19 ▼ Opening an Existing Document

We've shown you already how to create a document from scratch and how to save it to disk. Once a document is stored, you also can return to it at any time to make changes or additions.

Assumptions

- You have previously created a document that is stored on disk.

Exceptions

- This process opens a new document separate from any documents already open. If you want to merge information from a disk file, use **Insert File...** instead of the procedure described here.

Steps

1. Use **File Open... (Ctrl+O)** to display the File Open dialog shown in Figure 3.1.

> **TIP**
> You can highlight any filename in the list, then click on **View...** to open a small document window that shows the contents of any file you select. This lets you step through the list of files and see what is available without having to open the documents.

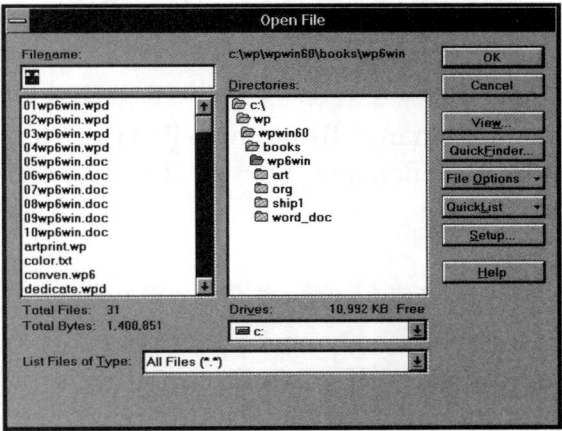

Figure 3.1   File Open... dialog.

2. Select a disk location where the file you want to retrieve is located by pulling down the list of available drives in the **D**rives: field of this dialog.

3. By default WordPerfect displays all files in the current directory. You can narrow the list by pulling down the file type list from the List Files of **T**ype: field in this dialog. A sample list is shown in Figure 3.2.

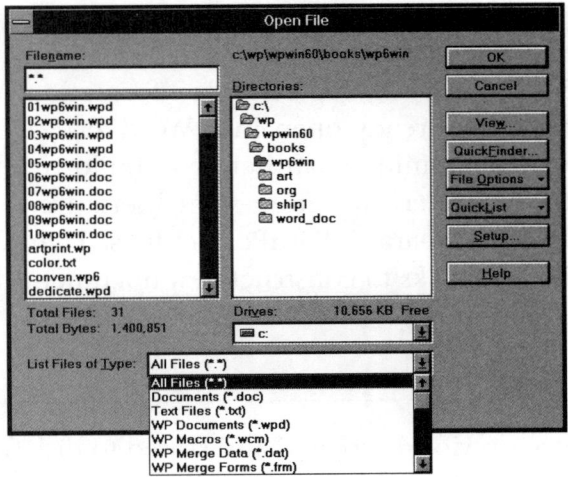

Figure 3.2   List Files of Type: list from the File Open dialog.

4. Select a directory from the Directories: list in this dialog. You can double-click on any listed directory to display additional directories beneath the selected directory.

5. Choose a filename from the Filename: list, or enter a name in the Filename: field of this dialog from the keyboard.

What To Do If

- If you can't find a document you think exists, try a different drive or directory. If you still can't find a document you want, use the QuickFinder feature, described on page 52.

See Also

- Using QuickFinder, p. 52.
- Using the WordPerfect File Manager, p. 48.
- Inserting Files into Existing Documents, below.

20 ⎇ Inserting Files into Existing Documents

Most of the time when you call up a file from disk you'll want to install it in a separate editing window in WordPerfect. However, there are times when existing on-disk information needs to be merged with a file already open in a WordPerfect editing window. In fact, this technique can help you build repetitive documents easily. Simply create letter, sales literature, or company report modules as separate WordPerfect files. Then you can use them as building blocks to construct new documents by merging appropriate modules.

Assumptions

- You have previously created and stored to disk files that you want to merge with information in a WordPerfect editing window.

- The insertion point is at the location in the open document where you want on-disk data to appear.

_____ **Exceptions**

- None.

_____ **Steps**

1. Use **Insert File...** to display the Insert File dialog shown in Figure 3.3. (This is basically the same dialog you see when loading or saving a file.)

2. Select a disk location where the file you want to insert is located by pulling down the list of available drives in the **D**rives: field of this dialog.

3. By default WordPerfect displays all files in the current directory. You can narrow the list by pulling down the file type list from the List Files of **T**ype: field in this dialog. A sample list is shown in Figure 3.4.

4. Select a directory from the Directories: list in this dialog. You can double-click on any listed directory to display additional directories beneath the selected directory.

TIP
You can highlight any filename in the list, then click on **View**... to open a small document window that shows the contents of any file you select. This lets you step through the list of files and see what is available without having to merge the document to find out what is in it.

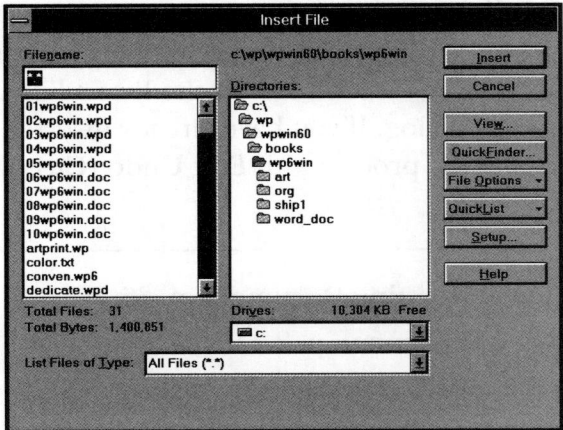

Figure 3.3   Insert File... Insert File dialog.

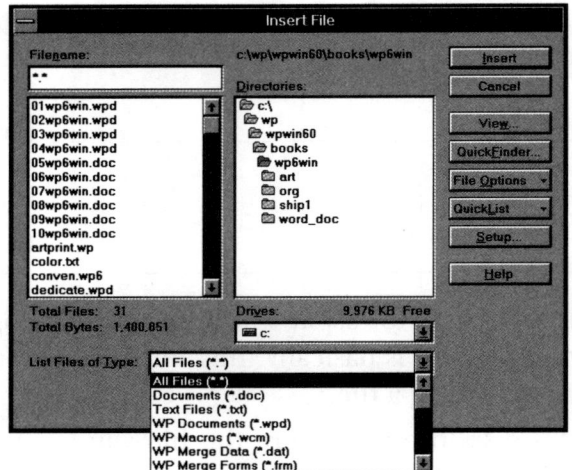

Figure 3.4   List Files of Type: list from File Open dialog.

5. Select a filename from the File**n**ame: list, or enter a name in the File**n**ame: field of this dialog from the keyboard.

6. Click on **OK** to accept the selected file. (You can also double-click on the chosen filename and skip the **OK** step.)

7. Click on **OK** when the Insert File Into Current Document? Confirmation dialog appears.

What To Do If

*   If you change your mind about inserting a file into the current document, click on **No** on the Insert File Into Current Document? dialog. If you have already inserted the file, you can reverse the process with **E**dit **U**ndo (**Ctrl+Z**).

See Also

*   Opening an Existing Document, p. 36.
*   Creating a Document, p. 2.
*   Using the WordPerfect File Manager, p. 48.
*   Using QuickFinder, p. 52.

Entering Document Summary Information   21

As you work with a broader range of documents, as the number of documents you have stored on your system increases, and when more than one person uses the same files, it becomes more important to store file summary data along with the filename. By filling out the summary screen, and setting other features we discuss in this section, you will find it much easier to locate specific documents or a range of documents that contains specific information.

Assumptions

- Automatic Document Summary entry is disabled. When you want to fill out a document summary dialog you have to specifically call up the dialog for each file from the File menu.

- The document for which you want to enter summary information is the current document (it is displayed in a WordPerfect editing window).

Exceptions

- You can tell WordPerfect to present the Document Summary dialog automatically with the **F**ile **Pr**eferences... **S**ummary dialog.

Steps

1. Use **F**ile Document Summary... to display the Document Summary dialog shown in Figure 3.5.

2. Type as much information into the fields of the Document Summary dialog as you wish. At the least you should enter a descriptive name and a subject. Notice that WordPerfect fills in some of the information for you. For example, the system knows who the current user is, and the creation

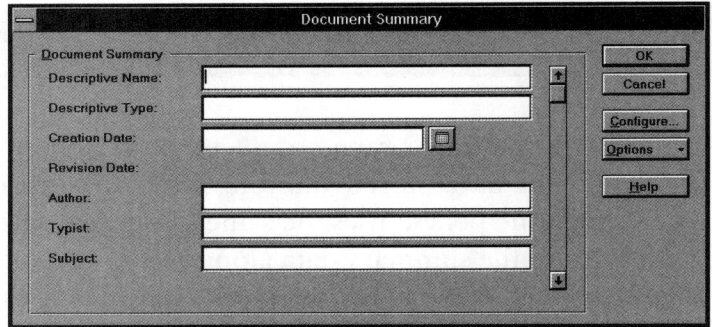

Figure 3.5 Document Summary dialog.

date and revision dates are entered from file information.

3. Use the vertical scroll bar to display all of the fields in the dialog.

4. Click on **OK** to save the changes.

What To Do If

• If you want to make additions or changes to any document summary, simply reissue the **File Document Summary...** command to display the dialog again. Edit or add to the fields as desired.

See Also

• Configuring the Document Summary Dialog, below.
• Storing a Document, p. 7.

Configuring the Document Summary Dialog

You have several options for configuring how the Document Summary information is entered and displayed. We'll show you how to use them in this section.

Specifying Document Summary on Save/Exit

22

If you find that you are entering document summary information for the majority of the documents you create, the best course is to make document summary entry automatic. You can configure WordPerfect to present the Document Summary dialog when you save a document for the first time or when you exit WordPerfect.

Assumptions

- None.

Exceptions

- None.

Steps

1. Use **F**ile **P**references... to display the Preferences dialog shown in Figure 3.6.

2. Choose **S**ummary from this dialog to display the Document Summary Preferences dialog.

3. Click on **C**reate Summary on Save/Exit to turn on the display of the Document Summary dialog when a document is first saved.

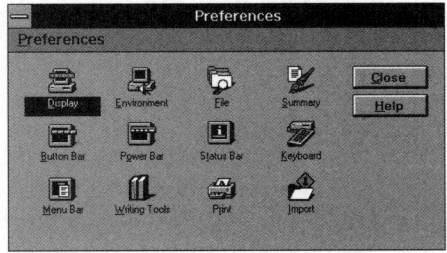

Figure 3.6   Preferences dialog.

4.   Click on **OK** to close the dialog and effect the changes.

What To Do If

- If you decide you'd rather call up the Document Summary dialog for each document on your own, simply repeat steps 1 to 4 and turn off the **C**reate Summary on Save/Exit toggle.

See Also

- Entering Document Summary Information, p. 41.

23   Enabling Descriptive Name Display

When you load or save a file or insert a file into an existing document, you use WordPerfect's File Manager display. By default, this display shows only the names of files in the Filename: window of the File Manager dialog. You can also use the Document Summary dialog to turn on a descriptive name display in the File Manager.

Assumptions

- You have entered some document summary information into your WordPerfect documents.

TIP
You can also turn on this feature from inside the File Manager. Select **S**etup... from the File Manager menu. Then select an option that includes Descriptive Names from the **S**how: field.

Exceptions

- If there is no information in the summary fields, then part of the File Manager screen will be blank if you turn on the descriptive name display.

Steps

1.   Use **F**ile Preferences... **S**ummary to display the Document Summary Preferences dialog.

2. Click on the **U**se Descriptive Names: field to turn on this option. An "X" should appear in the box beside this field.

3. Click on **OK** to make this change effective.

What To Do If

- If you want to turn off Descriptive Name display, reissue the **F**ile **P**references... **S**ummary... command and click in the **U**se Descriptive Names: field to toggle off this option.

See Also

- Using the WordPerfect File Manager, p. 48.
- Specifying Document Summary on Save/Exit, p. 43.

Setting Default Document Type

24

Among the settings you can include on the Summary Preferences dialog is a default document type. You can use Document Type to help you organize your files and to help find them in groups when you use the QuickFinder features of the File Manager.

Assumptions

- You want to use Document Type to help categorize your files and the majority of files falls into one category.

Exceptions

- This setting applies to all documents created after you make the change, but the Descriptive Type information on existing documents is not affected.

Steps

1. Use **F**ile **P**references... to display the Preferences dialog.

TIP

Remember to change this default each time you start working with a different type of document. Remember, this setting is for all new documents, so if you change the default as you start working with a new group of documents, you automatically create a type definition for them.

2. Choose **S**ummary... from the icons on the Preferences dialog.

3. Type the default document type in the **D**efault Descriptive Type: field. You can enter up to 40 characters in this field.

4. Click on **OK** to accept the change.

What To Do If

- You can easily change the default definition by repeating steps 1 to 4 above, but remember that if you have already created documents using this default, the Descriptive Type for these documents won't change. You can open each document that you want to change and use **F**ile Document Summary... to change the Descriptive Type.

See Also

- Using the WordPerfect File Manager, p. 48.
- Enabling Descriptive Name Display, p. 44.

25 / Setting the Default Subject Text

Part of WordPerfect's document management capability lets you create a subject in the summary fields automatically from information stored in each document. The summary create routine will search the active document for the Subject Text, then copy the text immediately following the Subject Search Text into the Subject: field of the document summary.

The default search text is **RE:** because many official documents use a heading somewhere on the first page that uses RE:. If your document headings include another label for the document subject, such as **SUBJECT:**, then change RE: on the Preferences dialog to SUBJECT:.

When you use **F**ile Document Summary... to create a summary for the active document, you can click on **O**ptions, then choose **E**xtract Information From Document. WordPerfect searches the first page of the document for the Subject Text, then copies up to 150 characters (or to the first hard return, whichever comes first) immediately following the search text into the **S**ubject: field of the summary. At the same time, the first 400 characters of the document are copied into the **A**bstract field.

_____ **Assumptions**

- You want to change the default Subject Text for automatic Subject and Abstract entries in document summaries.

_____ **Exceptions**

- If the default Subject Search Text doesn't appear on the first page of your document, then the document summary routine won't find the subject and won't be able to copy to subject out of the document and into the Subject: field of the summary.

_____ **Steps**

1. Use **F**ile Preferences... **S**ummary... to display the Summary Preferences dialog.
2. Type the new default Subject Search Text in the proper field of this dialog.
3. Click on **OK** to effect the change.

_____ **What To Do If**

- If you want to change this default, simply repeat steps 1 to 3 above, entering a new search text default. Remember, however, that this setting affects only new documents as they are created. The summary fields for existing documents will not be changed.

See Also

- Specifying Document Summary on Save/Exit, p. 43.
- Enabling Descriptive Name Display, p. 44.
- Setting Default Document Type, p. 45.

Using the WordPerfect File Manager

You use the WordPerfect File Manager every time you open a new file, save a file, or use Insert File to merge data from two files. In addition, you can use the features of the File Manager to manage and maintain WordPerfect files and other disk files. In this section we describe features of the File Manager that go beyond file opening or saving support. For basic File Manager operation, see the preceding File Open and Insert File sections, as well as the File Save discussion in Chapter 1. If you are familiar with WordPerfect 5.2 for Windows, you know that the File Manager was a separate, stand-alone utility. In WordPerfect 6 for Windows, however, there is no separate File Manager utility. The File Manager is used for other, internal operations.

26 Setting Up the File Manager

WordPerfect's File Manager is installed with certain default settings. You can do about everything you need to do with File Manager using these default settings. However, you also can set up the File Manager for your own needs.

Assumptions

- None.

Exceptions

- None.

Steps

1. Use File **O**pen... **(Ctrl+O)** to display the File Open File Manager dialog shown in Figure 3.7. Notice that this dialog has five basic areas: File**n**ame:, **D**irectories:, Drives:, List Files by **T**ype:, and a Command, Setup, and Utilities section (the buttons).

2. Click on **S**etup... to display the File Manager Open/Save As Setup dialog, shown in Figure 3.8.

3. Click on the **S**how: bar and hold down the left mouse button to pop up the list of options on what file information is displayed with the File Manager. You can select from four options:

   - Filename only
   - Filename, size, date, time

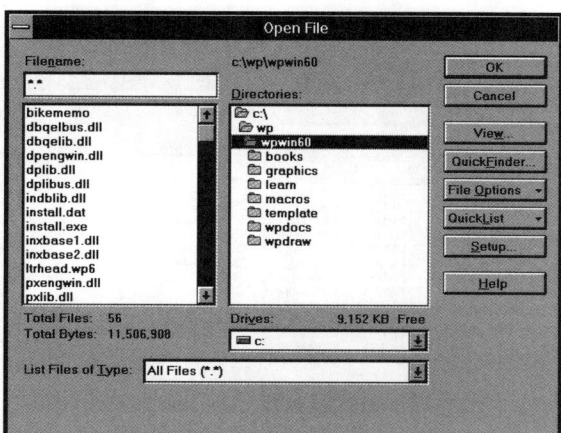

Figure 3.7   File Open (File Manager) dialog.

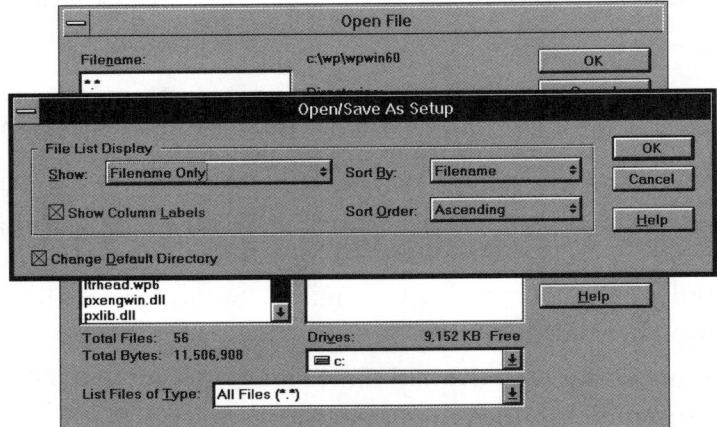

Figure 3.8   File Manager Open/Save As Setup dialog.

- Descriptive name, filename (requires entries in Document Summary)
- Custom columns

The WordPerfect default is Filename only, which you can see in Figure 3.7. The Custom Columns display is shown in Figure 3.9.

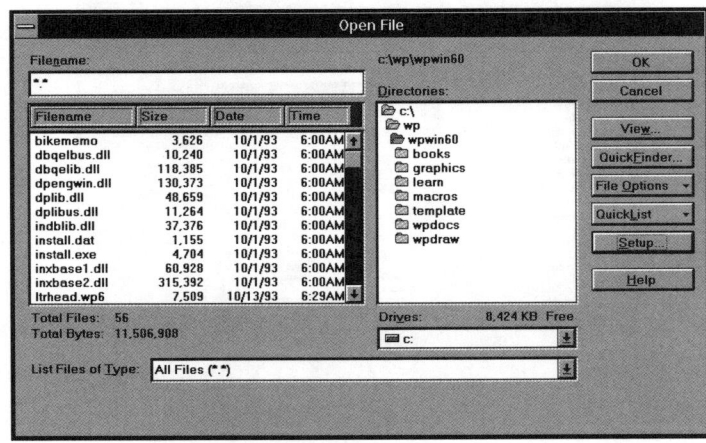

Figure 3.9   Custom Columns display in File Manager.

4. Select the option you want to implement by moving the mouse pointer up and down the list. Release the mouse button to choose an option.

5. Click on the Sort **B**y: bar and hold down the left mouse button to pop up the list of options for sorting the files displayed in the File Manager. You have up to six choices:

- **F**ilename
- **E**xtension
- **S**ize
- **D**ate/Time
- Descriptive **N**ame (only available with Custom Columns and Descriptive Name, Filename directory displays)
- Descriptive **T**ype (only available with Custom Columns directory displays)

Filename is the WordPerfect default.

6. Specify **A**scending or **D**escending sort in the Sort **O**rder: field.

7. Click on **OK** to accept the changes and display the new File Manager dialog.

8. Click on the Change Default directory box to enable or disable automatic default directory changes as you work with the File Manager. With this box checked, each time you specify a new directory for searching, it becomes the automatic default. If this box is not checked, then the directory that was current when you disabled this feature remains the default each time you access the File Manager.

What To Do If

- If the File Manager display you create is not what you wanted, simply click on **S**etup... again and make any required changes.

See Also _____

- Opening an Existing Document, p. 36.
- Storing a Document, p. 7.
- Using QuickFinder, below.

Using QuickFinder

Part of WordPerfect's File Manager is a feature called "Quick-Finder." This is actually an index feature that can speed up file searches when you want to find specific file types. An *index* is a secondary file frequently used in database searches. An index holds information extracted from a main file so that when you search for specific information, the software can search the much shorter index rather than the longer main file. Index files speed up data searches considerably.

The QuickFinder index is a full-text database that includes every word contained in the files and directories you want to set up for QuickFinder searches. How can this be more efficient than simply searching the files themselves? Because an index contains each unique word only once, along with a pointer to the files that contain each word.

You can access the QuickFinder from the File Open..., File Save As..., and File Insert... commands, all of which display the basic WordPerfect File Manager screen. The basic process for using QuickFinder is:

- Create a QuickFinder index.
- Establish search options.
- Conduct a QuickFinder search.

Each of these procedures is discussed in detail in the following sections.

Creating a QuickFinder Index	**27**

You can create multiple QuickFinder indexes with different names and holding different files. This is one more way to organize your word processing data and a way to help you find files quickly when you need to. And the QuickFinder can index files created by some other applications, including previous versions of WordPerfect and programs that create ASCII files.

Assumptions

- You have previously created files in WordPerfect or other applications that you want to index through the Quick-Finder.

Exceptions

- None.

Steps

1. Use **F**ile **Q**uickFinder... to display the QuickFinder dialog shown in Figure 3.10.

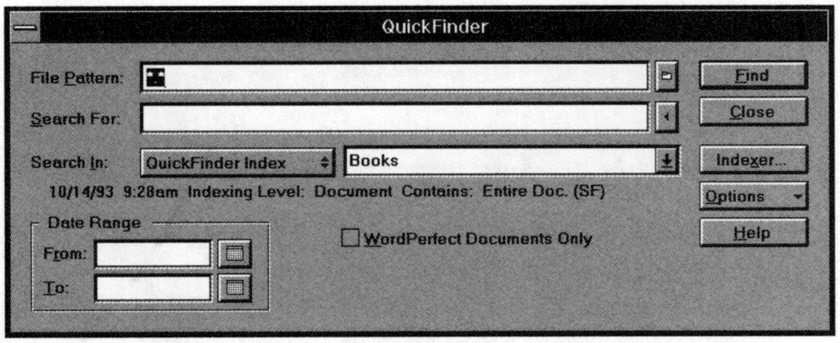

Figure 3.10   QuickFinder dialog.

> **TIP**
> An index name should be a descriptive name that will tell you at a glance what types of file information it contains. You can use a name with up to 40 characters for each index. And you can create multiple indexes, if you wish.

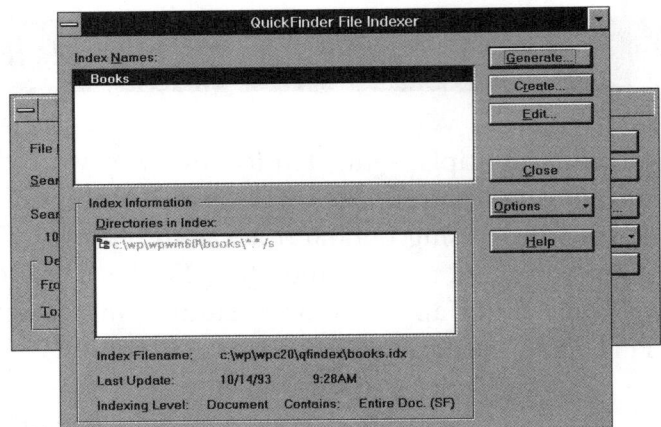

Figure 3.11 QuickFinder Indexer dialog.

2. Click on In**dex**er... to display the QuickFinder Indexer dialog shown in Figure 3.11.

3. Click on **C**reate... to display the Create Index Name dialog.

4. Type the name of the index you want to create.

5. Click on **OK** to accept the name and display the Create Index dialog shown in Figure 3.12.

6. Click on **O**ptions on the Create Index dialog to display the Options dialog shown in Figure 3.13.

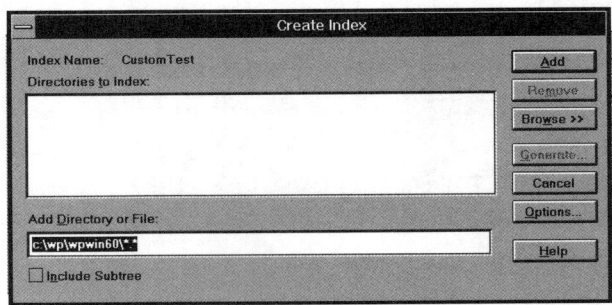

Figure 3.12 Create Index dialog.

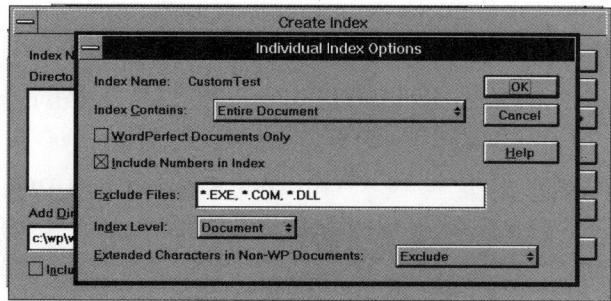

Figure 3.13   Individual Index Options dialog.

7. Click on the Index **C**ontains: field to choose how much information will be indexed. The WordPerfect default is Entire Document, but you also can specify Entire Document—Summary Fields, Text Only, Summary Fields Only, and Filename Only.

8. Click on **W**ordPerfect Documents Only if you want the indexer to include only information from WordPerfect files. If this box is not checked (the default) index information will be built from all files in the specified directories, except that the files specified in **Ex**clude Files: will be bypassed.

9. Click on the **I**nclude Numbers in Index if you want to turn off this default feature.

10. Edit the **Ex**clude Files: field if you want to change or add to the excluded files list before the index is generated.

11. Click on the In**d**ex Level button to pop up the level menu. The Document level is the WordPerfect default, but you also can specify Hard Page, Page, Paragraph, Sentence, or Line. This setting specifies the area to search for word patterns, limiting the area to the entire document, for example, or within a single page, and so on.

12. Click on the **E**xtended Characters in Non-WP Documents button to pop up additional choices. The WordPerfect default is **Exclude**, but you can also select from Interpret as ANSI and Interpret as ASCII.

13. Click on **OK** to accept these settings and return to the Create Index dialog.

14. The next step is to create a list of directories to be included in the index. Click on **A**dd to accept WordPerfect's suggested directory.

15. Edit the Add **D**irectory or File: line to specify another directory or file. You can use **Browse >>** to search for directories to include. For each directory you choose, click on **In**clude Subtree to include any subdirectories under the main directory in the index building process.

16. When all of the files and directories you want included in this index have been selected, click on **G**enerate... to build the index.

17. Click on **OK** on the Index Completed dialog to return to the QuickFinder File Indexer. You can either design another index at this time, or select **C**lose to return to the QuickFinder main dialog.

What To Do If

- You can manipulate existing indexes with the Options... menu on the QuickFinder File Indexes dialog. For example, you can select an existing index, then use **O**ptions... **D**elete... to remove it, **O**ptions... **R**ename... to rename it, and so on.

- If you forget what information is included in any index, use Indexer... **O**ptions... **I**nformation... to display full details about the selected index.

See Also

- Establishing QuickFinder Search Options, p. 57.
- Saving a QuickFinder Search, p. 60.

Establishing QuickFinder Search Options 28

Building a database and index is only part of the total picture of information handling. You go through these steps to be able to access the data you have stored. The same is true in WordPerfect. Your database consists of the document files you create and the index is created with the QuickFinder utilities. Then you are ready to specify search criteria so that you can locate the documents you want.

Assumptions

- You have previously built a QuickFinder index (see p. 53).

Exceptions

- None.

Steps

1. Use **F**ile **Q**uickFinder... to display the QuickFinder dialog shown in Figure 3.14.

2. Click on the **S**earch In: field to display the popup menu. The WordPerfect default is a QuickFinder Index, but you

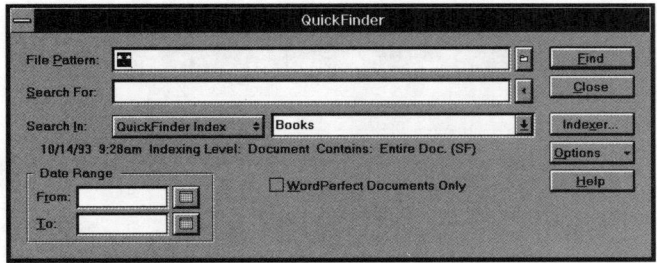

Figure 3.14 QuickFinder dialog.

also can tell QuickFinder to search a specific directory, subtree, or disk.

3. If you are searching a QuickFinder index, specify the index name in the field to the right of the Search In: field. You can click on the down arrow to the right of the Index Name: field to display a list of available indexes.

4. Narrow the search, if you wish, by specifying a file pattern in the File Pattern: field. You can use the WordPerfect File Manager to help with this specification by clicking on the file folder icon to the right of this field.

5. Narrow the search further by entering information in the **S**earch For: field. To get some help on this specification, click on the left-facing triangle at the right of this field to display the list shown in Figure 3.15. Each of these choices includes another menu level. Select any of these to help you build a search specification.

6. Keep adding information to search for until the complete search specification has been built.

7. Click on the **W**ordPerfect Documents Only box if you want to exclude non-WordPerfect files from the search.

8. Specify a Date Range, if you want to narrow the search by date.

9. Click on **O**ptions to display the Options popup list shown in Figure 3.16.

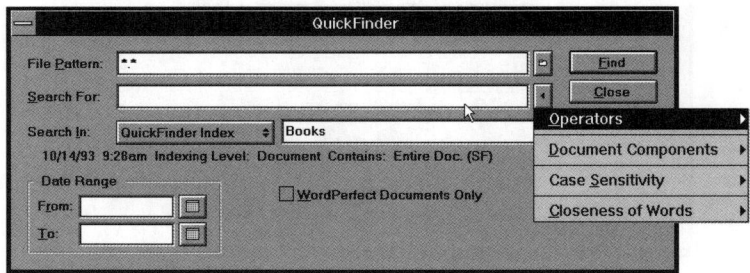

Figure 3.15   Search For: prompt popup menu.

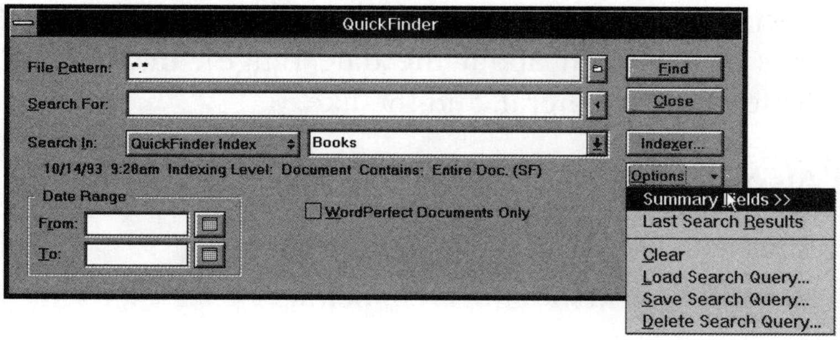

Figure 3.16   QuickFinder Options popup list.

10. Select Summary **F**ields>> to display the Summary Fields dialog shown in Figure 3.17. You can specify information in any of these fields to help you find specific documents.

11. Choose **S**ave Search Query... to save the current Quick-Finder specifications so you can use it again later.

12. Click on **F**ind to begin the search.

What To Do If

* If a document that you believe is on file doesn't show up in the search, try restructuring the search by making it less

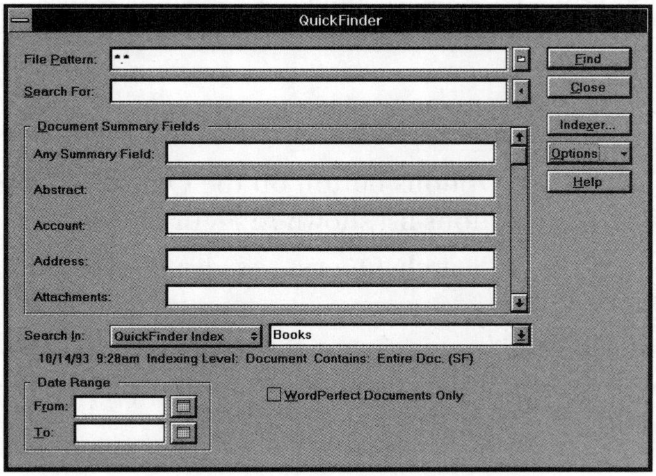

Figure 3.17   QuickFinder Summary Fields dialog.

restrictive. Remove the date restriction, for example (you may be mistaken about the date range), making the file pattern more general, and the like.

See Also _____

- Reusing a QuickFinder Search, p. 61.
- Saving a QuickFinder Search, below.

29 | Saving a QuickFinder Search

As with most database products, WordPerfect's file search facility supports saving previous search criteria. Then you can conduct the same search again by simply calling up the stored search.

Assumptions _____

- You have designed a search criteria using the File Quick-Finder... dialog. See the preceding description of this process.

Exceptions _____

- None.

Steps _____

1. Click on the **O**ptions button on the QuickFinder dialog to display the options list shown in Figure 3.18.
2. Choose **S**ave Search Query... to display the Save Search Query dialog.
3. Enter a search name in the Search **N**ame: field of this dialog. You can enter a name with up to 40 characters in this field.

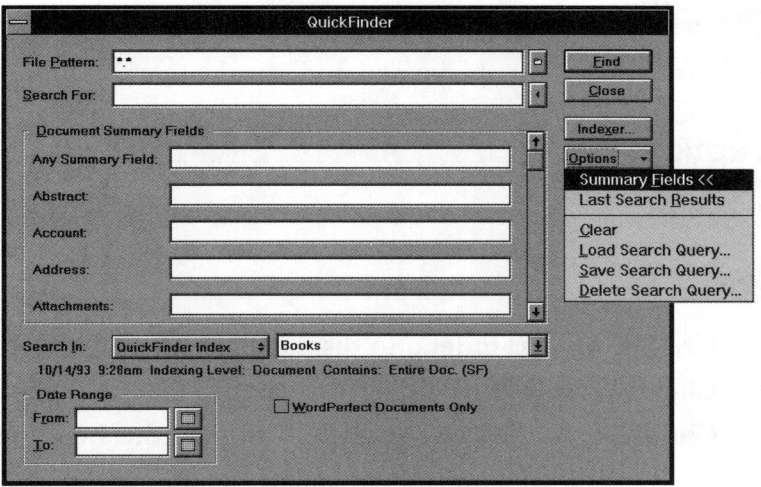

Figure 3.18   QuickFinder Options popup list.

_____ **What To Do If**

- If you need to change the search criteria, simply redo the
search and save the search specifications again using the
same name as before.

_____ **See Also**

- Creating a QuickFinder Index, p. 53.
- Establishing QuickFinder Search Options, p. 57.
- Reusing a QuickFinder Search, below.

Reusing a QuickFinder Search   30

Once you have saved a search criteria, you can reuse it at will by
simply calling it up and running it against the current index.

Assumptions

- You have previously created and saved a search scheme.

Exceptions

- None.

Steps

1. Use **F**ile **Q**uickFinder... to display the QuickFinder dialog.
2. Click on **O**ptions to display the options list.
3. Choose **L**oad Search Query... to display the Load Search Query dialog.
4. Select a saved search from the list and click on **L**oad.
5. Click on **F**ind to start the search.

What To Do If

- If you need to modify the basic search you can do it from the QuickFinder dialog after you load the saved search.

See Also

- Saving a QuickFinder Search, p. 60.
- Establishing QuickFinder Search Options, p. 57.
- Creating a QuickFinder Index, p. 53.
- Managing QuickFinder Search Results, below.

31 | **Managing QuickFinder Search Results**

After you have conducted a search you have several options for manipulating the found data.

Assumptions

- You have completed a search and one or more files have been found that meet your search criteria. The Search Results list will look similar to the one in Figure 3.19.

Exceptions

- None.

Steps

1. Select a file from the list and click on View... to view the contents of the file. The words you specified in your search will be highlighted. You can use the mouse or cursor movement keys to step through the file list, viewing each file in succession.

2. Use File Options to display the file options list. Use these commands to copy a file, move it, rename it, change its attributes or print the file. You can also use the Print List... option to print the list of found files.

3. Use Sort Setup... to display the Search Results Sort Setup dialog, shown in Figure 3.20. Select options from the By: and Order: fields to adjust the sort order of the found files list.

> **TIP**
>
> Prior to printing the search results you can use the mouse to grab field titles at the top of the Search Results: list to move them around, changing the appearance of the report.

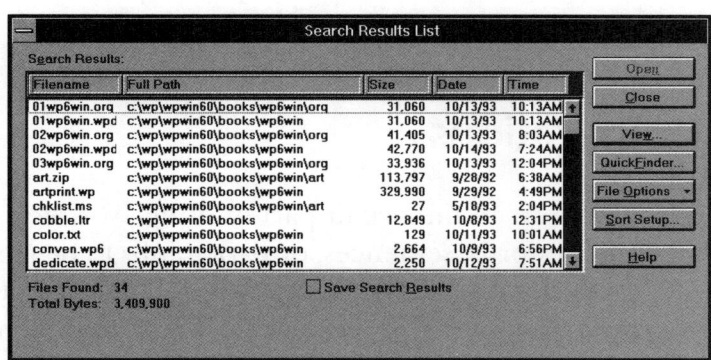

Figure 3.19   Sample Search Results list.

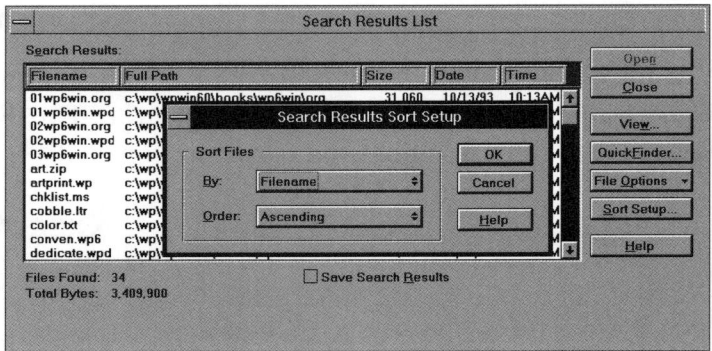

Figure 3.20   Search Results Sort Setup dialog.

What To Do If

- If you don't see a file you expected, click on **QuickFinder...** from the Search Results list screen to return to the QuickFinder dialog. Simply restructure the search as necessary (see the preceding steps) until you get the results you want.

See Also

- Saving a QuickFinder Search, p. 60.
- Establishing QuickFinder Search Options, p. 57.
- Creating a QuickFinder Index, p. 53.

Block Operations

Block operations are an important part of using WordPerfect. A block is a series of words, sentences, or paragraphs to be manipulated as a group. In WordPerfect, a block is defined by a reverse video screen that shows what information is included in the block. Blocked information within a document can be copied, deleted, moved, formatted, and so on. A block of text can be marked with the mouse or the keyboard.

We'll show you in this section how to mark blocks of WordPerfect information, then how to use these blocks in several ways.

Marking a Block 　32

Assumptions

- The document you want to mark is loaded and current.
- The area of text you want to mark is visible on the screen.

Exceptions

- None.

Steps

To mark a block with the mouse:

1. Position the mouse pointer at the beginning of the block.
2. Hold down the left mouse button.
3. Drag the highlight across the text, tables, and graphics you want to mark as a block.

   OR

1. Place the mouse pointer in the left margin of a sentence you want to mark.
2. Click three times. The first time you click, the mouse pointer is moved to the new location. The second click marks the word closest to the pointer and the third click marks the whole sentence that contains the word just marked.
3. Click again quickly to mark the entire paragraph.

> **TIP:**
> You can mark the paragraph adjacent to the mouse pointer with four rapid clicks: one to place the pointer, one to mark the word, one for the sentence, and one to mark the paragraph.

To use the keyboard:

1. Move the insertion point to the beginning of the block.
2. Hold down the **Shift** key.
3. Move the cursor with the arrow keys, marking the block as you go.

What To Do If

- If you wait too long to issue the last click, the marking is removed from the text. Simply start the process over again, or use the conventional method of holding down the left button and "painting" the section of the document you want to mark.

See Also

- Copying a Block, below.
- Moving Information, p. 67.

33 ▽ Copying a Block

Once you have a block of a document marked, you can do a number of things with it, including copying the block to another location within the same document or to another document. The copy process leaves the original material where it was and places a copy of it at the new location. When you copy a block in WordPerfect you use a feature of Windows called the Clipboard. This is a special section of memory that holds information from a document temporarily until you replace it with something else.

Assumptions

- The block of text you want to copy has been marked.

_____ **Exceptions**

- None.

_____ **Steps**

1. Select **E**dit and choose **C**opy (**Ctrl+C**).
2. Move the insertion point to the location in the current document (or another document, if you are copying the text to another file) where you want the copied text to appear.
3. Select **E**dit and choose **P**aste (**Ctrl+V**), or press **Shift+Ins**.

_____ **What To Do If**

- If the format of the block you copied is not what you want in the new location, select the new material and change the format as required. You can also try using Reveal Codes (**Alt+F3**) to display the moved formatting codes so you can delete them.

_____ **See Also**

- Moving Information, below.
- Marking a Block, p. 65.

> **TIP**
>
> When you copy a block of a document it looks as if nothing has happened. The block remains marked and nothing changes on the screen. What has happened is that the marked portion of your document has been copied to the Clipboard.

_____

Moving Information **34**

Moving data within a document or from one document to another is similar to copying information. Again, you use the block operation described above and move data temporarily to the Clipboard before copying it back to a new document location.

Assumptions

- The block of information you want to move has been marked.

Exceptions

- None.

TIP
When moving (or copying) text, the information remains in the Clipboard even after you have used **Edit Paste** to place it in a new location. So, if you want to make multiple copies of the data, simply reposition the insertion point and use **Edit Paste** (**Ctrl+V**) to copy it to a second location. You can do this as often as you like to place multiple copies of the same information into the same or different documents.

Steps

1. Select **E**dit and choose **C**ut (**Ctrl+X**).
2. Move the insertion point to the location in the current document (or another document, if you are copying the text to another file) where you want the copied text to appear.
3. Select **E**dit and choose **P**aste (**Ctrl+V**), or press **Shift+Ins**.

What To Do If

- Use Reveal Codes (**Alt+F3**) to display formatting codes for the new block to delete any unwanted codes.
- If you change your mind about moving the block after you have cut the block but before you have pasted it to the new location, use **Edit U**ndo (**Ctrl+Z**) to put the block back where it was.
- If you change your mind about moving the block after you have pasted it to a new location, mark the block in its new location and press **Del** to delete it at the new location. Reposition the insertion point to the original location and use **Edit P**aste (**Ctrl+V**) or **Shift+Ins** to restore the original block.

See Also

- Copying a Block, p. 66.
- Marking a Block, p. 65.

Paragraph Formatting

Much of the document formatting you do in your work with WordPerfect is paragraph-oriented. This includes the spacing automatically placed between paragraphs, borders and shading, indenting, and more. We will show you how to conduct each of these paragraph formatting procedures in this section.

Paragraph—Indenting First Line   35

One manuscript style dictates that the first line of each new paragraph will be indented. You can easily press the tab key each time you start a new paragraph, of course, but if you want every paragraph to start with an indented line, it is easier to format it that way in the first place.

Assumptions

- The insertion point is located where you want the new paragraph formatting to take effect.

Exceptions

- None.

Steps

1. Use **L**ayout **P**aragraph **F**ormat... to display the Paragraph Format dialog shown in Figure 3.21.

2. Click on the up arrow beside the First Line Indent: field, or click anywhere inside the field to enter the amount of first line indent you want. If you want to emulate a standard tab indent, select 0.5," which is the standard tab spacing.

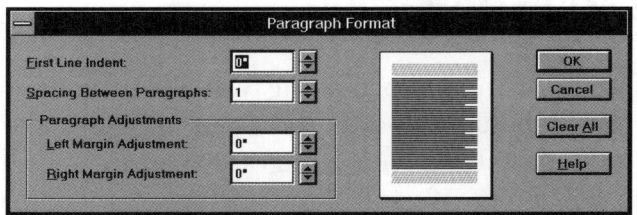

Figure 3.21   Paragraph Format dialog.

3.   Click on **OK** to make the change effective and return to your document.

What To Do If

- If the first line indent doesn't take effect where you want it, use Reveal Codes to locate the indent code. Delete it, reposition the insertion point, and go through the steps again to reset the first line indent code.

See Also

- Paragraph—Spacing Between Paragraphs, below.
- Paragraph—Adjusting Margins, p. 72.

36   Paragraph—Spacing Between Paragraphs

If you learned to type on a typewriter instead of a computer, you're probably used to pressing Return twice to put a blank line between paragraphs. You don't have to do this with WordPerfect; the software puts in the extra line for you, if you tell it to. Moreover, you don't want to do it yourself, for a couple of reasons. For one thing, you save a lot of keystrokes if you let WordPerfect handle between-paragraph spacing for you. You save one press of the Return key with each paragraph in your document. But in addition to that, it is better to set up an automatic paragraph spacing because when, or if, you send your document to someone else to manipulate it in a page layout package such as PageMaker or Quark, it is a lot easier to manage if there are few hard codes in the document.

_____ **Assumptions**

- The insertion point is positioned where you want the paragraph formatting change to occur.

_____ **Exceptions**

- None.

_____ **Steps**

1. Use **L**ayout **P**aragraph **F**ormat... to display the Paragraph Format dialog shown in Figure 3.21.
2. Click on the up-facing arrow to the right of the Spacing Between Paragraphs: field to change the default value of zero. You can also click in the field to select it and then enter a value directly from the keyboard. The default is 1 line. Change this to 1.5 lines for a slightly wider space than normal, or to 2.0 to set double-space paragraph spacing.

> **TIP**
> If you're careful not to compress things too much, you can reduce the spacing to less than 1 line. This can be useful to force a long document to fit on a page, or simply to give your document a closed-up appearance. If you set this value too low, however, the text will become difficult to read.

_____ **What To Do If**

- If you accidently set the incorrect paragraph spacing, simply place the insertion point anywhere within the paragraph where you changed the spacing before and reissue the **L**ayout **P**aragraph **F**ormat command and enter the correct value. The new setting will overlay the old setting.

_____ **See Also**

- Paragraph—Indenting First Line, p. 69.
- Paragraph—Adjusting Margins, p. 72.

Paragraph—Adjusting Margins

Normally when you set margins you want the settings to apply for the entire document. At times when you want to offset the left or right margins, or both, within one or a few paragraphs, you can use the margin adjust features of WordPerfect's paragraph formatting.

Assumptions

- The insertion point is within the paragraph for which you want to adjust margins. Use the mouse to select several adjacent paragraphs for change.

Exceptions

- This procedure is generally for a small segment of a document, a few paragraphs at most. For longer segments, use the Layout Margins command.

Steps

1. Use **L**ayout **P**aragraph **F**ormat... to display the Paragraph Format dialog.
2. Enter values for left and right indents in the Paragraph Adjustments section of this dialog.
3. Click on **OK** to make the changes effective.

What To Do If

- Adjust the additional margins you have set by simply repeating the steps above with the insertion point positioned anywhere within the same paragraph. Any new settings you enter will replace the original ones.

_____ **See Also**

- Adjusting Margins, p. 17.
- Paragraph—Spacing Between Paragraphs, p. 70.

| Paragraph—Borders and Shading | **38** |

WordPerfect includes a number of features to help you emphasize paragraphs or other blocks of data. Among the things you can do to enhance the appearance of text is to place a border around it and place some type of shading behind the text. These features are set at the paragraph level in WordPerfect.

_____ **Assumptions**

- The insertion point is located within the paragraph you want to border or shade, or you have selected multiple paragraphs for border and shading.

_____ **Exceptions**

- This procedure is best used on text material. You can treat a graphics image as a paragraph and use shading or borders with it, but there are other techniques for emphasizing graphics material (see Chapter 6).

_____ **Steps**

1. Use **L**ayout **P**aragraph **B**order/Fill... to display the Paragraph Border dialog shown in Figure 3.22.

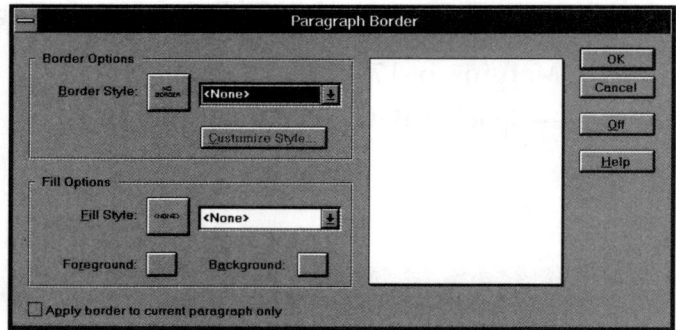

Figure 3.22   Layout Paragraph Border/Fill (Paragraph Border) dialog.

2. Click in the **B**order Style: field to pull down the Border Type menu shown in Figure 3.23. Select the type of border you want from this list.

3. Click in the **F**ill Style: field to pull down the shading options list. Choose a shading value from the list. Notice the sample window shows you how the portion of your document formatted this way will appear.

4. Click on **OK** to finish the paragraph formatting.

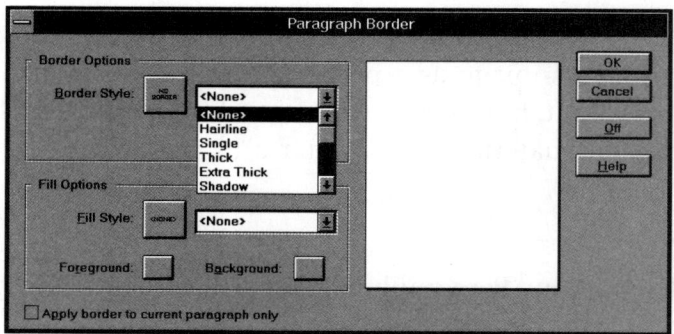

Figure 3.23   Paragraph border type pull-down list.

What To Do If

- To change a border or shading specification, simply place the insertion point inside the paragraph you want to change, reissue the **L**ayout **P**aragraph **B**order/Fill... command, and make any desired changes. The new settings will replace the original ones.

See Also

- Paragraph—Bulleted Lists, p. 79.
- Paragraph—Setting Indents, below.

Paragraph—Setting Indents   39

Use Indent to move an entire paragraph one tab stop to the right, beginning where the indent command is inserted (see Task 11 for illustrations).

Think of an indent as a temporary left margin. When you press Tab, the line of text from the insertion point onward is moved to the right to the next established tab stop. Subsequent lines of text revert to the left margin. An indent code, on the other hand, moves the line of text to the right to the next established tab stop, but subsequent lines of text follow this new margin until a hard return is entered.

Indents are useful for emphasizing a block of text, and for constructing bulleted lists or hanging indents (see the following sections on hanging indents and bulleted lists).

Assumptions

- The insertion point is located where you want the indent to take effect.

Exceptions

- In WordPerfect the indent code is inserted at the location of the insertion point, not at the beginning of the paragraph. Make sure you have placed the insertion point where you want the indent to begin before issuing the Indent command.

Steps

- Use **Layout Paragraph Indent (F7)** to insert an indent code.

What To Do If

- If you misplace an indent, simply position the insertion point at the first character in the indented text and press Backspace to erase the code.

See Also

- Paragraph—Bulleted Lists, p. 79.
- Paragraph—Hanging Indents, below.
- Setting Paragraph Indents, p. 18.

40 ⌄ Paragraph—Hanging Indents

A hanging indent is a block of text where the first line starts one tab stop to the left of the body of the text. The hanging indent code actually is two codes, an indent code followed by a back tab. Use the back tab by itself to back up a line of text one tab stop. (We show you how to use the back tab code on page 78.)

Assumptions

- The insertion point is positioned where you want the hanging indent code inserted.

Exceptions

• The hanging indent takes effect at the insertion point. If you want the hanging indent to start at the beginning of the paragraph, make sure the insertion point is at the beginning of the first line of the paragraph before you give the Hanging Indent command.

Steps

• Use **L**ayout **P**aragraph **H**anging Indent (**Ctrl+F7**) to insert the hanging indent code.

What To Do If

• A misplaced hanging indent code is easily replaced. Simply position the insertion point to the left of the first character in the hanging indent group and press **Backspace** twice to remove both the back tab and the indent codes.

See Also

• Paragraph—Setting Indents, p. 75.
• Paragraph—Double Indent, below.

> **TIP**
> You can create a hanging indent for existing text, or you can position the insertion point and insert the hanging indent code before you start typing text.

Paragraph—Double Indent   41

As the name implies, double indent involves inserting two indent codes, but it doesn't result in a left-margin indent two tab stops over. Rather it produces a paragraph indented one tab stop from the right margin as well as from the left. Use the double indent to offset a paragraph for emphasis, such as when you want to present a lengthy quote within a document.

Assumptions

- The insertion point is positioned within the paragraph you want to format with double indent.

Exceptions

- The double indent takes effect at the location of the insertion point. If you position the insertion point in the middle of a paragraph, only the portion of the paragraph after that location will be formatted with double indent. To format the entire paragraph with double indents, position the insertion point at the beginning of the first line in the paragraph.

Steps

- Use **Layout Paragraph Double Indent** (**Ctrl+Shift+F7**) to insert the double indent code.

What To Do If

- You can remove a misplaced double indent code easily by positioning the insertion point to the left of the first character in the indent block and pressing **Backspace** to erase the code.

See Also

- Paragraph—Setting Indents, p. 75.
- Paragraph—Hanging Indents, p. 76.

42 Paragraph—Back Tab

Use Back Tab to move the insertion point to the left to the next tab stop. If the insertion point is already at the left margin, then

Back Tab positions the insertion point left one tab position into the margin.

Assumptions

- The insertion point is positioned where you want the back tab code inserted.

Exceptions

- The back tab code takes effect at the location of the insertion point. If you want a back tab at the beginning of a paragraph you must position the insertion point at that location.

Steps

- Use **L**ayout **P**aragraph Back **T**ab to insert the back tab code.

What To Do If

- To remove a misplaced back tab code, position the insertion point to the left of the first character after the back tab code and press **Backspace** to erase it. Use Reveal Codes if necessary to help you locate the embedded code.

See Also

- Paragraph—Setting Indents, p. 75.
- Paragraph—Hanging Indents, p. 76.
- Paragraph—Double Indent, p. 77.

Paragraph—Bulleted Lists 43

A bulleted list is a good way to present a series of ideas in a manner that makes it easy to pick them out. A bulleted list consists of a "bullet" character and a hanging indent code combination. The bullet traditionally is a small- to medium-sized round dot; however, you can use any character as a bullet. A heart, for example, could be used for a Valentines Day list or promotion, or you could use a small graphic of a car when generating a list of automobile-related information.

There are three ways to construct a bulleted paragraph: (1) Use the bullet list icon on the tool bar, (2) use the Insert menu to place one of the standard bullets, or (3) use **Ctrl+Shift+B.** In addition, you can construct your own bullet list by combining a hanging indent with your own graphics symbol to serve as a bullet.

Assumptions

- The insertion point is located within the paragraph where you want the bullet and hanging indent to appear.

Exceptions

- The bullet list codes are inserted at the beginning of the current paragraph, not at the location of the insertion point.

Steps

TIP

If you want to type a bullet list from the keyboard, click on **cc** on this dialog and a new bullet and indent code will be inserted at the beginning of the next line each time you press **Return.**

Using the Insert menu:

1. Use **I**nsert Bullets & **N**umbers... to display the dialog shown in Figure 3.24. You can also click on the bullet list icon on the tool bar to display this same dialog.

2. Select the type of bullet you want to insert. The standard choices are small circle, large circle, diamond, square, and triangle.

3. Click on **OK** to insert the bullet code, which consists of a paragraph format code and a bullet character code. You can see a sample bullet code in Reveal Codes (**Alt+F3**) in Figure 3.25.

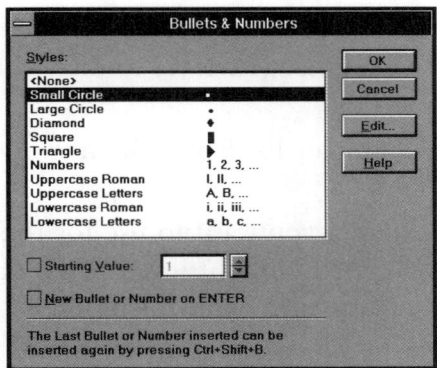

Figure 3.24   Bullets & Numbers dialog.

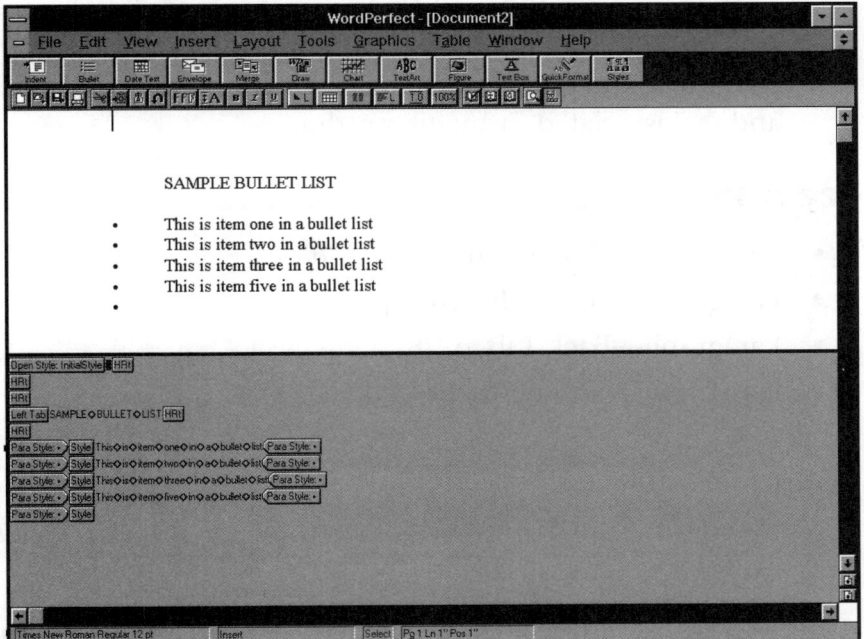

Figure 3.25   Sample bullet list in Reveal Codes.

TIP

You can double-click on the type of list you want to build, bypassing the need to click on OK to insert the code. You can also use the **Ctrl+Shift+B** to repeat the last bullet command.

Custom Bullet List:

1. Use Insert Character (**Ctrl+W**) to display the WordPerfect Characters dialog.

2. Select the character list from which you want to choose a character.

3. Select a character you want to use for the bullet and double-click on it, or highlight it and click on Insert to place the special character in your document.

4. Use Layout Paragraph Indent to insert an indent code after the bullet character.

5. Type the text you want to include in the bulleted list.

What To Do If

- You can remove a misplaced bullet code with the Backspace or Del keys, even if Reveal Codes is turned off. Simply position the insertion point beside the bullet character in your document and press **Backspace** or **Del** to remove the bullet and the associated formatting codes.

See Also

- Paragraph—Hanging Indents, p. 76.
- Paragraph—Setting Indents, p. 75.
- Paragraph—Back Tab, p. 78.
- Paragraph—Numbered Lists, below.

44 Paragraph—Numbered Lists

A numbered list is similar to a bulleted list, and a little like an outline. The numbered list inserts a sequential number at the head of paragraphs, then adds an indent code, like a bullet. Use numbered lists in conjunction with or instead of bulleted lists to add emphasis to your lists of information.

_____ **Assumptions**

- The insertion point is positioned where you want the numbered list to appear.

_____ **Exceptions**

- None.

_____ **Steps**

1. Use **I**nsert Bullets & **N**umbers... to display the Bullets & Numbers dialog shown in Figure 3.26.

2. Choose the type of numbers you want to insert. You can select from regular numbers, Uppercase Roman Numerals, Uppercase Alphabet, Lowercase Alphabet, and Lowercase Roman Numerals.

3. To specify the first number in the current list, click on Starting **V**alue: on this dialog, then enter a value in the

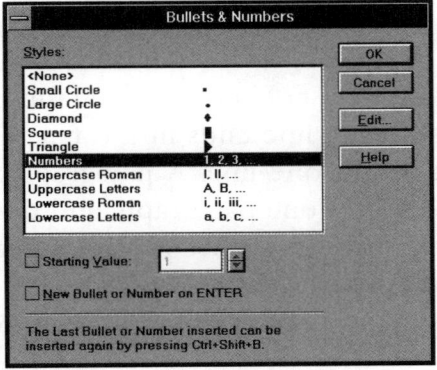

Figure 3.26 Bullets & Numbers dialog.

box beside this field (or click on the up and down arrows beside this box to select a value).

4. Click on OK to accept the changes and insert a number into your document.

What To Do If

- If you are building a numbered list and decide to add a line between two existing numbers, you can do so easily. Simply position the insertion point to the left of the lower number, press **Enter** twice, then press **Ctrl+Shift+B** to insert a number. The numbers in the list after the new inserted number will automatically update so the numbering sequence is correct.

See Also

- Paragraph—Bulleted Lists, p. 79.
- Paragraph—Setting Indents, p. 75.
- Paragraph—Hanging Indents, p. 76.

45 Sorting a List

WordPerfect's sorting ability is strong. You can sort information in a table, or a simple list of items, or even full paragraphs. A line sort assumes that each line ends in a carriage return and each record consists of just one line. A paragraph sort assumes that each record consists of one paragraph, and that each paragraph ends in a double carriage return. A Merge Record sort assumes each record ends in an {END RECORD} merge code and a Table Row sort can be done only on information inside a WordPerfect table.

Assumptions

- You have previously entered information you want to sort.

Exceptions

- If you are sorting paragraphs, they must be separated by a double carriage return (two hard lines).
- Make sure to save the current file before attempting a sort. That way if the results are not what you want, it is easy to load the original file and start over.

Steps

1. Use the mouse or cursor keys to mark (select) the block of text you want to sort.
2. Use **T**ools **S**ort... **(Alt+F9)** to display the Sort dialog shown in Figure 3.27.

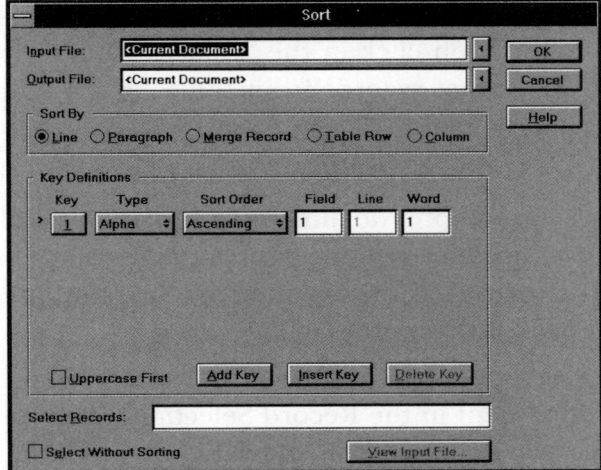

Figure 3.27   Sort dialog (Tools Sort...).

TIP

The key field specifies where the sort should begin on the line. Fields are separated by tabs or indents on a line of text. If you are doing a paragraph sort that uses the first line as the key, for example, and each paragraph has an indented first line, then the sort would begin in Field 2, not Field 1. The tab at the beginning of the line creates a second field on that line.

3. Specify the source and destination files. For most sorts you probably will use the current document for both, but you can sort a file on disk and copy the sorted version to a second file, if you wish. Or you can use the current document as the source, but place the sorted version in another file on disk.

4. Specify the type of sort: line, paragraph, merge record, table row, column.

5. Specify the sort key in the next part of this dialog. A sort key tells WordPerfect how to sort the information: numeric or alphanumeric sort, ascending or descending sort, which word in which field on which line of each record serves as the key.

6. Add or insert a key for additional levels of sorting, if you wish. WordPerfect displays only a single key by default, but you can specify up to nine keys if necessary. For example, you might want to sort a company list first by city or zip code, then by product type, and finally by company name. To do this would require three different key definitions.

7. Specify record selection in the last field on this dialog, if you wish. If you click in the "Select without sorting" box, you can extract records from the source document without sorting them.

8. Click on **OK** or press **Enter** to start the sort process.

9. If you have a long document with many records and you want to produce a document that contains only certain records extracted during the sort, use the Record Selection: field at the bottom of this dialog.

10. To select specific records you must enter a record selection statement in the Record Selection: field. WordPerfect selects records based on the value of specified keys. Keys are identified by the term KEY#, where # is a number from 1 to 9. To specify a selection based on key 1, for example, use the term KEY1. To select by comparing values in key 2, use KEY2, and so on.

11. Use standard computer compare symbols to design a record selection statement. Use an equals sign (=) to specify a value that is the same as another, for example, and use the plus symbol (+) for the logical OR and the asterisk (*) for the logical AND. The comparison symbols you can use in record selection are shown in Table 3.1.

For example, you could tell WordPerfect to extract only those records that contain the city name "Knoxville" and the business type "Publishing." Assuming the city name is in field 3 and the business type in field 6, the Record Selection statement would look like this:

KEY3=Knoxville * KEY6=Publishing

To find *any* company in Knoxville and *any* company with a business type of publishing, use this selection statement:

KEY3=Knoxville + KEY6=Publishing

When you complete a sort that includes record selection criteria, the resulting document contains only the records that meet the selection criteria. You should always back up a file—or at least make double sure you have stored it to disk—before conducting

Table 3.1	Record Selection Compare Symbols
Symbol	Description
+	OR
*	AND
=	Exactly the same as
<>	Not equal to
>	Greater than
<	Less than
>=	Greater than or equal to
<=	Less than or equal to

a sort. When you extract records, it is especially important to save the original document, because after the sort you won't have all of the records you started with.

What To Do If

- If you have trouble with a paragraph sort you probably have forgotten to place double carriage returns between paragraphs. A series of paragraphs that are not double-spaced (have one blank line between paragraphs) will not sort properly.

- If you don't get the results you expected, use **E**dit **U**ndo to reverse the sort operation. Just make sure you haven't entered any other commands since the sort was completed.

See Also

- Marking a Block, p. 65.

46 Setting Tabs

Tabs are "set" or specified in WordPerfect at any interval you wish so that each time you press the Tab key on the keyboard the insertion point jumps to a predefined location.

A tab is a specific amount of space within a document. With a typewriter, a tab is generally assumed to be the equivalent of five spaces. In electronic word processing, however, the tab is usually measured in inches or centimeters to account for proportionally spaced characters. In a proportional typeface, each character doesn't require as much space on the page as every other character, so setting a tab at five "spaces" is inaccurate and would cause variations in how text lined up on a page.

By default, WordPerfect is installed with tabs installed at half-inch intervals across the page. You can see these tab symbols on the ruler bar when it is displayed.

You can change the position of any of these preset tabs simply by dragging them along the horizontal bar to a new location.

Add tabs to the ruler by dragging a copy of the appropriate tab symbol from the icon and button bar above the ruler. To remove a tab, drag its symbol off of the ruler.

You don't have to use the ruler to set tabs, of course, but this is definitely the easiest way to do it.

Assumptions

- The ruler bar is displayed.
- The insertion point is located where you want the change in tab settings to take place.

Exceptions

- To set tabs without the ruler, use **L**ayout **L**ine **T**ab Set... to display the dialog in Figure 3.28.

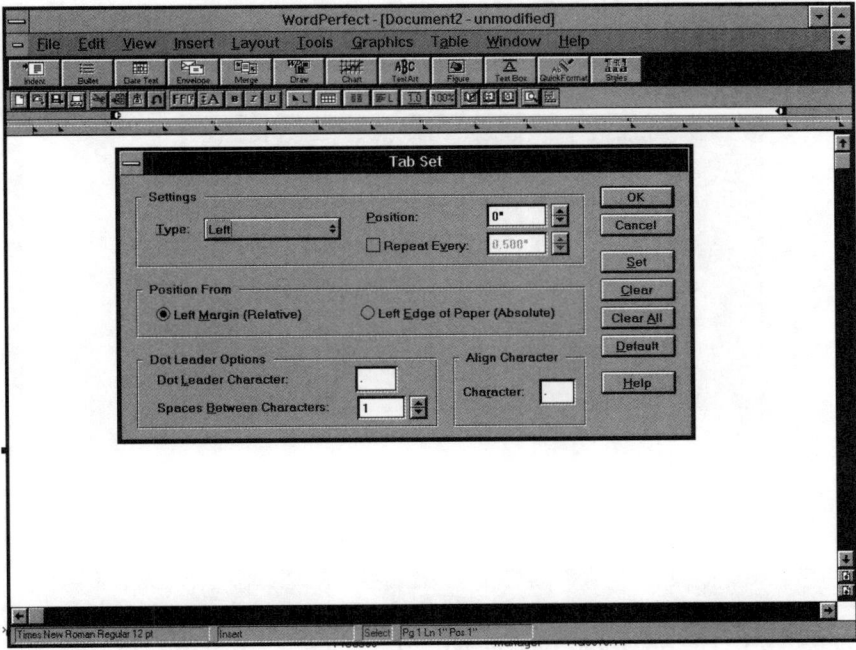

Figure 3.28   Layout Line Tab Set... dialog.

Steps

1. Click on the tab symbol on the power bar and hold down the left mouse button to pull down the menu shown in Figure 3.29.

2. Move the mouse up and down the list and release the left button when you have selected the type of tab you want to insert.

3. Click on the ruler bar where you want a new tab inserted.

4. Drag the symbol onto the ruler where you want a new tab to appear.

5. To change the location of a tab symbol already on the ruler, drag it from where it is to where you want it to be. A dotted line appears on the document to show you where the tab will be set (see Figure 3.30).

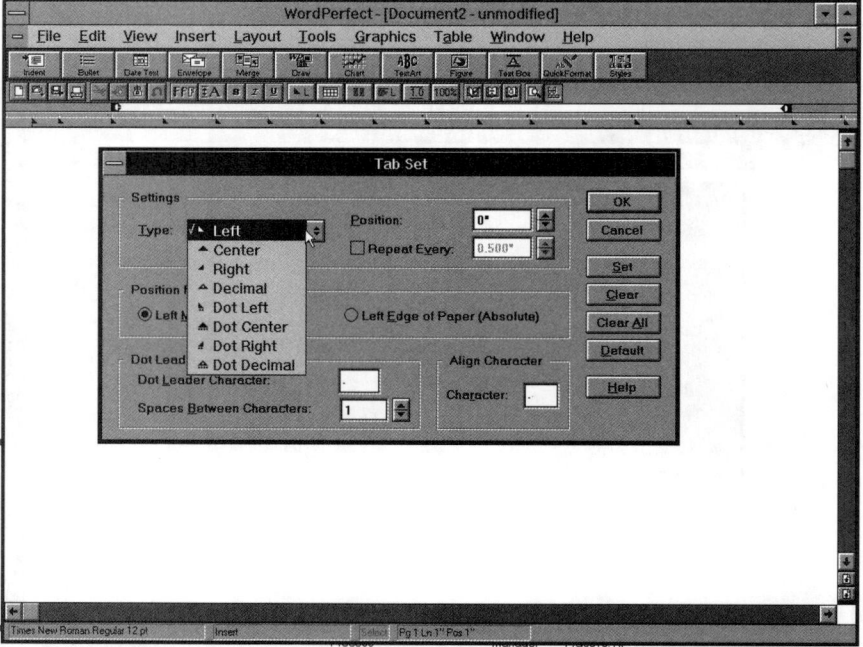

Figure 3.29 Pull-down Tab Type menu.

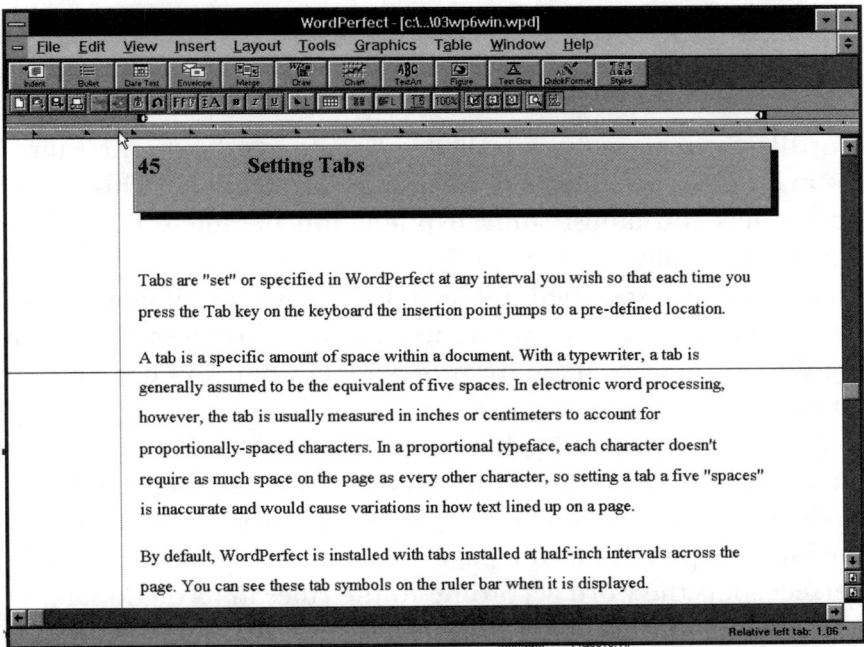

Figure 3.30 **Dragging a tab symbol on the ruler with dotted line.**

6. To remove an existing tab, drag it off of the ruler bar.

_____ **What To Do If**

- If the wrong type of tab is set, it means you had the wrong tab type selected on the power bar. Go back to step 1.
- If you try to move a tab already placed on the ruler bar but the tab type set on the power bar is different from the type you are moving, you will set a new tab instead of moving an existing tab. Set the tab type to be the same as the tab you are moving first.

_____ **See Also**

- Adjusting Margins, p. 17.

47 / Hyphenation

WordPerfect can automatically hyphenate words when required to maintain specified margins and justification. This menu option lets you adjust some hyphenation parameters. Hyphenation is normally off in WordPerfect, because you don't need it unless you have specified full or right justification. When you use proportional fonts with these justifications, however, the resulting document appears more professional when you use hyphenation.

WordPerfect uses a hyphenation dictionary to know where to place hyphens. And the "Hyphenation Zone" settings tell Word-Perfect when to hyphenate a word. When a word near the end of the line completely fills the page area defined by this zone, Word-Perfect splits the word according to the rules in its dictionary.

The left and right hyphenation zones are measured relative to the right margin. The left zone is measured from the margin toward the left edge of the page and the right zone is measured from the margin toward the right edge of the page.

A word is wrapped to the next line if it starts inside the left zone, even if it extends over the right zone. However, if a word begins to the left of the left zone, extends through the hyphenation zone, and crosses the right zone, the word is hyphenated.

The smaller the hyphenation zone, the more words are likely to be hyphenated; the wider this zone, the fewer words are likely to be hyphenated. The width of the zone is measured from the left zone margin to the right zone margin.

Assumptions

- The insertion point is located where you want the hyphenation change to take effect.

Exceptions

- None.

Steps

1. Use **L**ayout **L**ine Hyphenation... to display the Hyphenation dialog shown in Figure 3.31.
2. Specify the left and right hyphenation zone or accept WordPerfect's defaults.
3. Toggle Hyphenation on.
4. Click on **OK** to exit the dialog.

What To Do If

- Use Reveal Codes to locate the hyphenation code if you want to remove an existing code. This is actually two codes, one to turn hyphenation on (Hyphen on) and the other to specify what type of hyphenation to enable (Style). Remove both of these codes and repeat the preceding steps 1 to 4 to correct hyphenation settings.

See Also

- Using the Spell Checker, p. 130.
- Setting Language, p. 140.

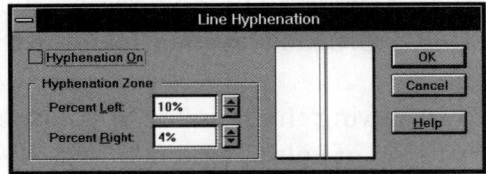

Figure 3.31   Hyphenation... dialog.

48 Using Columns

A graphics-oriented product such as WordPerfect for Windows offers distinct advantages when you begin using special page formatting such as graphics images within a document and fonts and columns. In fact, WordPerfect for Windows now gives you support for on-screen column management that is much easier and more intuitive than any previous release of this product.

There are two steps to using columns in WordPerfect: defining the column structure, then turning columns on. The text in your document from the code to the end will be displayed in columns until you issue a Columns Off code.

Multicolumn pages can add a level of professionalism and reader interest that can be valuable additions to your message and its presentation. Many word processors have handled columns in the past, but until they started using graphics screens so that you could see on the screen what the final printout looks like, it was usually very difficult to work with columns.

Generally you can accept the WordPerfect defaults for columns, specifying only the number of columns you want on a page. The default for the number of columns is 2, but you can specify 3 or 4 on a standard 8 ½ × 11-inch page and get fairly satisfactory results.

The Define Columns dialog will accept up to 24 columns on a page but, obviously, that many columns on a standard sheet of paper would not be practical. The only reason such broad limits are even supported is probably to plan for future hardware and software capability.

In addition to specifying the number of columns, you can tell WordPerfect what type of columns to use. When you are designing a newsletter or multicolumn pages for a long report, you probably will accept the default of newspaper-style pages. This column style is sometimes called "snaking" columns, which means that the text starts in the left column and when the bottom of the page is reached, the text starts again at the top of the next column. If more than two columns appear on a page, the process is repeated until the end of the page is reached. Then the text appears in the first column on the next page, and so on. Figure 3.32 shows a typical newspaper column page layout.

WordPerfect also offers a newspaper column style called "Balanced," which places the columns on the page so that all columns are the same length.

You can also use columns to print lists of information that should stay together, such as inventory and price information, company names and addresses, book titles and descriptions, and the like. For this application, select parallel columns on the Column Define dialog.

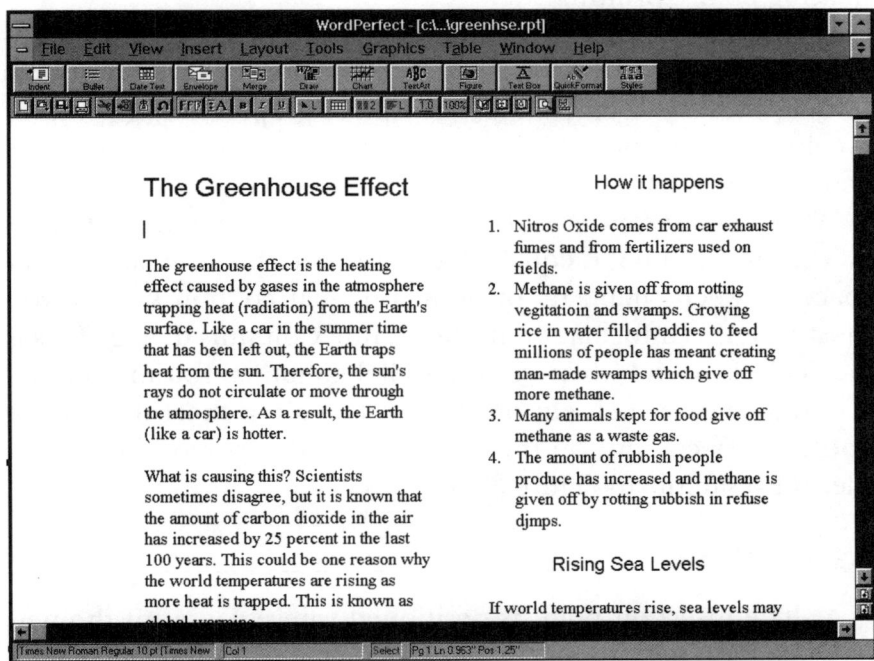

Figure 3.32 Typical newspaper column page layout.

If the parallel columns include information of unequal length—a left column with one line and a matched right column with three lines, as when you have a book or other item in the left column and a description in the right—use Parallel with Block Protect mode. This mode tells WordPerfect not to separate information in the parallel columns even if at the end of the page, the left-column data will fit on the page and the right column information won't. Instead, both columns of information are moved to the next page to keep the parallel data together.

You can either establish the multiple columns and then enter text, or type the text first and then turn on multicolumn display. This is the easiest way of working with columns. Although WordPerfect does a good job of displaying information in multiple columns on the screen, this type of graphics display slows down screen updates considerably. It is easier to work with the full page width, then turn on columns and do only fine-tuning of the formatting before printing.

Once you get data into columns, you can use most of the usual WordPerfect formatting features, including right or full justification, fonts, and so on. You also can place graphics images within a column or in the middle of two columns so the image spans across two columns.

When you accept WordPerfect defaults in defining columns, all columns will be of equal width and have the same amount of space between them. If you want unequal column widths, you must type this information in the Define Columns dialog. This is particularly useful when using parallel columns. You may want a relatively narrow column on the left to hold a short item name and a wider column on the right for the description, for example. See a sample in Figure 3.33.

Assumptions

- The insertion point is positioned where you want the new column definition to take effect.

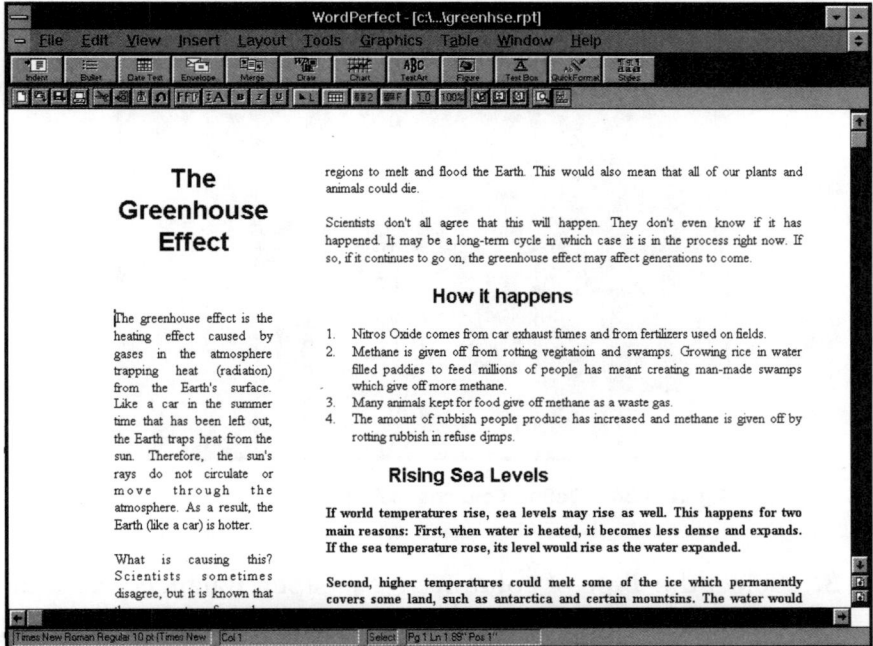

Figure 3.33 Two-column layout: narrow on left and wide on right.

Exceptions

- Column definitions are paragraph-oriented. When you enter a column definition and column on command, the changes take effect at the beginning of the current paragraph and remain in effect until you turn off columns or change the column definition.

Steps

1. Use **L**ayout **C**olumns Define... to display the Columns dialog shown in Figure 3.34.
2. Enter the number of columns you want in the Number of **C**olumns: field.

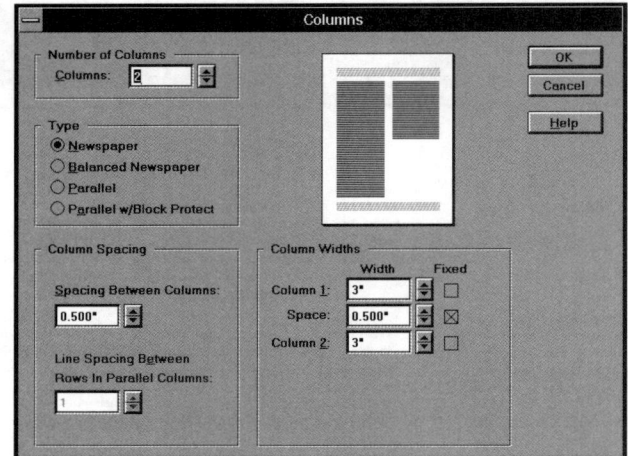

Figure 3.34   Define Columns dialog.

3. Select the Type of columns: **N**ewspaper, **B**alanced Newspaper, **P**arallel, or **P**arallel with **B**lock Protect.

4. Change Column Spacing settings if you don't want to accept WordPerfect's defaults.

5. Change Column Width settings if you don't want to accept WordPerfect's defaults.

6. Click on **OK** or press **Enter** to accept the changes.

What To Do If

- You can change a column definition by simply repeating steps 1 to 6. The new definition will replace the existing one.

- Once you have defined columns you can move the insertion point from column to column by simply clicking in the column you want to use, or by pressing **Ctrl+G** and making a selection from the dialog box that is displayed. You can also use these keystroke combinations:

Alt+Home	Top of current column
Alt+End	Bottom of current column

| Alt+Left Arrow | To the previous column (to the left) |
| Alt+Right Arrow | To the next column (to the right) |

See Also

- Using Vertical Lines, p. 194.
- Setting Column Borders and Fill, below.
- Creating Tables, p. 126.

Setting Column Borders and Fill ◣ 49

Once you have set a column format, you can set borders and shading for the columns just as you can for individual paragraphs. The column shading and borders settings transcend paragraphs and apply to the current columns.

Assumptions

- You have previously defined multiple columns and turned on columns.
- The insertion point is positioned within the columns you want to border or shade.

Exceptions

- The borders and fill (shading) used in this procedure applies to all columns. If you have a three-column definition, for example, and place the insertion point at the beginning of the first column, when you turn on a border or shading, all three columns will carry the border or shading attribute.

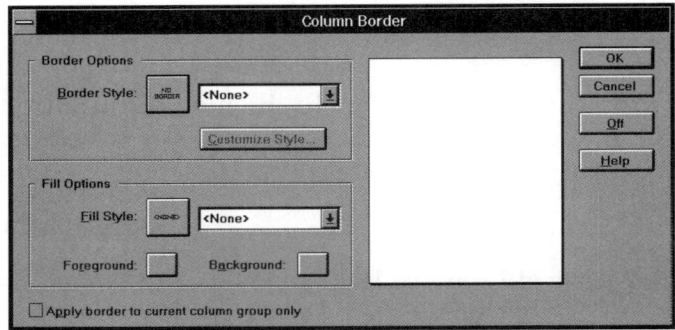

Figure 3.35   Column Border dialog.

Steps

1. Use **L**ayout **C**olumns **B**order/Fill... to display the Column Border dialog shown in Figure 3.35.

2. Pull down the Border Type menu by clicking on the down arrow beside the Border Style: field.

3. Click on one of the border types in the list to select it.

4. Pull down the Fill Type List menu by clicking on the down arrow to the right of the Fill Style: field.

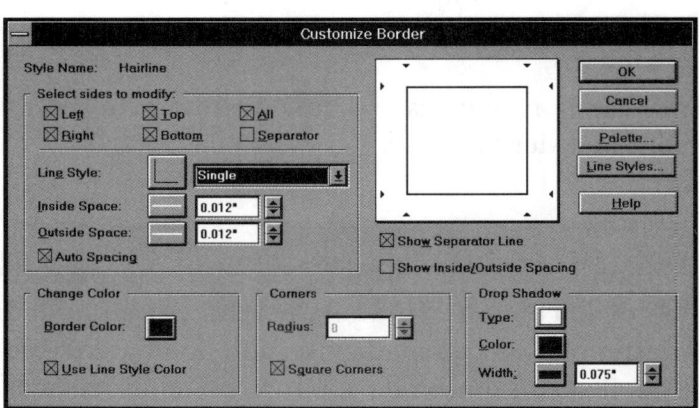

Figure 3.36   Column Border Customize dialog.

5. Click on one of the fill types in the list to select it.

6. Click on **OK** to set the column border and fill options.

_____ **What To Do If**

- You can remove a border and shading combination easily. Place the insertion point within the shaded or bordered area you want to clear, use **L**ayout **C**olumns **B**order/Fill and click on **O**ff on the Border/Fill dialog.

_____ **See Also**

- Paragraph—Borders and Shading, p. 73.
- Using Columns, p. 94.

> **TIP**
> To place vertical lines (rules) between columns, choose "Column Between" from the pull-down Border Style list on the Column Border dialog.

Using Outlining

When you turn on Outlining in a WordPerfect document, a paragraph style code and an outlining style code are placed in the document at the beginning of the current paragraph. From that point on, until an outline off code is inserted or you move into another existing paragraph, you are operating in Outline mode, even if you close the Outline tool bar that appears when you turn on outlining.

When WordPerfect encounters a hard return, an auto paragraph number code is inserted in the document. The level of this number changes with the left-to-right position of the insertion point.

As you create an outline in WordPerfect you can turn on Outline mode and have the program automatically insert the proper outline level symbols as you use Tab to indent the text. To use this automatic outlining feature, press hard return at the end of each line that ends a level entry. WordPerfect inserts a paragraph number code at the beginning of the new line. If the next line of the outline is for the highest level (I, II, III, and so on), just start typing. To write a line at the next outline level (A, B, C, etc.), press **Tab** once. For the third level, press **Tab** twice, and so on. You can have up to eight outline levels.

50 ◢ Turning on Outlining

The first step in using outline in WordPerfect is to turn on the Outline feature bar. Then you have control of several outlining features.

Assumptions

- The insertion point is positioned where you want outlining to begin.
- You are creating an outline with new text, not existing text.

Exceptions

- When you first open the Outline feature bar to turn on outlining, WordPerfect assumes you want to number paragraphs. To turn on Outline mode, pull down the menu list in the type field to the left of the Close button and choose **Outline**.
- You can place an outline code at the beginning of existing text by turning on outlining and then clicking on the "Previous Level" arrow at the left of the Outline feature bar. A top-level code will be inserted, and you can create additional outline numbers by entering a carriage return anywhere within the current paragraph.

> **TIP**
>
> Pressing Tab in Outline mode moves the text to the right one tab stop, but it also increments the outline level. To insert a tab in outline text, use Layout Paragraph Indent (**F7**) or press **Ctrl+Tab**. To insert a back tab in an outline, press **Ctrl+Shift+Tab**.

_____ **Steps**

1. Use **T**ools **O**utline to turn on the Outline feature bar shown in Figure 3.37.

2. Type the new text you want for this outline entry.

3. Press Carriage Return **(Enter)** to move to the next line and to increment the outline number by one.

4. Remove the Outline feature bar by clicking on **C**lose at the right side of the bar.

_____ **What To Do If**

*   During outline entry, if you mistakenly move the outline level too far to the right, don't use Backspace to back up. If you do, you will erase the paragraph number code for that line. Instead, press back tab **(Shift+Tab)**. The back tab code is not actually inserted in the document; WordPerfect uses this keystroke combination to recognize a request to back up the outline one level.

*   The paragraph number codes that produce the various outline levels are hidden codes that you can view with Reveal Codes, however you can delete them by pressing Backspace. If you delete a paragraph numbering code, the outline identifier on that line disappears. To correct the problem, use Backspace repeatedly until that blank line disappears, press Enter again, and the paragraph number code should be reinserted on that line.

Figure 3.37 Outline feature bar display.

See Also

- Defining Outlines, below.
- Paragraph—Bulleted Lists, p. 79.
- Paragraph—Numbered Lists, p. 82.

51 ▼ Defining Outlines

When you first turn on the Outline feature bar, certain WordPerfect outlining defaults are selected. For example, WordPerfect assumes you want to use paragraph numbering. You can see that by the "Paragraph" notation in the Number Type: field at the right-hand side of this feature bar. In addition, all levels of the outline will be displayed, and the next paragraph number will be the next one in sequence based on the last number entered (if any). You can change these defaults from the Outline feature bar.

Assumptions

- The insertion point is positioned where you want the new outline definitions to take effect.

Exceptions

- The configuration options described in this section affect all of the current document that is set in Outline mode, unless you have defined multiple outlines within the same document (see What To Do If).

Steps

1. Click on the **O**ptions button to display the options menu shown in Figure 3.38.

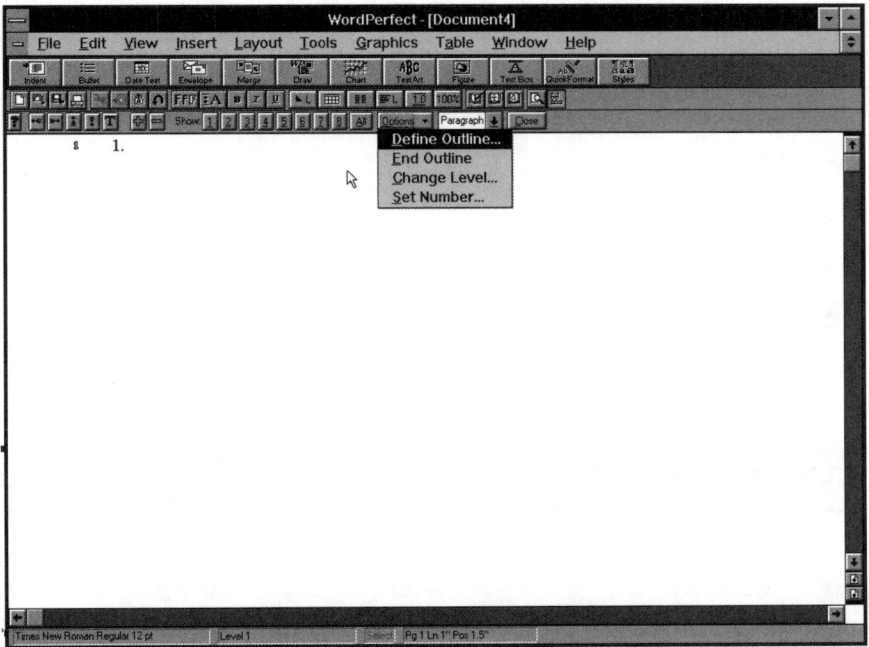

Figure 3.38   Outline Options menu.

2. Choose **D**efine Outline... to display the Outline Define dialog.

3. Choose **O**utline from this list to establish conventional outlining. Choose one of the other definitions to use another type of outlining.

4. Click on **OK** to close this dialog. The new outline type should appear in the Type: field to the left of the **C**lose button on the Outline feature bar.

_____ **What To Do If**

• You can have multiple outline definitions within the same document. Simply click on the Start New Outline button on the Outline Define dialog. This lets any previous out-lines stay the way they are while setting the new definitions for outlines that follow.

See Also

- Turning on Outlining, p. 102.
- Paragraph—Bulleted Lists, p. 79.
- Paragraph—Numbered Lists, p. 82.

Using Outlining

Once you have turned on the Outline feature bar and have con-figured outlining to appear the way you want, you can access several additional features from the feature bar.

Assumptions

- You have turned on the Outline feature bar display.
- You have made any necessary changes to outline configura-tion with the **O**ptions **D**efine Outline menu.

Exceptions

- None.

Steps

1. Use the left and right level arrows at the left of the Outline feature bar to insert outline or number codes at various levels. If you click on the left arrow, a numbering code at the previous level is inserted for the current paragraph; if

you click on the right arrow, a paragraph number at the next level is inserted.

2. Use the up and down arrows to move the current paragraph up or down in the outline. The paragraph where the insertion point resides moves up or down one paragraph for each click on the up or down arrow button. The outline level remains the same during the move.

3. Click on the Text symbol (**T**) to toggle between Outline and standard (body) Text mode. If the current paragraph is a part of an outline, then when you click on this icon the paragraph reverts to standard text and the paragraph numbering is removed. If the current paragraph is standard text, when you click on this icon, an outline number of the next sequential level is inserted.

4. Click on the plus (+) or minus (−) symbols to change the level of outline display. When you click on the minus sign, all levels of the outline below the current one are hidden. When you click on the plus sign, all levels of the outline are displayed. Figure 3.39 shows an outline fully displayed; Figure 3.40 shows the same outline with some levels hidden.

5. Use the level buttons to specify which levels of the outline should be displayed. If you click on All, then all levels will show; if you click on 2, then only the first two outline levels will be visible, click on 3 to display the first three levels, and so on.

6. Click on **C**lose to remove the Outline Options bar. The outline definitions and codes previously entered remain in your document.

What To Do If

- You can easily change the level of any outline item. Simply click on the left or right arrows on the feature bar to move the current paragraph up or down a level.

WordPerfect - [c:\...\fig0339.wpd - unmodified]

File　Edit　View　Insert　Layout　Tools　Graphics　Table　Window　Help

Indent | Bullet | Date Text | Envelope | Merge | Draw | Chart | TestArt | Figure | Text Box | QuickFormat | Styles

Show: 1 2 3 4 5 6 7 8 All | Options ▾ | Outline | Close

```
    I.      Introduction
    II.     Chapter 1 -- Basic WordPerfect
            A.      What is WordPerfect
            B.      Differences
            C.      Strengths
            D.      Limitations
    III.    Chapter 2 -- The WordPerfect Screen
            A.      Windows Program Manager
            B.      The WordPerfect Applications Window
            C.      WordPerfect Icons
            D.      The Main WordPerfect Screen
                    1.      Title Bar
                    2.      Menu Bar
                    3.      Button Bar
                    4.      Power Bar
                    5.      Feature Bar
                    6.      Status Bar
                    7.      Scroll Bars
    IV.     Chapter 3 -- Starting WordPerfect
            A.      Launching from Program Manager
            B.      Loading a Document
            C.      Starting a New Document
```

Times New Roman Regular 12 pt　　Level 1　　Pg 1 Ln 1" Pos 1.5"

Figure 3.39　Complete Outline display.

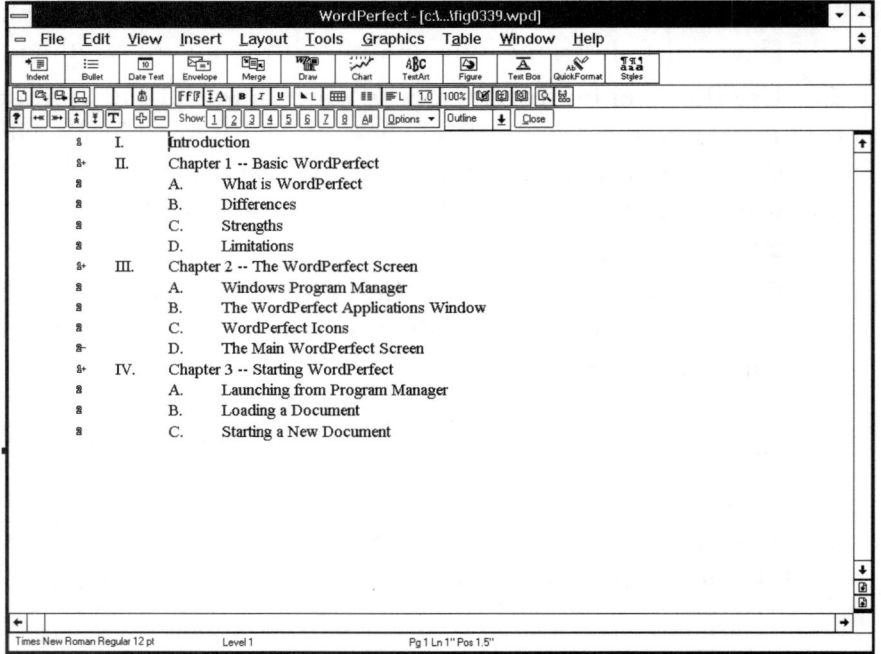

Figure 3.40　Outline with some levels hidden.

See Also

- Turning on Outlining, p. 102.
- Defining Outlines, p. 104.

Marking Text for Tables of Contents 53

Among the powerful features of word processors such as Word-Perfect is the ability to construct a complete table of contents. You open the Table of Contents feature bar, mark the text you want to appear in the TOC list, and specify a level. You repeat this process for each TOC entry, then use a separate utility to generate the list at the location of the insertion point.

Assumptions

- You have previously entered text for a document that you want to mark with table of contents entries.

Exceptions

- None.

Steps

1. Use **T**ools Table of **C**ontents to display the Table of Contents feature bar shown in Figure 3.41.

2. Select the text you want to include in the current table of contents entry.

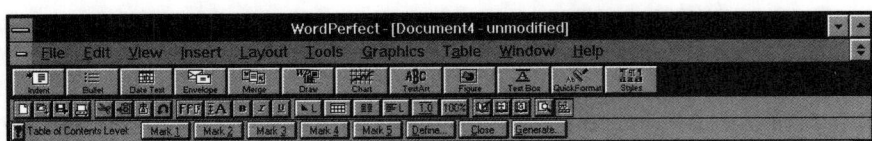

Figure 3.41   Table of Contents feature bar.

3. Specify a TOC level by clicking on one of the level buttons: Mark **1** through Mark **5**.

4. Repeat steps 2 and 3 for every block of text you want to use in the table of contents.

5. Click on **C**lose to close out the Table of Contents feature bar.

What To Do If

- Use Reveal Codes (**Alt+F3**) to display the TOC codes if you need to remove any existing codes.

See Also

- Marking Text for Other Lists, p. 122.
- Marking Text for Indexes, below.
- Marking Text for Tables of Authorities, p. 114.

54 Marking Text for Indexes

A variation of the Table of Contents list is the Index list, also well supported in WordPerfect. The procedure is similar to creating a Table of Contents: Display the feature bar, mark the text you want to include in the list, click on Heading to specify the main entry, click on Subheading to specify the subordinate entry. You do this for each item you want included in the index, then generate the list.

Assumptions

- You have previously entered text that you want to include in an index entry.

Exceptions

- None.

Steps

1. Use **T**ools Inde**x** to display the Index feature bar shown in Figure 3.42.

2. Mark the text you want to include in the current index entry.

3. Click on **H**eading: to transfer the marked text into the Heading list. This makes the marked text the main index entry.

4. Click in the **S**ubheading: field to activate it, then type any text you want for the Subheading. This becomes the index entry beneath the Heading entry.

5. Click on the **M**ark button to mark the selected text with the heading and subheading specifications you just entered.

6. Repeat steps 2 through 5 for each word or phrase you want to include in the index for the current document.

7. Position the insertion point where you want the index to appear when it is generated and click on **D**efine... on the Index feature bar. The Define Index dialog shown in Figure 3.43 is displayed.

8. Click on the arrow beside the Position: field to display the Position menu. Hold down the left mouse button and move the mouse to select one of these options. The sample in the middle of the dialog shows how the index will appear.

9. Click on Page **N**umbering... to display the Page Number Format dialog. Accept the WordPerfect default of docu-

> **TIP**
>
> You can build a separate concordance document that speeds up index generation. The concordance file is a standard WordPerfect document that simply lists all of the words and phrases you want WordPerfect to locate in the current document and include in the index. Enter one word or phrase per line. You can specify the concordance file to use when you define the index.

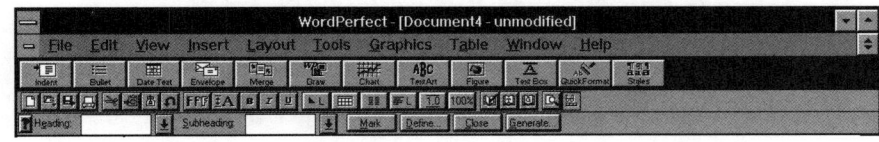

Figure 3.42   Index feature bar.

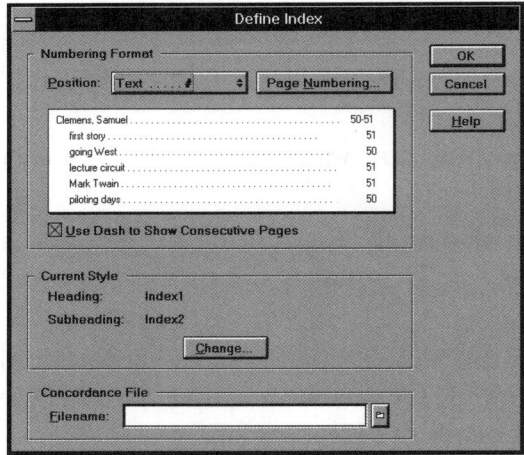

Figure 3.43   Define Index dialog.

ment page numbering or define a number scheme of your own.

10. Click on **OK** to close the Page Number Format dialog.

11. Click on **C**hange in the Current Style area of this dialog to display the Index Styles dialog shown in Figure 3.44 if you

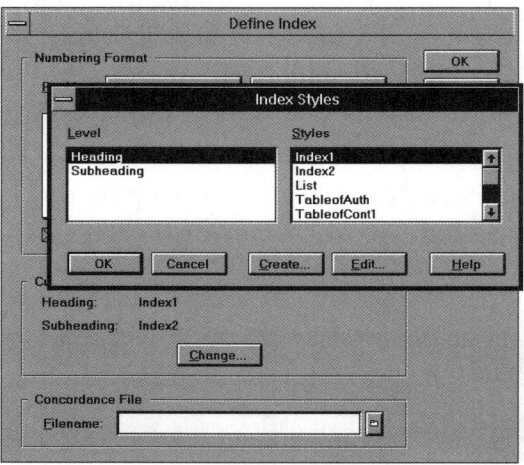

Figure 3.44   Index Styles dialog.

want to change the default index styles. The WordPerfect default is Index1 for the Heading entries and Index2 for the Subheading entries.

12. You can select different styles for the Heading and Subheading entries, edit any existing entry, or define a new style from this dialog. If you select Edit from this dialog, you can view the current settings for the selected style (see Figure 3.45).

13. Make any changes you wish on this dialog, then click on **OK** to close the dialog and return to the Index Styles dialog. Click on **OK** again to return to the Define Index dialog.

14. Enter the complete path and filename for the concordance file for this document, if you are using one.

15. Click on **OK** to close the Define Index dialog and return to your document.

16. Click on **C**lose to remove the Index feature bar.

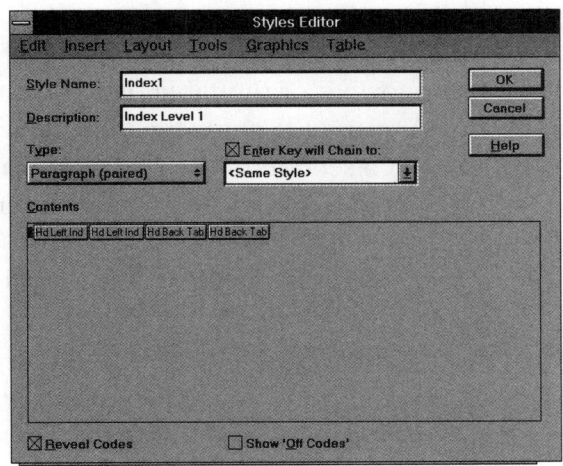

Figure 3.45   Styles Editor dialog.

What To Do If

- Use Reveal Codes (**Alt+F3**) to display the index codes you already have entered. You can then remove any you do not want to keep.

See Also

- Marking Text for Tables of Contents, p. 109.
- Marking Text for Other Lists, p. 122.

55   Marking Text for Tables of Authorities

A table of authorities lists sources or authorities used for background for your document. Strictly speaking, a table of authorities is used to list where citations of specific legal cases and statutes appear in a brief. However, you can use a table of authorities as another list type. For example, you could design a table of authorities as a bibliography or as an informal list of sources for the current document.

There are four basic steps to creating a table of authorities (ToA): (1) Design the format of the table, (2) mark the text you want to tie to each ToA entry, (3) enter the text (details) for each entry, and (4) define each section of the table. Of course, as with all WordPerfect lists, you must generate the table after all the definitions and table text are complete.

For example, if you are designing a ToA for legal references, you might have some of these section names:

- Cases
- Constitutional Provisions
- Statutory Provisions

- Miscellaneous

  If, on the other hand, you are creating a bibliographic reference and you want to categorize the references with the ToA form, you might have these section names:

- Books
- Periodicals
- Speeches
- Movies and Other Media
- Unpublished Documents
- Other References

To design your ToA, simply decide on the section names and the order you want them to appear in the final ToA. You don't do this inside WordPerfect; rather, you do it in your head or on a piece of paper before you start marking the ToA entries in your document.

Assumptions

- You have designed the ToA so that you know what sections will be included and the order in which they will appear in the final table.

Exceptions

- None.

Steps

1. Use **T**ools Table of **A**uthorities to turn on the Table of Authorities (ToA) feature bar shown in Figure 3.46.

2. Position the insertion point where you want the ToA reference to appear in your document.

3. Click on C**r**eate Full Form... to display the Create Full Form dialog (if you have previously entered the full-text information for this Authority, then skip steps 3 to 8).

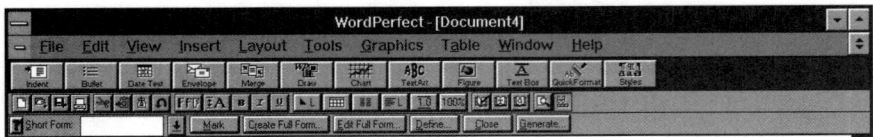

Figure 3.46 Table of Authorities feature bar.

4. Enter the Section **N**ame: for this entry (or use the pull-down list at the right of this field to select the Section Name).

5. Enter the Short **F**orm: name for this entry (or use the pull-down list at the right of this field to select the Short Form text).

6. Click on **OK** to close this dialog and display the full-form feature bar and ToA editor.

7. Type the full text for this entry, using whatever format is appropriate for your document and ToA type. Legal entries, for example, will take one format, bibliographic entries another format, and so on. Figure 3.47 shows a sample bibliographic entry.

8. Click on **C**lose to close the ToA entry editor and return to your document. The Short Form text you specified on the Full Form dialog will appear in the Short Form field on the ToA Feature bar. After you have created the first Full Form entry for a particular entry, you need only pull down the Short Form name for it for subsequent entries of the same authority.

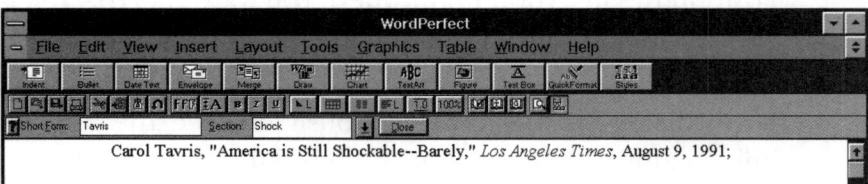

Figure 3.47 Sample bibliographic ToA entry.

9. Click on the **M**ark button on the feature bar to insert a ToA code in your document at the location of the insertion point.

10. Repeat steps 2 to 9 for all of the ToA entries you want in your document.

11. Position the insertion point where you want the ToA to appear in your document.

12. Click on the **D**efine... button to display the Define Table of Authorities dialog shown in Figure 3.48. The first time you use this command the dialog is blank.

13. Click on Cre**a**te... to display the Create Table of Authorities dialog shown in Figure 3.49. This dialog creates the specifications of a section of completed ToA. If you were using our bibliographic example, you would need to use Create six times, once for each section name.

14. Enter a name for this section format in the **N**ame: field of this dialog.

15. Click on the up and down arrows to the right of the Position: field to display the popup menu. Hold down the left mouse button and select one of the display types from the list. The sample entries in the window below this field shows you how the selected format will appear in the final ToA.

16. Click on the Pa**g**e Numbering... button to display the Page Numbering dialog. Change any entries in this dialog you wish.

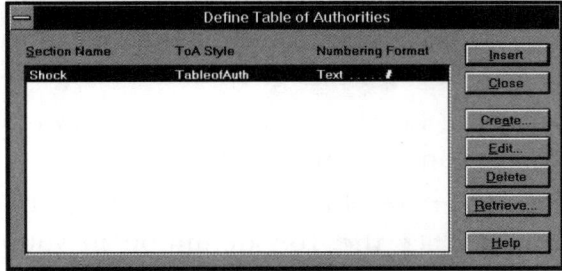

Figure 3.48   Define Table of Authorities dialog.

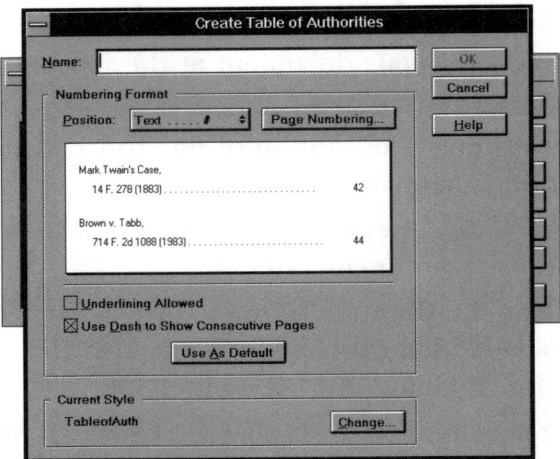

Figure 3.49   Create Table of Authorities dialog.

17.   Click on **OK** to close the Page Numbering dialog.

18.   Click in the **U**nderlining Allowed box to toggle this option on or off. The WordPerfect default is off; click once in this box to turn Underlining Allowed on.

19.   Click in the Use **D**ash to Show Consecutive Pages box to toggle this option on or off. The WordPerfect default is on; click once in this box to turn off the Dash for consecutive pages in the final ToA list.

20.   Change these defaults, if you wish, by clicking on the Use **A**s Default button.

21.   Click on the **C**hange... button if you want to change the default document style for the ToA.

22.   Click on **OK** to close this dialog and return to the Define Table of Authorities dialog.

23.   Repeat steps 13 to 22 as often as necessary to create all of the ToA section definitions required.

24.   Click on **I**nsert to close the Define Table of Authorities dialog and place the ToA definition in your document.

When you generate tables, this is where the ToA will appear.

_____ **What To Do If**

- You don't have to create all of the ToA entries at once. After you have made a pass at your document, you can repeat the process at any time to add more references.

- Use the Create Table of Authorities dialog from the Define dialog to add new section names as you need them.

- If you decide later that you have misplaced the ToA definition code (the place where the ToA will appear when the document is generated), use Reveal Codes or Edit Find to locate the code, delete it, and use **D**efine... again to insert the code in a new location.

_____ **See Also**

- Marking Text for Other Lists, p. 122.
- Marking Text for Cross-References, below.
- Marking Text for Tables of Contents, p. 109.

Marking Text for Cross-References   **56**

Cross-references are used in WordPerfect documents to refer the reader to other parts of the document (_See Chapter 12_, or _Refer to Figure 4.32_, for example). A cross-reference consists of two parts, the Reference and the Target. The Reference is the direction to the reader to read another part of the document; the Target is the location in the document where you are referring the reader.

To use cross-references in WordPerfect, you must complete three steps:

1. Mark the Reference.
2. Mark the Target.
3. Generate the Document.

Cross-reference entries can be useful in a document to help the reader find additional information about a given topic. The cross-reference process is conducted in two steps, because you may know you want to create a reference early in the document, but you don't know where the target will appear until later. When you create the reference, a question mark appears until you have marked the corresponding target and generated the document.

Assumptions

- The insertion point is positioned where you want to create a cross-reference.

Exceptions

- The cross-reference mark is like an index or table of contents mark. The references to locations don't appear until the document is generated. Therefore, the process described here is not complete until you generate the document.

Steps

TIP

If the target is a graphics object, use Reveal Codes (**Alt+F3**) to locate the actual code that defines the object, position the insertion point to the right of the code, and then issue the Mark Target instructions.

1. Type the introductory text for the cross-reference. This could be "See Page" or "See Figure" and the like. Leave one space after the reference. WordPerfect will fill in the correct page, figure, or other reference when the document is generated.

2. Use **T**ools Cross-**R**eference to display the Cross-Reference feature bar shown in Figure 3.50.

3. Click on the **R**eference button to display the Reference Type menu. Choose from among **P**age, **S**econdary-Page, **C**hapter, **V**olume, Paragraph/**O**utline, **F**ootnote, **E**ndnote,

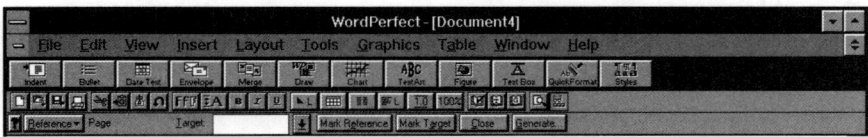

Figure 3.50   Cross-Reference feature bar.

Caption **N**umber, Counter.... This tells WordPerfect what type of object will be referenced.

4. Click in the **T**arget: field to activate it, then type a target name for this reference. If you have already created a target that fits this reference, pull down the list and choose the appropriate target from the list.

5. Click on Mark **R**eference on the feature bar. WordPerfect inserts a reference code in your document at the insertion point and displays a question mark, indicating that a cross-reference code exists. The actual reference (page number, figure number, etc.) will be added when the corresponding target is entered and the document generated.

6. Move the insertion point to the location of the corresponding target for this reference. (If the target has not yet been written, delay this step and the next one until the target area exists.)

7. Make sure the correct target name is displayed in the **T**arget: field on the Cross-Reference feature bar and click on Mark **T**arget to insert a target code that corresponds to the previously entered reference code.

8. Click on Close to close the Cross-Reference feature bar.

What To Do If

- To move a cross-reference code, turn on Reveal Codes (**Alt+F3**) to locate the code and use **Backspace** or **Del** to remove it. Reposition the insertion point and step through the reference create process just described.

See Also

- Generating Documents, p. 124.
- Defining Outlines, p. 104.
- Marking Text for Other Lists, below.

57 ▽ Marking Text for Other Lists

WordPerfect handles lists of various kinds well. The process involves marking text with codes for a particular type of list, then using an intrinsic WordPerfect utility to scan the document and create the lists. You can customize the features of your lists, creating lists for graphics objects, text boxes, figure captions, or anything else in your document. You can maintain multiple lists within the same document by simply giving each list a separate name.

Assumptions

- None.

Exceptions

- You can define and mark several lists within the same document, but the lists don't appear until you generate the document.

Steps

1. Use **T**ools **L**ist to display the List feature bar.
2. Use **D**efine... Create... from the feature bar to display the Create List dialog shown in Figure 3.51.
3. Enter a name for the list in the **L**ist: field of this dialog. This is the name you will use later to mark text in your document.

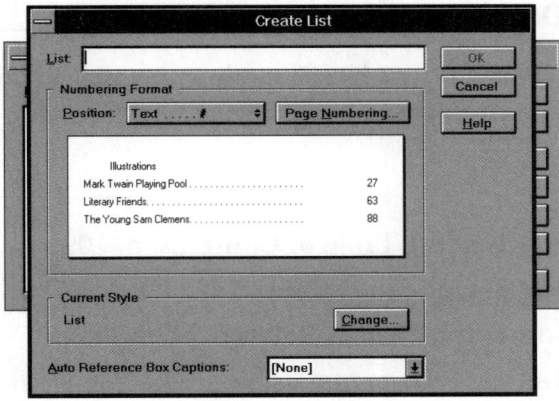

Figure 3.51   Create List dialog.

4. Make any changes to the Numbering Format or Style areas of this dialog you wish. For most applications you can accept WordPerfect's default settings.

5. Pull down the list in the **A**uto Reference Box Captions: field to select a caption type for automatic list generation if you are creating a list of captions for standard WordPerfect objects. For example, if you are creating a list of captions for graphics boxes, choose Graphics from this list, and WordPerfect will mark each caption automatically as it is created. You won't have to mark them yourself to generate the list.

6. Click on **OK** to close this dialog and return to the Define List dialog. Click on **OK** again to return to your document.

7. Select the text you want included in the list mark.

8. Pull down a menu of list names from the List: field and choose a name. These names are ones you created with the **D**efine... **C**reate... command.

9. Click on **M**ark to insert a list code for the selected text.

10. Repeat steps 7 to 9 for each item in the document you want to include in this list.

11. Click on **C**lose to close the List feature bar.

What To Do If _____

- Use Reveal Codes (**Alt+F3**) to locate any list codes you want to delete or move.

See Also _____

- Marking Text for Table of Contents, p. 109.
- Marking Text for Indexes, p. 110.
- Marking Text for Cross-References, p. 119.
- Generating Documents, below.

58 ▼ | Generating Documents

After a document has been marked for one or more lists you create the actual lists by "generating" the document. Document generation launches a WordPerfect utility that scans the entire document looking for list definition codes and for marked text that corresponds to the defined lists. During several passes of a document, the generating utility compiles the various lists and inserts them in the document at the location of the definition marks.

Assumptions _____

- You have previously defined one or more lists and you have marked the text within the document to be included in these lists.

Exceptions _____

- None.

Steps _____

1. Use **T**ools **G**enerate... (**Ctrl+F9**) to display the Generate dialog shown in Figure 3.52.

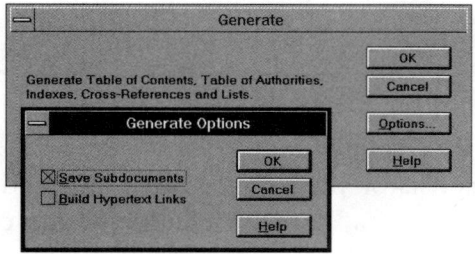

Figure 3.52   Generate dialog.

2. Click on **O**ptions... if you want to deactivate saving subdocuments. This saves generation time when you are working with subdocuments. Click on **B**uild Hypertext Links on the Options dialog to build hypertext links during generation.

3. Click on **OK** to close the Options dialog, if it is open, then click on **OK** on the Generate dialog to begin generating tables of contents, tables of authorities, indexes, cross-references, and lists.

What To Do If

- If you notice errors in any generated list, correct the marking within the document and then regenerate the lists. The existing lists will be replaced.

- If you need to move a generated list, you can use Reveal Codes to remove the list definition, place a new definition at the proper location, and regenerate the list. Alternately, you can use cut and paste to move an existing list.

See Also

- Marking Text for Tables of Contents, p. 109.
- Marking Text for Indexes, p. 110.
- Marking Text for Tables of Authorities, p. 114.
- Marking Text for Other Lists, p. 122.

TIP

Even if you plan to place the table of contents or other lists at the head of your document, place all definition marks at the end of the document. This will force all lists to be placed at the end, maintaining proper page numbering. If lists are generated at the head of a document, then page numbering during subsequent generation takes into account the extra pages added with each list. You can select a list, cut it from the original location, and paste it to a new location at the head of your document, if you wish.

Creating Tables

Tables in WordPerfect are an excellent way to enter related information such as lists or prices. Anytime you need to place information side-by-side in a WordPerfect document, consider using a table. Once the table is created and inserted in your document, you can move the insertion point into the table and type information as you would inside the WordPerfect document, except that the lines of the table will separate data fields, keeping information associated properly.

Assumptions

- The insertion point is positioned where you want the table inserted in your document.
- The power bar is displayed. If it is not, use **View** **P**ower Bar to turn it on.

Exceptions

- This procedure describes table creation using the power bar tables icon. You can also use **T**able **C**reate... (**F12**) to design a table.

Steps

1. Click on the tables icon on the power bar to pull down a sample table like the one in Figure 3.53.
2. Hold down the left mouse button and use the mouse pointer to define the table. Each square on the sample, pull-down table represents one cell in the table you are creating.
3. Release the left mouse button. The table you just described will be placed into the document at the insertion point (see Figure 3.54).

TIP

Be sure to add at least one extra row to each table to hold the column titles. In fact, it is easier to add several more rows and columns than you think you need. You can always delete any extra ones after you have entered information into the table.

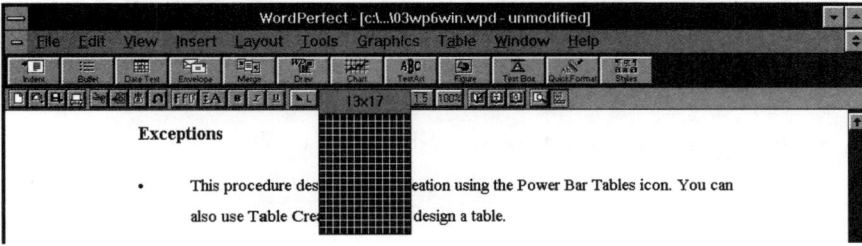

Figure 3.53 Table pull-down from ruler.

_____ **What To Do If**

• If you run out of room on a table, you can add more rows and columns easily. Place the insertion point where you want to add cells and use **Table Insert...** to display the insert dialog.

TIP

Click in any table cell to place the insertion point in it. You can also press **Tab** to move from cell-to-cell from the left to the right or back tab (**Shift+ Tab**) to move from cell-to-cell right to left.

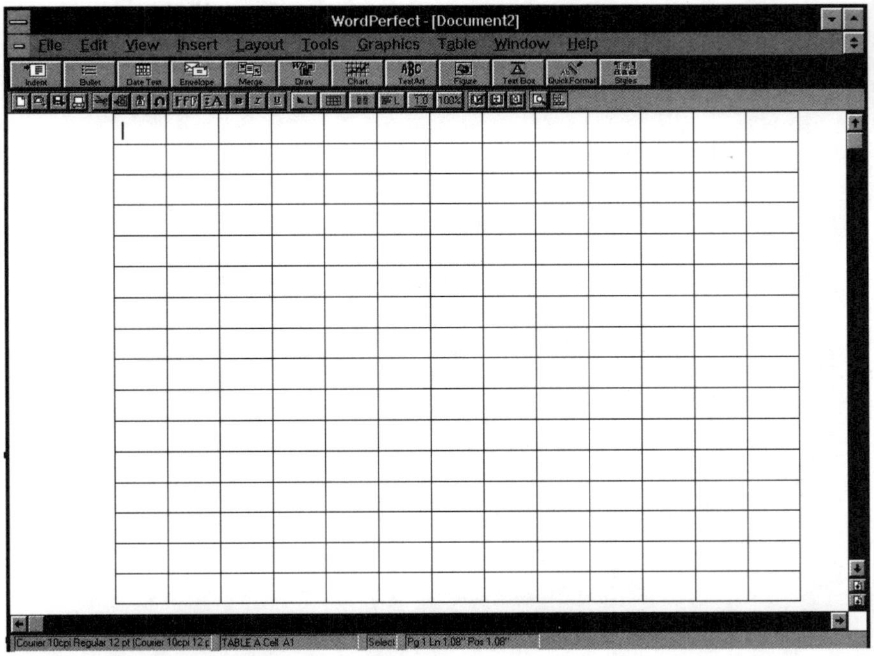

Figure 3.54 Designed table inside document.

- Use **T**able **D**elete... to remove unwanted table cells.

See Also

- Paragraphs—Borders and Shading, p. 73.

Chapter
4

PROOFREADING

Entering text and formatting it are only the first steps in producing a finished document. Before you're ready to send that report to the boss or your latest paper to the teacher, you should spend some time checking and proofing your document. In this chapter we show you some of WordPerfect's facilities that help you do that.

60 Using the Spell Checker

Using the WordPerfect speller won't guarantee a flawless document (the speller can't tell you that you meant "their" and not "there," for example), but it will find common typographical errors and misspellings. WordPerfect comes with a capable dictionary and you can add words of your own that fit your particular discipline or personal needs.

Assumptions

- You have created a document that is finished, or nearly so, and you want to check the spelling.
- The document you want to spell is the current document.

Exceptions

- None.

Steps

1. Use **Tools Speller... (Ctrl+F1)** to display the Speller dialog shown in Figure 4.1.

2. Click on **Check** to pull down the Check Options menu if you want to change the WordPerfect default of Document (spell check the entire document). Click on one of the menu choices to change the speller's checking method. You can choose from among:

> **TIP**
> Double-click on a selected word in your document when the speller pauses and you can change the text directly in your document, add text and conduct other editing procedures. If you watch carefully as the speller scans your document, you can also detect other problems and correct them as you correct spelling.

Figure 4.1   Speller dialog.

- **W**ord
- **S**entence
- **Pa**ragraph
- **P**age
- **D**ocument
- To **E**nd of Document
- **S**elected Text
- **T**ext Entry Box
- **N**umber of Pages...

3. Use the Dictionaries menu to select a supplemental dictionary if you want to use other than the WordPerfect default.

4. Use the Speller Options menu to specify how WordPerfect conducts its spell checking. These are toggles. A check mark beside an entry indicates it is enabled. Choose from these options (options preceded by * are WordPerfect defaults):

*Words with Numbers	Treats words with combined letters and numbers as possible errors.
*Duplicate Words	Treats repeated words (such as *the the*) as an error.
*Irregular Capitalization	Treats irregular capitalization (such as WordPerfect) as an error.

Exhaustive Checking	Available only with some language selections. Turns on exhaustive spell checking when limited checking is normally used.
*Auto Replace	Causes the speller to automatically replace subsequent occurrences of a misspelled word after you have specified the first change; so if you have consistently misspelled a word, after you correct it the first time, the speller automatically changes the rest of the words in the current document.
*Document Dictionary	Enables or disables a supplementary dictionary associated only with the open document.
Beep on Misspelled	Causes the computer to beep whenever the speller detects a word not found in its dictionary.

5. Click on **S**tart to begin spell checking your document. WordPerfect starts at the beginning of the file and checks the spelling word-by-word.

6. When WordPerfect finds a word in your document that is not in its dictionary, the word is selected, the word closest to it is displayed in the Replace **W**ith: field, and additional words are shown in the Sugg**e**stions: window. Click on one of the Speller dialog buttons:

Replace	To replace your word with the Replace **W**ith: word
Skip **O**nce	To skip the selected word in your document this time only
Skip **A**lways	To skip the selected word in your document this time and every

TIP

The speller automatically adds new words to the wp-spelus.sup supplemental dictionary file. You can click in the Add **T**o: field to change the supplementary dictionary file. This would let you create separate supplementary dictionary files for each user or for each type or group of words.

other time it is encountered in your document. This choice also causes WordPerfect to flag the selected-word as "correct" and will point out changes in the word later, such as when you use it with an initial capital letter.

Add — To add the selected word in your document to your personal dictionary so that when the word is encountered later in other documents, WordPerfect will know it as a correct word.

Suggest — To select a different set of words from the dictionary to display in the Suggestions: window. Select one of the existing words in this window before clicking on the Suggest button.

7. Click on **C**lose at any time to stop the spell checking or click on **OK** when the speller tells you the document spell checking is complete and asks whether you want to close the Speller dialog.

_____ **What To Do If**

- If you spell-check a document, then add more text, you can check just the new text by selecting the text before launching the speller.

_____ **See Also**

- Using the Thesaurus, p. 134.
- Using the Grammar Checker (Grammatik), p. 136.

Using the Thesaurus

An adjunct to the spell checker is the thesaurus, which helps you decide on the proper word for a particular application or to help you choose an alternate word for one you have already used.

Assumptions

- You have selected a word or placed the insertion point on a word within the current document. This is the word the thesaurus will check automatically when it is started.

Exceptions

- None.

Steps

TIP
You can double-click inside your document with the Thesaurus dialog open to return to document editing and leave the Thesaurus dialog open while you conduct additional editing. Return to the thesaurus by clicking anywhere in the Thesaurus dialog.

1. Use **T**ools **T**hesaurus... **(Alt+F1)** to display the Thesaurus dialog. Figure 4.2 shows a sample Thesaurus display with some alternative words suggested.

2. To get more information, double-click on one of the words in the first window. WordPerfect conducts a thesaurus lookup on that word and offers suggestions in the next window. You can select one of these words to create a third display in the third window and so on. Use the left and right buttons to scroll to different suggestion windows.

3. Highlight the word you want to use instead of the selected word in your document and click on **R**eplace to insert the thesaurus word into your document instead of the original.

4. Type additional words in the Word: field and click on **L**ook Up to have WordPerfect search the thesaurus for new words.

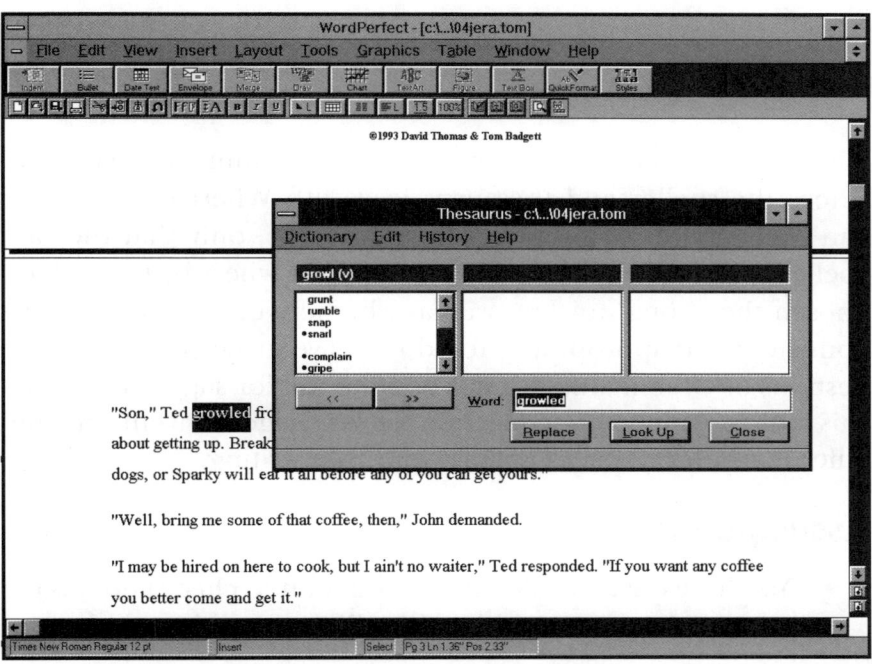

Figure 4.2   Sample document with Thesaurus display.

5. Click on **C**lose to close the Thesaurus dialog.

_____ **What To Do If**

- If the word you selected isn't in WordPerfect's thesaurus file, the suggestion windows are blank and the selected word appears in the Word: field. Try entering a similar word you know to see if it is in the thesaurus file.

_____ **See Also**

- Using the Spell Checker, p. 130.
- Using the Grammar Checker (Grammatik), p. 136.

TIP

Use the Thesaurus menu for additional features. Change the Thesaurus file with Dictionary, for example. The Edit menu lets you conduct standard editing operations on the word or words in the Word: box of the Thesaurus dialog, and History displays a history of the words you have selected in the thesaurus. Redisplay information on previous words by selecting it from the History list.

Using the Grammar Checker (Grammatik)

The WordPerfect grammar checker—Grammatik—picks up where the speller and thesaurus leave off. Whereas the speller can't tell whether you meant their or there, only that they are spelled correctly, Grammatik will tell you when you may have chosen the wrong word, as well as whether your writing appears consistent and appropriate. You don't have to agree with the suggestions of Grammatik, but it is good to ask for suggestions from this utility, which is a collection of language conventions and rules that you can check against your own writing.

Assumptions

- You have created a document you want to check and it is the current document within a WordPerfect editing window.

Exceptions

- None.

Steps

> **TIP**
> Select Custom 1, Custom 2, or Custom 3 and then Edit to create your own writing style settings.

1. Use **Tools Grammatik... (Alt+Shift+F1)** to display the Grammatik dialog shown in Figure 4.3.

2. Use the Check menu to specify what portion of the document you want Grammatik to check. You can choose from:
   - Sentence
   - Paragraph
   - Document
   - To End of Document
   - Selected Text
   - Text Entry Box

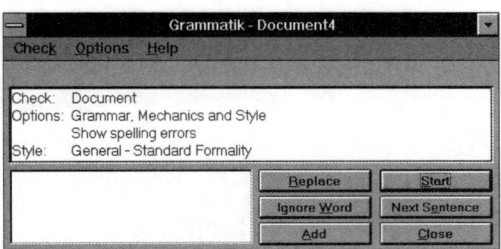

Figure 4.3   Grammatik dialog.

3. Use **O**ptions **W**riting Style... to display the Writing Style dialog shown in Figure 4.4.

4. Select the writing style that best matches the style of your document. Documents intended for different audiences are written in a different style: A formal business letter doesn't use the same style as a child's fictional story, for example.

5. Select a formality level: Standard (the WordPerfect default), Formal, or Informal.

6. Click on the **E**dit button to display the Writing Style Settings dialog shown in Figure 4.5. Turn on or off as many of these toggle settings as you want to fine-tune the writing style settings. Note that you have different selections for

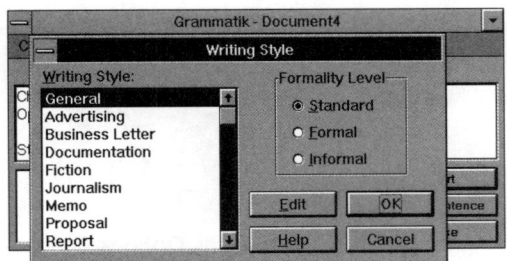

Figure 4.4   Grammatik Options Writing Style dialog.

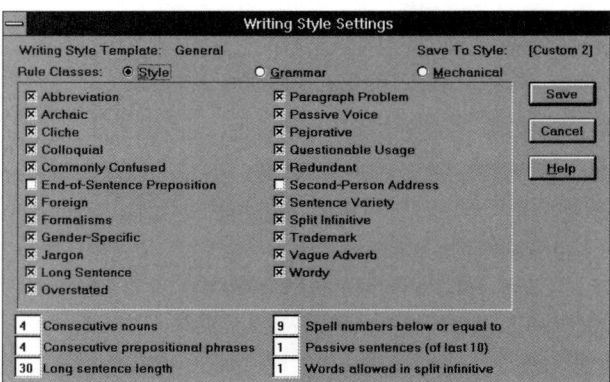

Figure 4.5   Writing Style Settings dialog.

Style, Grammar, and Mechanical settings. View each of
these lists and make changes as desired.

7. Click on Save to store your writing style changes to the
    selected Writing Style.

8. Click on **OK** to close the Writing Style dialog and return to
    the Grammatik dialog.

9. Use **O**ptions **C**hecking Options... to display the Options
    dialog shown in Figure 4.6. Turn off or on as many of
    these option toggles as you wish.

10. Click on **OK** to close the Options dialog and return to the
    Grammatik dialog.

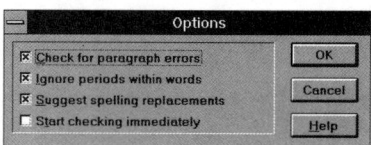

Figure 4.6   Grammatik Options
             Checking Options
             dialog.

11. By default Grammatik is linked to the speller so it can display spelling errors. Disable this feature by displaying the **O**ptions menu and clicking on **S**how Spelling Errors. You may want to disable Show Spelling Errors if you have previously spell-checked the document and if you have a number of specialty words that won't appear in the standard dictionary. Disabling this feature can speed up Grammatik.

12. Use the **O**ptions menu again to specify the Proofreading mode. Select from the following:

Grammar, Mechanics, and Style	Checks all three areas of your document: grammar, mechanics, and style.
Grammar and Mechanics	Uses only grammar and mechanics rules during checking, side-stepping style checks.
Statistics	Scans the document for word and sentence structure information, then offers statistics on readability.

13. Click on **S**tart to begin grammar checking your document.

14. When Grammatik pauses to suggest a different word, click on **R**eplace to put the Grammatik word into your document in place of the highlighted word, or click on Next Sentence to continue checking without making a change to the document.

15. Note Grammatik's suggested changes for each section of your document. You can click on the highlighted word to make the document active and make changes before clicking on Re**s**ume to continue grammar checking.

16. Click on Ignore **W**ord (or phrase) if you want Grammatik to ignore the highlighted word in the rest of your document.

17. Click on **A**dd if you want Grammatik to add the highlighted word to its check file.

18. Click on **C**lose to stop the grammar checker at any time, or answer OK when Grammatik tells you the grammar check is complete and asks if you want to close the dialog.

What To Do If

• If you have run Grammatik and then add more text, you can check the new text by selecting it prior to launching the grammar checker.

• You may want to use different writing style settings for the same document. The Grammatik results may be different.

See Also

• Using the Spell Checker, p. 130.
• Using the Thesaurus, p. 134.

63 Setting Language

When you select a language from the Language dialog, WordPerfect inserts a language code in your document at the location of the insertion point. Everything from that point forward, until a new language code supersedes it, will operate in the chosen language.

In addition, you can select a block of text before invoking the Language facility, and WordPerfect inserts a language code for the selected language at the beginning of the block and a language code for the previous language at the end of the block.

Note that selecting another language with this facility does not remap the keyboard to include special characters for that language. Use the **F**ile **P**references **K**eyboard facility to define a new keyboard layout that contains the characters you need.

Assumptions

- The insertion point is positioned where you want a new language to take effect.

Exceptions

- None.

Steps

1. Use **T**ools **L**anguage... to display the Language dialog shown in Figure 4.7.

2. Select the language you want. Use the scroll bar to view the entire list.

3. Click on **D**isable Writing Tools if you want to disable the speller, thesaurus, and grammar checker for the portion of the document that uses the new language.

4. Click on **OK** to close the dialog and return to your document.

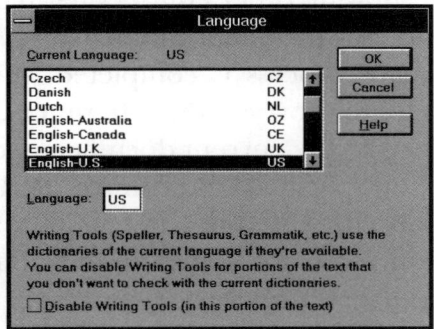

Figure 4.7   Language dialog.

What To Do If _____

- To change the selected language, use Reveal Codes **(Alt+F3)** to locate the language code. Erase it and then repeat steps 1 to 4 to specify a different language.

See Also _____

- Using the Spell Checker, p. 130.
- Using the Thesaurus, p. 134.
- Using the Grammar Checker (Grammatik), p. 136.

64 ▼ Comparing Documents

As you work with WordPerfect documents it is easy to generate more than one copy of the same one. Especially as several people work with the same document, you may need to know which documents are identical and which have been changed. In addition, when you are editing documents you may want to save an original version and open a new copy for editing. Then when you conduct a document compare WordPerfect automatically marks new and deleted text, showing other editors what has been changed. To do this, you will use Document Compare.

After the compare process is completed, the current document contains codes to show you the differences, if any. Anything that has been added to the current document—compared to the other document you specified—is redlined. Redlining is used to show additional text in edited documents. On a color monitor this text appears in red color. When you print a redlined document, redline text has vertical lines in the margin beside it.

Anything that has been deleted from the current document is shown with strikeout characters through it. Text that has been moved is marked with the phrases: THE FOLLOWING TEXT WAS MOVED ahead of the moved phrase and THE PRECEDING TEXT WAS MOVED after it.

Once you have viewed the marked changes to the current document, you can remove the markings with the **T**ools **D**ocument Compare **R**emove Markings procedure.

_____ **Assumptions**

- One of the documents you want to compare is loaded and is selected as the current document.

_____ **Exceptions**

- None.

_____ **Steps**

1. Use **F**ile Compare Document **A**dd Markings... to display the Add Markings dialog shown in Figure 4.8.

2. Enter the name of the file you want to compare to the current document in the **C**ompare Current Document To: field.

3. Choose the type of comparison to make in the Compare by: area of this dialog. The choices are:

   - Word
   - Sentence
   - Phrase
   - Paragraph

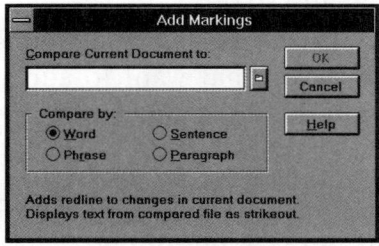

**Figure 4.8   File Compare Document
Add Markings... dialog.**

4. Click on **OK** to start the compare process.

What To Do If

- Remove the markings in your documents with the **File** Com-pare Document **R**emove Markings... command sequence.

See Also

- Redline (Editing Marks), p. 151.
- Strikeout (Editing Marks), p. 153.

65 Using Document Comments

Document comments let you insert nonprinting comments in your documents. You can use these comments to remind you to look for more information on a topic, to document a source, to tell other editors what you have done or what needs to be done, and the like.

If the documents you create in WordPerfect are long-lived and are edited or reviewed over a long period of time, or if more than one person has access to the documents, the Comments facility can be useful.

You can use comments to mark missing information, to remind you to expand some data, to list additional sources for information, to justify a comment or observation, to ask an edi-tor to do something, and so on.

You can use comments to store temporary information or short paragraphs that you may want to add to a document but that you don't want in the document now.

Assumptions

- The insertion point is positioned where you want a com-ment to appear.

Exceptions

- Comments appear on the WordPerfect screen, but they don't print when you print the document. Use the Insert Comment Convert to Text sequence to insert a comment into the document as text. Then you can print comments with the body text.

Steps

> **TIP**
> Click on the comment icon in your document to view the full text of the comment.

1. Use Insert Comment Create... to display the Comment Create editing window. This looks like a standard Word-Perfect document with a Comment feature bar.

2. Enter the comment text.

3. Use the feature bar buttons to insert additional information:

   - Initials (as entered in Preferences)
   - Name (as entered in Preferences)
   - Date (System date)
   - Time (System time)

4. Click on **OK** and WordPerfect inserts the comment at the insertion point. A comment icon appears in the margin of your document (see Figure 4.9).

What To Do If

- Remove comments by turning on Reveal Codes (**Alt+F3**) to locate the comment code. Use **Backspace** or **Del** to remove it.

- Change an existing comment with the Insert Comment Edit command sequence. You can also use Next and Previous on the Comment feature bar to access existing comments.

See Also

- Using Reveal Codes, p. 146.

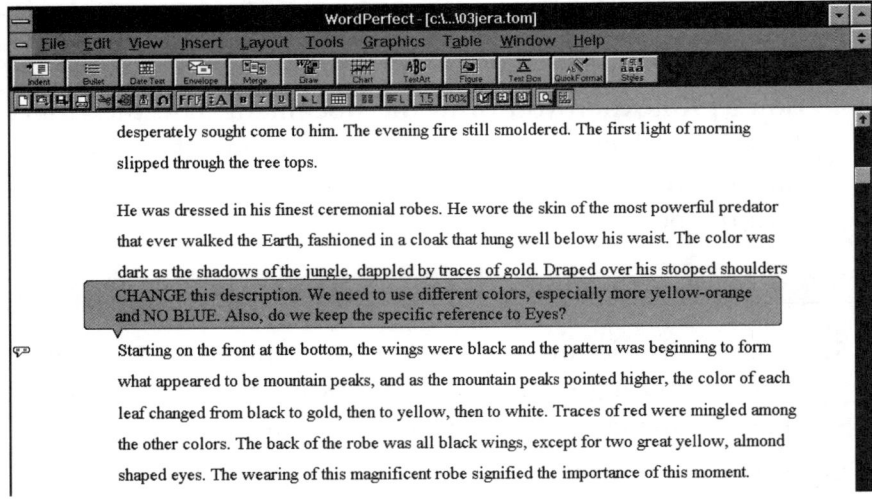

Figure 4.9   WordPerfect document with comment inserted.

- Redline (Editing Marks), p. 151.
- Strikeout (Editing Marks), p. 153.

66 ▸ Using Reveal Codes

WordPerfect does what it does—that is, sets fonts, changes character attributes, adjusts page margins, and so on—by embedding special hidden codes within a document. Normally as you type information into a document you don't see these codes. Word-Perfect displays fonts and attributes on the screen pretty much as they will print on a printer.

As you edit a document, however, it is sometimes useful to see these codes so you can find out precisely where they are and what they are. Most WordPerfect codes take effect from where they are in the document for the rest of the document, unless you change the setting with another code.

Particularly if you are marking a table of contents, an index, or other list entries, you likely will need to see these special codes on occasion to make sure the proper text has been marked.

Although the Reveal Codes feature can be quite useful during editing and formatting, it can take awhile, at first, to get used to reading the codes. Each code has its own abbreviation, surrounded by square brackets. The symbol for hard return, for example, is **[HRt]**, and soft return is **[SRt]**, and a left-aligned tab shows up as **[Left Tab]**.

Other codes are more complicated, depending on what they do. The codes for text attributes are straightforward. To establish attributes such as Bold or Underline, you insert a code to turn an attribute on and all of the text you type following the code takes on this attribute until you insert a code to turn it off. These are paired codes, one for **on** and one for **off**.

Assumptions

- None.

Exceptions

- Many WordPerfect codes are displayed in shortened format until you place the cursor to the left of the code, then the code box expands, showing the full code.

Steps

1. Use **V**iew **R**eveal **C**odes (**ALT+F3**) to split the Word-Perfect screen and show document codes as shown in Figure 4.10.

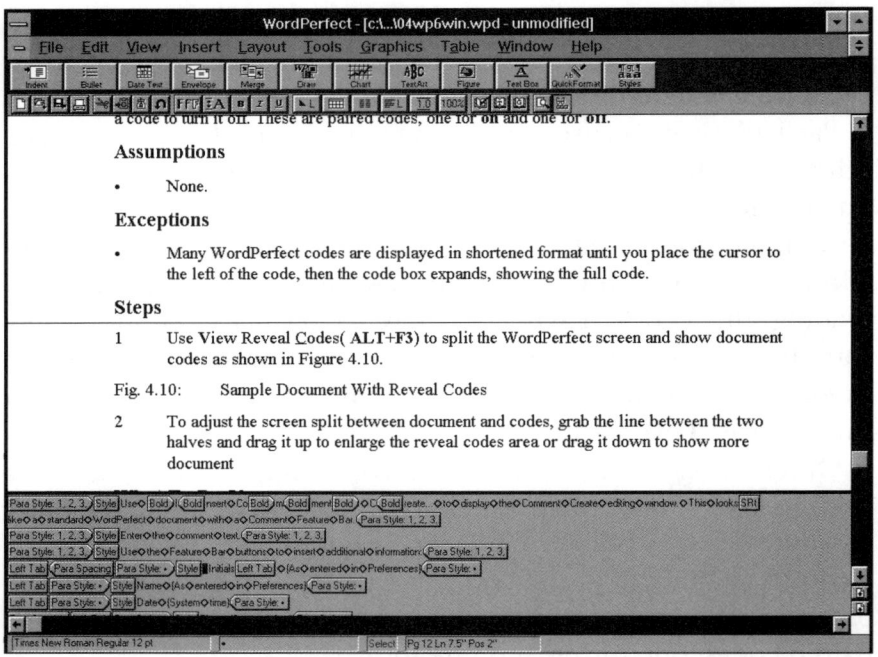

Figure 4.10   Sample document with Reveal Codes.

2. To adjust the screen split between document and codes, grab the line between the two halves and drag it up to enlarge the reveal codes area or drag it down to show more document.

What To Do If

- Document navigation can be quite slow with Reveal Codes enabled. If you need to move to another part of your document, turn off Reveal Codes first to speed up the process.

See Also

- Working with Hidden Text, p. 150.
- Show Symbols (¶), p. 149.

Show Symbols (¶) | 67

Sometimes you don't need to see all of the codes in your document, but it can be helpful to see the end of paragraph (Carriage Return/Linefeed) symbol (¶) and some other codes. This can help you in placing graphics and other boxes, setting fonts, formatting paragraphs, and the like.

Assumptions

- None.

Exceptions

- This procedure turns on only paragraph codes and some additional formatting character codes. To see all formatting codes, use **View Reveal Codes (Alt+F3)** instead.

Steps

1. Use **View Show ¶ (Ctrl+Shift+F3)** to turn on paragraph codes. This will show codes whenever there is a space, a hard return, a tab, or an indent in your document. (See Figure 4.11.)

2. Use **View Show ¶ (Ctrl+Shift+F3)** again to toggle off Show ¶.

What To Do If

- None.

See Also

- Using Reveal Codes, p. 146.
- Working with Hidden Text, p. 150.

> 68→ →   **Show·Symbols·(¶)** ¶
>
> ¶
> Sometimes·you·don't·need·to·see·all·of·the·codes·in·your·document,·but·it·can·be·helpful·to·see·the
> end·of·paragraph·(Carriage·Return/Linefeed)·symbol·(¶)·and·some·other·codes.·This·can·help·you
> in·placing·graphics·and·other·boxes,·setting·fonts,·formatting·paragraphs,·and·the·like. ¶
>
> **Assumptions** ¶
>
> •Ӿ   None. ¶
>
> **Exceptions** ¶
>
> •Ӿ   This·procedure·turns·on·only·paragraph·codes·and·some·additional·formatting·character
>   codes.·To·see·all·formatting·codes,·use·View·Reveal·Codes·(**Alt+F3**)·instead. ¶
>
> **Steps** ¶
>
> 1Ӿ   Use·View·Show·¶·(Ctrl+Shift+F3)·to·turn·on·paragraph·codes.·This·will·show·codes
>   whenever·there·is·a··Space,·a·Hard·Return,·a·Tab,·or·an·Indent·in·your·document.·(See
>   Figure·4.11) ¶
>
> Fig.·4.11:→   Sample·Document·With·Show·¶·Enabled ¶
>
> 2Ӿ   Use·View·Show·¶·(Ctrl+Shift+F3)·again·to·toggle·off·Show·Symbols. ¶

Figure 4.11   Sample document with Show ¶ enabled.

---

68   Working with Hidden Text

You can use hidden text in your document to enter editor's notes or instructions, comments, reminders, or anything else you don't want to appear as part of the main document. You can toggle hidden text off and on to enter it, view it, or edit it.

Assumptions _____

- The insertion point is positioned where you want the hidden text to appear.

Exceptions _____

- Hidden text won't print with the rest of your document unless View Hidden Text is enabled.

Steps

1. Use **V**iew Hidden Text to turn on viewing hidden text.
2. Use **L**ayout **F**ont... to display the Font dialog.
3. Click on Hidd**e**n in the Appearance section of this dialog.
4. Click on **OK** to enable Hidden Text and return to your document.
5. Type the note or comment you want hidden. The text you enter will be surrounded by hidden code marks (you can see these marks in Reveal Codes).
6. Press the right arrow or use the mouse to set the insertion point outside the hidden code marks.
7. Use **V**iew Hidden Text to turn off hidden text view, hiding the text you just entered.

TIP

You can convert existing text to hidden text by selecting the text, then use the **L**ayout Font Hidden sequence to format the selected text as hidden.

What To Do If

- If you change your mind about formatting the new text as hidden, simply select it and use **L**ayout **F**ont Hidd**e**n to toggle off the hidden appearance attribute, returning the text to body text. Or, you can use Reveal Codes to display the hidden text marks and delete them.

See Also

- Using Reveal Codes, p. 146.

Redline (Editing Marks) | 69

Redlining is used in editing a document to show that text has been added. You can mark any text as redlined in WordPerfect with the **L**ayout **F**ont... **(F9)** Appearances command sequence.

Or, you can save an original copy of your document and open a copy for editing. Then use **F**ile **C**ompare Document to have WordPerfect automatically compare the original with the new and add redlining for new text.

Assumptions

- You have selected text you want in redline format or you have positioned the insertion point where you want new text to be in redline format.

Exceptions

- None.

Steps

1. Use **L**ayout **D**ocument **R**edline Method... to display the Redline Method dialog if you want to change WordPerfect's default of selecting the printer-dependent method.
2. Choose Mark **L**eft Margin, Mark **A**lternating Margins, or Mark **R**ight Margin.
3. Click on **U**se as Default if you want to change the default redlining method.
4. Click on **OK** to return to your document.

What To Do If

- Turn off redline characters by selecting the strikeout text, then using **L**ayout **F**ont... **(F9)** to change the character attributes.

See Also

- Comparing Documents, p. 142.
- Strikeout (Editing Marks), p. 153.

- Working with Hidden Text, p. 150.
- Using Document Comments, p. 144.

Strikeout (Editing Marks) ▷ 70

Strikeout characters are used in editing a document to show that text has been deleted. You can mark any text as strikeout in WordPerfect with the **L**ayout **F**ont... **(F9)** Strikeout command sequence. Or, you can save an original copy of your document and open a copy for editing. Then use **F**ile **C**ompare Document to have WordPerfect automatically compare the original with the new and add strikeout formatting for deleted text.

Assumptions

- You have selected the text you want in strikeout format.

Exceptions

- None.

Steps

1. Use **L**ayout **F**ont... **(F9)** to display the Font dialog.
2. Click on Strikeout in the Appearances section of this dialog to turn on the strikeout attribute.
3. Click on **OK** to close the dialog and return to your document.

What To Do If

- Turn off strikeout characters by selecting the strikeout text, then using Layout Font... (F9) to change the character attributes.

See Also

- Comparing Documents, p. 142.
- Redline (Editing Marks), p. 151.
- Working with Hidden Text, p. 150.
- Using Document Comments, p. 144.

Chapter
5

Faxing with WordPerfect

PRINTING FROM WORDPERFECT 6.0 FOR WINDOWS

With most word processing applications, the ultimate goal is to produce a printed document. Once you have typed the text, designed the page to look like you want it, checked the spelling, and saved the document to disk, you are ready to print it.

As a Microsoft Windows product, WordPerfect uses Windows-based printer configurations and definitions. But WordPerfect also includes its own printer drivers and print manager. This offers additional flexibility in how you handle your print jobs, but it also injects a level of complexity to the print operation.

The good news is that when WordPerfect is installed, the default settings are more than adequate to let you print the documents you create. And, as you work with the program, add a new printer, or simply want to experiment, you can do that too. We'll cover all aspects of using your printer with WordPerfect in this chapter.

71 Installing a New Printer Driver

When you install WordPerfect, it assumes you will be using the printers you already have installed in Windows. You can also install additional printer drivers from inside WordPerfect, both into Windows and into a separate WordPerfect driver section.

Assumptions

- WordPerfect is installed and running.
- You want to install a new printer driver.

Exceptions

- You will need the WordPerfect distribution disks if you are installing a WordPerfect printer.
- You *may* also need the Microsoft Windows distribution disks if you are installing a Windows printer.

Steps

1. Use **F**ile **S**elect Printer... to display the Select Printer dialog shown in Figure 5.1.
2. Click on **A**dd Printer and select Word**P**erfect... or **Win**dows... .
3. If you are installing a Windows-based printer:

   - Click on **A**dd>> to display the **L**ist of Printers:.
   - Use the scroll bars to display the printer name you want to select.
   - Select the printer you want to install by clicking on the name.
   - Click on **I**nstall... .
   - If the driver for the selected printer is on your hard disk, the printer name appears in the Installed Printers: list at the top of this dialog.
   - If the driver for the selected printer is not on your hard disk, you will be asked to insert one of the Microsoft Windows distribution diskettes so the driver can be copied to the disk.

> **TIP**
>
> If you didn't install any WordPerfect printers when you first installed the software, then the required *.all and *.prs files won't be on your hard disk. Exit WordPerfect and launch the WP-Install utility from the WordPerfect Applications window in the Program Manager. Choose **C**ustom Installation and click on **P**rinters... . WordPerfect will ask you to insert a distribution disk so the printer files can be copied to the hard disk.

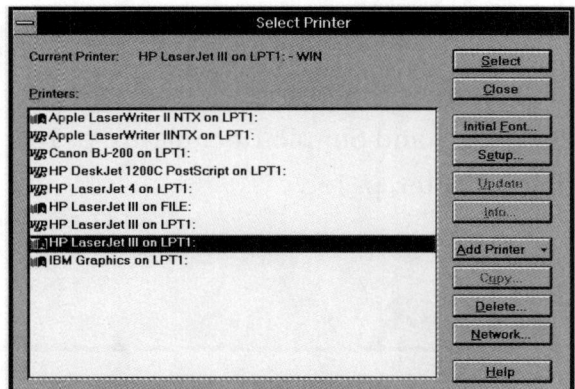

Figure 5.1   Select Printer dialog.

4. If you are installing a WordPerfect-based printer:

    -   Click on **Ad**ditional Printers (*.all) to view a list of all the available printers in WordPerfect in the **Pr**inters: window of this dialog.

    -   Click on **P**rinter Files (*.prs) to view a list of the Word-Perfect printer drivers already installed on your hard disk in the Printers: window of this dialog.

    -   Select a printer from the Printers: list window of this dialog.

    -   Click on **OK** to close this dialog and return to the Select Printer dialog. The new printer you specified should be listed in the Printers: window of this dialog.

What To Do If

-   If the printer you're using isn't on the WordPerfect or Windows printer list, you can still use it with WordPerfect. First, study your printer documentation to see which printers it emulates. A LaserJet printer from Hewlett-Packard is a common printer, for example, and most printers from other companies can act like a LaserJet. And, most impact (dot matrix) printers can act like an IBM Graphics printer or an Epson MX-series.

See Also

-   Printing Letters and Simple Documents, p. 160.
-   Selecting a Printer, p. 158.

72 Selecting a Printer

Once you have installed one or more printers, you can select them as the default for your printing in WordPerfect. For most of us, with a single printer attached to a single machine, this process will be done only once when the software is installed, and again if a new printer is added or the old printer replaced.

Assumptions

- You have previously installed one or more printers, either through Microsoft Windows or within WordPerfect.

Exceptions

- None.

Steps

1. Use **File P**rint... **(F5)** to display the Print dialog.
2. Click on **S**elect... to display the Select Printer dialog. All of the available printers (the ones you have installed) are listed in the Printers: window.
3. Double-click on the printer you want to use for the next output (or select the printer and click on **S**elect to return to the Print dialog).
4.. The name and description of the new printer appears at the top of the Print dialog. You can now set printing specifications and print your document.

What To Do If

- If the printer you want to select does not appear in the Printers: window, use **A**dd Printer to add a new one (see the preceding task, Installing a New Printer Driver).

See Also

- Installing a New Printer Driver, p. 156.
- Printing Letters and Simple Documents, p. 160.
- Printing Long Documents (Master Document Feature), p. 168.

Printing Letters and Simple Documents

Printing from WordPerfect is what using the software is all about. You can type and edit and refine as much as you like, but until you get the formatted document out on paper for other people to read, the work isn't worth much.

The Windows environment gives WordPerfect some excellent printing capabilities and the program itself includes impressive printing features. Assuming you have installed WordPerfect and have selected a printer and installed its drivers, printing from WordPerfect for Windows is as simple as calling up the print routine and letting the software do its work.

Assumptions

- The document you want to print is the current document.
- You have previously installed a printer driver to support the printer you are using.
- You have selected the printer you want to use from the WordPerfect Select Printer dialog.

Exceptions

- None.

Steps

1. Use **File P**rint... (**F5**) to display the Print dialog shown in Figure 5.2.
2. To accept WordPerfect defaults, click on **P**rint to start printing the entire document.
3. After the Print dialog box is displayed, you can change some of the default print settings. The options are:
    - Click on **C**urrent Page to print only the page where the insertion point rests.

> **TIP**
>
> When you specify multiple copies, you probably will get faster results if you let the printer generate them. Click on the double-ended arrow at the right of the Generated By: field. Choose **Prin**ter from the list. Now WordPerfect will send the document to the printer and include instructions for printing multiple copies. This frees up WordPerfect and the Windows Print Manager quicker and reduces traffic through your printer port.

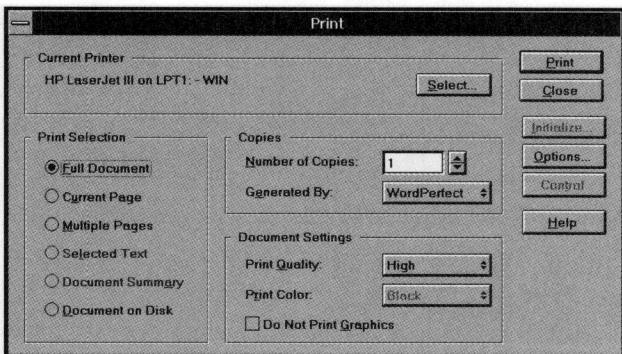

Figure 5.2   Print dialog box.

- Click on **M**ultiple Pages to print a range of pages. Specify which pages you want to print from the Multiple Pages dialog.

- Print a document you haven't loaded into memory by clicking on **D**ocument on Disk. Specify the name of the file from **D**ocument on Disk dialog.

- If you have selected a range of text before issuing the Print command, you can print this range by clicking on **S**elected Text in the Print dialog. If you haven't selected text in advance, the **S**elected Text option is not available.

- Specify the number of copies you want to print by entering a number in the **N**umber of Copies field of the Print dialog box. Click on the field, then type a number, or click on the up or down arrows to change the number from two to many thousands.

What To Do If

- If you change your mind about printing the current document after you have clicked on Print on the Print dialog, shrink the WordPerfect window by clicking on the minimize arrow at the upper right of the screen, then open the

WordPerfect Print Manager and click on **C**ancel Print Job on the WordPerfect Print Job dialog. (If your document is very short, the document will be printed before you can complete this process.)

See Also

- Installing a New Printer Driver, p. 156.
- Selecting a Printer, p. 158.

74 Printing Mailing Labels

WARNING

If you're using a laser printer, make sure the labels you select are designed for laser applications. Although standard copy machine labels *should* work in your printer, they may not. Buy laser printer labels! Also, you will be sorry if you try to use standard peel-off labels of the type designed for typewriter or tractor-feed applications. These labels can peel off inside your printer and stick to the drum. If this happens you'll probably have to replace the drum.

If you've tried printing mailing labels from WordPerfect for DOS (and many other DOS-based word processors), you know that it is not a pleasant task. What on the surface seems straightforward, what should be easy, can turn into a complicated, even impossible task. In WordPerfect for Windows 6, however, the process is much, much easier. Most of the work is done for you.

There are two types of label printing you may want to do: one or more labels with the same information, such as your own name and address for use as return address or identification labels, and several labels with different addresses, such as for use as mailing labels for a letter writing campaign.

Assumptions

- You have installed a printer driver for the printer you are using and you have selected this printer on the Select Printer dialog.
- You have the proper label stock for this printer. You'll need tractor feed labels for an impact printer and labels designed for laser applications for a laser printer.

_____ **Exceptions**

- This procedure is for creating "manual" labels, where you type each label on a WordPerfect editing screen. To use merge files to print labels, refer to the discussion of merge documents in Chapter 9.

_____ **Steps**

1. Use Layout Labels... to display the Labels dialog shown in Figure 5.3.
2. Select the type of label definitions you want to display by clicking on Laser, Tractor-Fed, or Both in the display area of this dialog. If you know you will be using a set of laser labels, click on Laser to reduce the number of label definitions you have to search to find your label set.
3. Use the scroll bar in the Labels: window to find the label definition you want to use.

> **TIP**
> If you can't find the labels you have, read the documentation with your labels carefully. Many companies list equivalent labels from other companies. You can also select labels in the Labels: window and note the Label Details to see if they match the labels you are using.

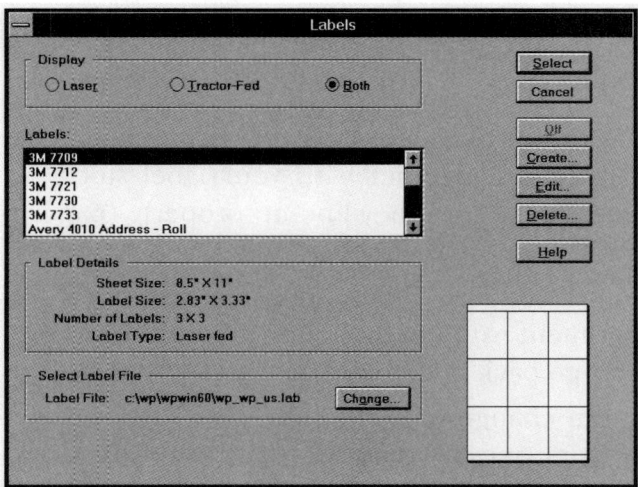

Figure 5.3   Labels dialog.

TIP

If you want to print multiple labels with the same address, select the text of the first label and use **Edit Copy** to place a copy of it on the Clipboard. Press **Enter** on the final line to open another label window, and use **Edit Paste** to copy the Clipboard information to this new label. Repeat this process until you have as many labels with the same information as you want. If you are printing laser labels, you will want to create one full page of labels to make the most use of your label stock.

TIP

You can use standard WordPerfect attribute and formatting commands on your labels. So, for example, if you want to enter a company name with larger type in boldface italics, simply select the text and use the **Layout Font...** **(F9)** command to set the attributes you want.

4. Click on the label name you want to use to select it from the **Labels:** list.

5. Click on **S**elect to select this label definition and display the label editing window.

6. Type the information you want for the first label. The label entry screen is in Page mode so you can see easily the layout of each label. When you press Enter on the last line of the first label, WordPerfect opens a second label. WordPerfect treats each label as a separate page, so the page number prompt on the status bar will show how many labels you have entered. If you are using Avery 5161 labels, for example, one full standard 8½" × 11" page is 20 labels.

7. Enter information for all of the labels you want to print. You can enter one page full of labels, multiple pages of labels, or only a partial page of labels.

8. Use **F**ile Save **A**s... to store your labels in a standard WordPerfect document file.

9. Use **F**ile **P**rint... **(F5)** to print the labels. Accept WordPerfect's default settings on the Print dialog.

What To Do If

- Try printing your laser labels on plain paper first. Hold up the printout, together with your label stock, to a strong light to make sure they line up properly (paper is cheaper for trial prints than labels).

- If your labels don't line up like you want, or if you'd like to experiment with additional or different fonts or attributes, simply go back to the editing screen and make the changes.

- You can change to a different label stock easily. Select the text from one of your labels and use **E**dit **C**opy. Use **F**ile **C**lose to close out the current document screen. Then use **L**ayout **L**abels to start over again. You can copy the existing text on the Clipboard into each label in turn after you have selected the new label stock you want to use.

See Also

- Using Merge Documents, p. 267.
- Installing a New Printer Driver, p. 156.
- Printing Letters and Simple Documents, p. 160.
- Storing a Document, p. 7.

Printing on Envelopes   **75**

Like printing to labels, printing on envelopes used to be an arduous task with most word processors. Now, WordPerfect for Windows makes the task relatively painless.

Assumptions

- You have typed a letter or other document that includes a name and address near the top of the first page.

Exceptions

- None.

Steps

1. Use **L**ayout Envelope... (or click on the Envelope button on the button bar) to display the Envelope dialog shown in Figure 5.4. If the current document "looks" like a letter to WordPerfect, then the "TO" address will appear in the Mailing Addresses window of this dialog.

2. If this is the first time you have used this procedure, enter your return address in the **R**eturn Addresses window. (Note that you can have multiple return addresses and multiple mailing addresses on file within WordPerfect. Click on **A**dd to add a new return address to the database.)

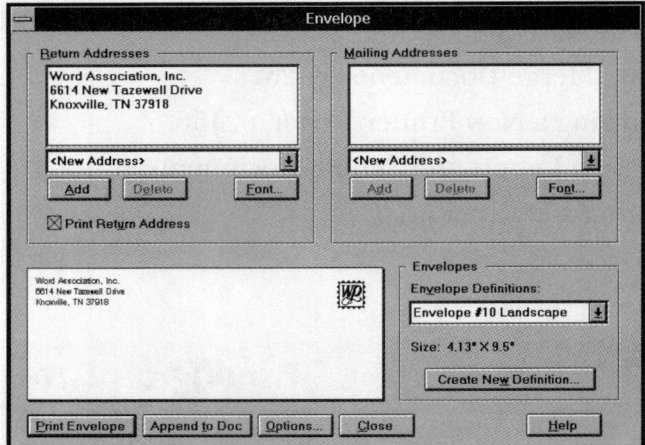

Figure 5.4   Envelope dialog (Layout Envelope...).

3. If you have multiple return addresses on file, use the pull-down list at the bottom of the Return Addresses window to select the return address you want to use for this letter.

4. You can click on **F**ont... to change the typeface used for the return address. You won't see your changes on the Envelope dialog, nor can you change the typeface on a line-by-line basis. The font you select applies to the entire return address.

5. Check the Mailing Address displayed in the **M**ailing Addresses window. If it is not correct, edit it or use the pull-down list to select another mailing address to use.

6. You can click on **A**dd to store the mailing address in the Mailing Addresses database if there is a chance you may want to use it again.

7. You can click on Fo**n**t... to change the typeface used for the mailing address. You won't see your changes on the Envelope dialog, nor can you change the typeface on a line-by-line basis. The font you select applies to the entire return address.

8. By default, WordPerfect assumes you want to print to a standard #10 business envelope. To change the default, pull down the list of available formats by clicking on the down arrow to the right of the Envelope Definitions: field. If you're printing to an unusual envelope format, use Create New Definition... to design your own envelope.

9. Click on **O**ptions to display the Envelope Options dialog shown in Figure 5.5. Make any changes you wish to this dialog, including toggling on or off the USPS POSTNET Bar Code option.

10. Click on **OK** to close the Envelope Options dialog. If you turned on the Bar Code toggle, a prompt for the bar code will appear beneath the Mailing Addresses window. Enter the five-digit zip code, the 10-digit zip+4 code, or the 11-digit Delivery Point Bar Code in the **B**ar Code: field (consult your postal manual or discuss this option with post office personnel for additional details).

11. Click on **P**rint Envelope to begin printing and return to your document.

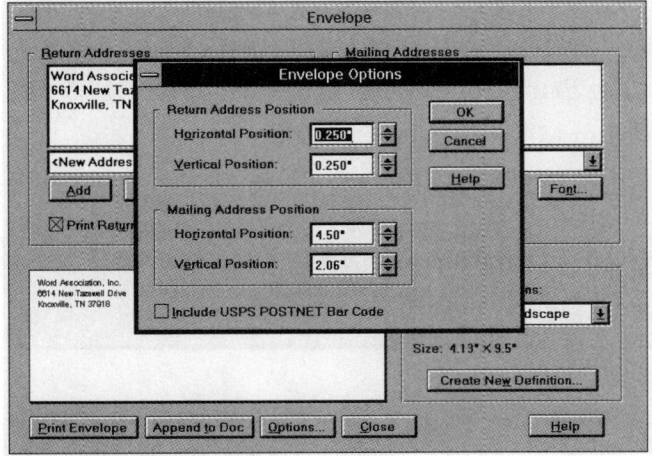

Figure 5.5   Envelope Options dialog.

12. Click on Append to Doc to insert the envelope format, the return address, and the mailing address at the end of your document. Once the form has been inserted into your document, you can add other font and attribute features. For example, you could specify a large font for the company name portion of the return address, leaving the rest of the return address in a smaller font.

13. To print the envelope after the form has been inserted into your document, position the insertion point within the envelope form at the end of your document, then use File Print and click on Current Page before starting the print job.

What To Do If

• WordPerfect selects certain defaults, such as landscape or portrait orientation, depending on the type of printer you have selected. You can change these defaults by creating a new definition. Click on create New Definition... on the Envelope dialog.

See Also

• Installing a New Printer Driver, p. 156.
• Setting Print Defaults, p. 188.
• Printing Mailing Labels, p. 162.

76 Printing Long Documents (Master Document Feature)

When you build long documents in WordPerfect, it frequently is more convenient to write smaller, individual documents and merge them together before you print them. This Master Document feature is particularly useful when you are writing a book, a lengthy report, or when several writers work on the same project. You can let each writer work with his or her own section of the project. When the individual documents are completed, you can use the Master Document feature to build a long document that includes all of the individual pieces.

The key to success with this feature is to make sure that no unwanted headers, footers, font codes, and the like appear in any of the subdocuments. If each document has its own headers and font settings, then different parts of the document will have a different appearance.

Assumptions

- You have previously created two or more documents that you want to merge into a single master document for printing.
- You have scanned each individual document, removing separate headers, footers, or other special codes that might disrupt printing or cause inconsistent document formatting.

Exceptions

- Building a master document from multiple individual documents doesn't change the originals unless you select to save each individual file when the master document is compressed.
- To print an expanded master document you must have enough disk space to store the expanded document twice: once for the master document and once for the print spooler (the temporary file WordPerfect uses to store the document as it is being sent to the printer). That makes three copies of the information, including the individual smaller documents.

TIP

To ensure that no unwanted codes exist in the expanded master document, use the Search facility (**F2**) to look for font codes, headers, or other codes that you feel might be in the individual documents. If you turn on Reveal Codes (**Alt+F3**) before starting the search, it is extremely easy to see what codes have been found and to delete them if necessary.

TIP

Although you can create headers and footers and build indexes and tables of contents without expanding the master document, you must expand it to print it.

Steps

1. Use **F**ile Master **D**ocument **S**ubdocument... to display the Include Subdocument dialog shown in Figure 5.6.

2. Choose a directory from the **D**irectories: list in this dialog.

3. Choose a filename from the File**n**ame: list, or type the name of a file in the Filename: field.

4. Click on **I**nsert to place a code for the specified document into the open WordPerfect editing window.

5. Press **Shift+Enter** to place a hard page code after the subdocument code. This starts each new chapter or document segment at the top of a new page.

6. Repeat steps 1 to 5 for each document you want to include in the master document.

7. Insert any define codes you need for tables of contents or other lists.

8. Generate the document.

9. Create any headers or footers you want at the top of the file so they will apply to all documents.

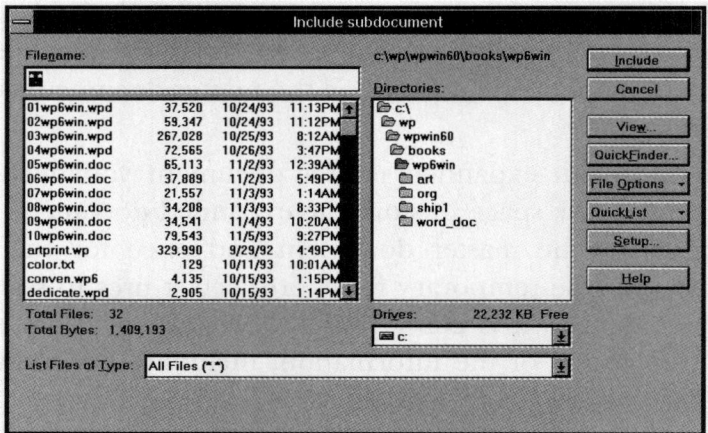

Figure 5.6   Include Subdocument dialog.

10. Use **File Save As**... to store the new master document.

11. If you want to print the entire document, use the **Tools Master Document Expand** sequence to pull all of the sub-documents into the current document. Then use **File Print**... to print the combined document.

_____ **What To Do If**

- If you don't have enough room on your hard disk to store the expanded document, compress it with **File Master Document Condense Master**... . Then you can save the master document definition and rebuild the expanded document again when you need it. Doing this also lets you use the latest versions of all files in master documents.

_____ **See Also**

- Printing Multiple Copies of a Document, below.
- Printing Portions of a Document, p. 172.

Printing Multiple Copies of a Document   **77**

Most of the time you'll probably want to print only one copy of the current document. But if you are sending out mailings, preparing an agenda for an upcoming meeting, or printing a stash of return address labels, you'll want to tell WordPerfect to print more than a single copy of your document. Obviously you could issue the **File Print**... command as often as necessary to produce the number of copies you need, but this is a slow process and requires too much user intervention. We'll show you an easier way here.

_____ **Assumptions**

- The current document is the one you want to print.

TIP

If you are using a laser printer, consider letting the printer handle multiple copies instead of WordPerfect. Do this by selecting **Printer** in the **Gen-erated By:** field of the Print dialog. If the software instead of the printer does the multiple copies, each page of the document must be generated inside WordPerfect and transmitted over a serial or parallel line to the printer once for each copy you want printed.

Exceptions

• None.

Steps

1. Use **File Print...** (**F5**) to display the Print dialog.
2. Use the up and down arrows to select the number of copies you want in the **Number of Copies:** field (or select the field and enter a number between 1 and 16,383).
3. Click on **OK** or press **Enter** to start the print process.

What To Do If

• If you change your mind about the number of copies or which document you want to print after you have closed the Print dialog, press **Esc** while the "Printing..." dialog is on the screen. This will cancel the print process.

See Also

• Setting Print Defaults, p. 188.
• Printing Portions of a Document, below.
• Selecting a Printer, p. 158.

78 Printing Portions of a Document

For small and medium-sized documents, you likely will choose to print the whole thing most of the time. However, during editing and revision, or if a few pages get wrinkled during collating, for example, you may want to print only one or a few pages of a document. Perhaps you only want to double-check the page layout of a complex document. Whatever the reason, you are bound to want to print less than the full document at some point. You have several options for printing only a portion of a document.

Assumptions

• The current document is the one you want to print.

Exceptions

• None.

Steps

1. Use **File Print...** (**F5**) to display the Print dialog.

2. Choose one of the partial document printing options in the Print Selection area of this dialog. The choices are:

   • **F**ull Document (the default)

   • **Cu**rrent Page (the fill page where the insertion point is located)

   • **M**ultiple Pages (one or more contiguous pages. Enter Px-Py in the dialog box after you click on **P**rint. *x* in this example is the starting page and *y* is the last page you want to print. See Figure 5.7. In addition to specifying a range of pages, you can narrow the print range by specifying a volume, chapter or secondary page range.)

> **TIP**
> There may be times when it is better to let WordPerfect produce multiple copies. When the printer does the job, each page is printed multiple times before the next page is printed. This produces a stack of page 1, on top of that is a stack of page two, and so on. When WordPerfect handles it, the entire document is printed multiple times, which produces multiple copies of the entire document.

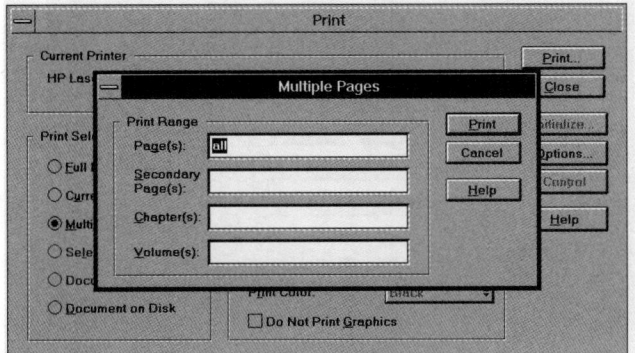

Figure 5.7 Multiple Pages dialog.

- Selected Text (available only if you have selected a portion of the document prior to entering the print routine)

- Document Summary (available only if the current document includes summary text)

- **D**ocument on Disk (to print a document not in memory: Provide the full path and other information on the Document on Disk dialog displayed after you click on **P**rint. See Figure 5.8.)

3. Click on **P**rint to begin printing the specified document portion. If you selected **M**ultiple Pages of **D**ocument on Disk, an additional dialog will be displayed. Answer the additional questions there before printing your document.

What To Do If

- If you specify the wrong range to print, press **Esc** before the print job is complete to cancel it. With short documents you won't be able to cancel the job before it is complete, in most cases. So, just start over again and specify a different range.

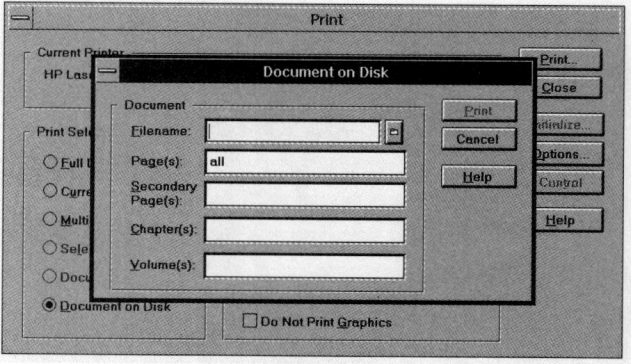

Figure 5.8   Document on Disk dialog.

_____ **See Also**

- Printing Letters and Simple Documents, p. 160.
- Printing Long Documents (Master Document Feature), p. 168.
- Printing to Disk, below.

Printing to Disk

Instead of sending a file to a printer, you can send it to a disk file. This process creates a data file that contains the information from your document in the format of the selected printer. You can transmit this file to another computer or take it to another location on floppy. This lets you print a document at another location that doesn't even have WordPerfect installed, for example, or you can use this technique to create a file for a printer you don't have, then take the file to another computer on diskette and print it on that printer.

The file that results from printing to a file usually is a standard DOS ASCII file that contains a series of commands to tell any compatible printer how to print your document, including text attributes and graphics.

_____ **Assumptions**

- The document you want to print is the current document.
- The printer you want to use to set the format of the document on disk has been selected. (You can make this selection as part of the print process if the printer you want to use is not the default printer.)

_____ **Exceptions**

- None.

> **TIP**
>
> To print a file generated with the WordPerfect print to disk routine, simply copy the file to the proper printer port: **Copy filename PRN.**

> **TIP**
>
> If you have difficulty in printing a document this way, the printer file WordPerfect generated may be in binary form, not ASCII. You cannot look at the file directly from DOS. To send a binary command file to a printer, add the /**B** switch to the command: **Copy filename PRN /B.**

TIP

If you print to disk frequently with this type of printer, use **Add>>** on the Printers dialog to install another version of this same printer. Specify LPT1 for one version of the printer and FILE: for the other. Then to print to disk you only need select a different printer from inside Word-Perfect. If you establish a separate printer definition for printing to a file, remember that all documents you print with this printer will go to the same file unless you change the destination on the Printer Setup screen. After printing a document with this printer definition, use DOS or the WordPerfect File Manager to rename the printer output file so it will not be overwritten by the next print job.

Steps

The process for printing information to a disk file is different for different printers. We will show you here how to print with a Post-Script printer selected and how to do the same thing with a Hewlett-Packard LaserJet printer. One of these procedures should cover your printer as well. You will see readily which procedure to use when you see the dialog boxes presented for your printer.

HP LaserJet:

1. Shrink the WordPerfect application window by clicking on the Minimize button at the upper right corner of the screen.

2. Open the Program Manager by double-clicking on the Program Manager icon, if it is not already open.

3. Locate the Main application window. Open it, if it is not already open.

4. Double-click on the Control Panel icon in the Main application window to open the Control Panel dialog.

5. Double-click on the printer icon within this dialog to display the Printers dialog shown in Figure 5.9.

6. Select HP LaserJet printer from the list of Installed Printers: in this dialog (if yours is not a LaserJet printer but you are using this procedure to print to disk, select your printer from this list).

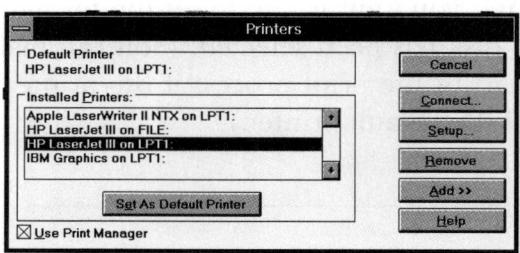

Figure 5.9 Control Panel Printers dialog.

7. Click on **C**onnect... to display the Connect dialog shown in Figure 5.10.

8. Use the scroll bar to the right of the Ports: window to locate the FILE: entry in this list. Select the **FILE:** entry.

9. Click on **OK** to return to the Printers dialog. The selected printer configuration is changed to show "on FILE:" instead of "on LPT1" as before.

10. Click on **C**lose to return to the Control Panel dialog.

11. Use **S**ettings **Ex**it to close the Control Panel and return to the Program Manager.

12. Double-click on the WordPerfect icon to return to the WordPerfect editing screen.

13. Use File **P**rint... **(F5)** to display the Print dialog. The current printer should be the one you just redirected to FILE: from LPT1. If it isn't, click on **S**elect... to choose this printer from the list.

14. Specify a Print Selection, if you don't want to print the entire document.

15. Click on **P**rint to display the Print To File dialog shown in Figure 5.11.

16. Enter the path and filename where you want the output to be stored.

17. Click on **OK** to start printing to disk.

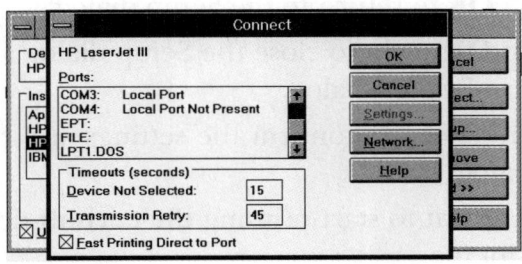

Figure 5.10   Control Panel Printers Connect . . . dialog.

TIP

You can make additional selections on the Print dialog if you wish. For example, you could specify a range of pages or tell WordPerfect to print only the current page.

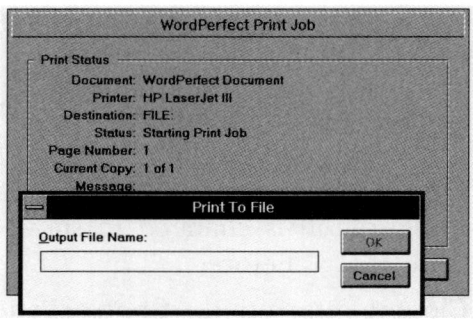

Figure 5.11   Print To File dialog.

TIP

When you have finished printing the current document to the file, repeat steps 1 to 10 to set printing again to the printer port instead of to a file. Otherwise the next time you print with the PostScript printer the information will go to the file you specified in this step instead of to the printer. Not only will you not get the hard copy output you expected, you will erase the previously created file.

PostScript Printer:

1. Use **F**ile **P**rint... to display the Print dialog.

2. Click on **S**elect... to display the Select Printer dialog.

3. If the PostScript printer is not selected, click on the name to select it.

4. Click on S**e**tup... to display the Setup dialog (the name of the chosen printer will appear at the top of this dialog).

5. Click on **O**ptions... to display the Options dialog.

6. Select Encapsulated PostScript **F**ile by clicking on the button beside this entry in the Print To section of this dialog.

7. Enter a complete path and filename in the **N**ame: field of this area of the dialog. Consider using an .EPS extension for this filename so you will know that the resulting file is in Encapsulated PostScript format.

8. Click on **OK** to return to the Setup dialog.

9. Click on **OK** again to close the Setup dialog and return to the Select Printer dialog.

10. Click on **S**elect to confirm the settings and return to the Print dialog.

11. Click on **P**rint to start printing the current document to a PostScript file.

What To Do If

- If you have forgotten to reset the printer destination from disk file and you don't want to print to disk after clicking on Print, choose **C**ancel from the Print To File dialog (HP LaserJet Printer) to return to your document.

See Also

- Printing Letters and Simple Documents, p. 160.
- Printing Long Documents (Master Document Feature), p. 168.

Printing to a Preprinted Form — 80

If you do much filling in of forms, you would be well served to purchase a program designed for that purpose, or to consult with your MIS department or an outside consultant to help you design templates and macros to make the job manageable in WordPerfect. However, for the occasional form—and if the form isn't too complicated—you can do it yourself. We'll show you the concept here.

Assumptions

- You have a preprinted form (or a form you have designed) that you want to fill in with WordPerfect.
- You have configured WordPerfect to use inch measurements. You can use this same procedure with other measurements, but you must change the figures we provide accordingly.

Exceptions

- This procedure is for a one-page form. You cannot advance the insertion point past a page break onto another page.

Steps

TIP

You could create a macro to prompt you for each field of this information, making it easier to fill out various versions of this form. See the discussion of macros in Chapter 8.

1. Use a ruler to measure your form and note the distances in inches for each field from the left edge of the page and from the top edge of the page. Write directly on the form the measurements you get (see Figure 5.12 for a sample form).

2. Use **Layout Typesetting Advance...** to display the Advance dialog, shown in Figure 5.13.

3. Click on the button beside **From Left Edge of Page** under Horizontal Position to enable that feature.

4. Enter the measurement from the left edge of the page for the first form information you want to enter in the **Horizontal Distance:** field of this dialog.

5. Click on the button beside From **Top** of Page under Vertical Position to enable that feature.

6. Enter the measurement from the top of the page for the first form information you want to enter in the **Vertical Distance:** field of this dialog.

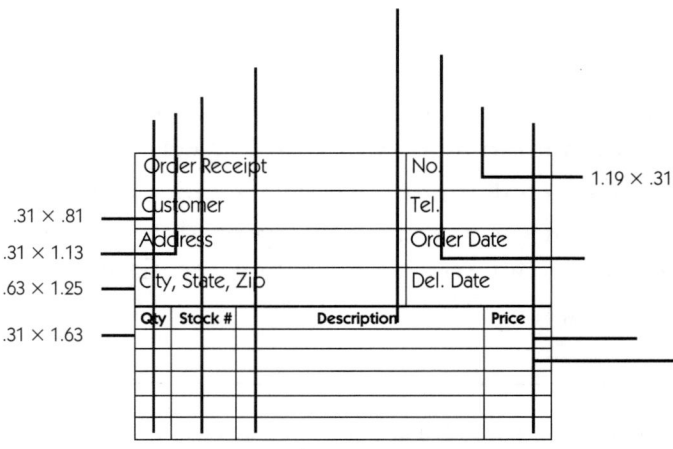

Figure 5.12   Hand-labeled sample form.

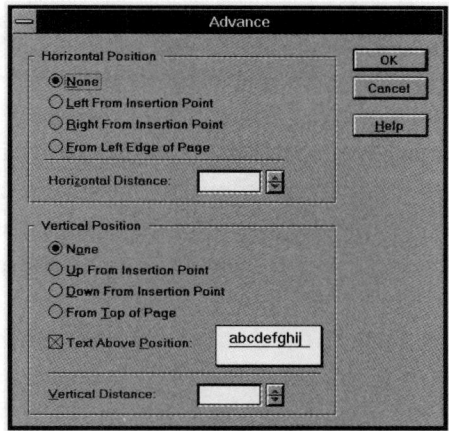

Figure 5.13   Advance dialog.

7. If you want the text to appear below the specified position instead of above it, click on the box beside the Text Above **P**osition: entry (see sample text in the box beside this entry).

8. Click on **OK** to close the dialog and return to your document.

9. Enter the text for the first field on your preprinted form.

10. Repeat steps 2 to 9 for as many information fields as you want to fill on the preprinted form.

_____ **What To Do If**

•   If you can't get the information to fit in the space provided on the preprinted form, try a different font. You may be able to reduce the size of the font enough to fit the information you want in the space provided.

_____ **See Also**

•   Using Macros, Chapter 8.
•   Printing Letters and Simple Documents, p. 160.

81 ▼ Using Color Output Devices

WordPerfect has evolved with the rest of the computer industry to support more sophisticated printing. For example, many of the sample images supplied with WordPerfect are in color, and it is fairly easy today to secure color art for inclusion in your Word-Perfect documents.

Obviously, to get the most out of color documents, you need a color printer, plotter, or other device. We give you some guidelines on using color output devices in this section.

Assumptions

- You have previously created a document that contains color material.
- You have installed a printer or plotter that supports color printing and it is the current output device.

Exceptions

- None.

Steps

> **TIP**
>
> If the printer you have selected does not support full color output then the Print Color: button is not available.

1. Use **File Print...** to display the Print dialog.
2. Click on the **Pr**int Color: button in this dialog to display the print color choices.
3. Choose **Full** Color.
4. Click on **Print** to begin printing the full-color document.

What To Do If

- If the Print Color: button is dimmed, use **Select...** to choose another printer that supports color.

See Also

- Selecting a Printer, p. 158.
- Printing Letters and Small Documents, p. 160.

Faxing with WordPerfect

The office (and even home) fax machine has become a standard fixture beside or nearby the computer. Many word processors, including WordPerfect, give you some utilities to make faxing easier. And, with fax modems, you can use your computer to send fax output directly from the computer, bypassing the print-and-fax process. We'll discuss WordPerfect's support for both of these options in this section.

Preparing a Fax Cover Sheet | 82

Depending on your faxing patterns, you may or may not need a cover sheet with the faxes you send. If the fax will be sent to a large mail room or secretarial pool in the recipient company before being sent to its ultimate destination, then a cover sheet of some kind is probably a good idea. If, on the other hand, you know the company on the other end of the line is relatively small, where everyone is likely to know everyone else, or you're sending a fax to a departmental machine that services a small group, then you can reduce transmission time, long distance charges, and paper by eliminating the cover sheet.

Assumptions

- None.

Exceptions

- None.

Steps

1. Use **File Template... (Ctrl+T)** to display the Template dialog shown in Figure 5.14.

2. Use the vertical scroll bar to locate the template called FAX1. Double-click on this name to load the template and load its associated macro. (Note that there are five supplied fax templates. Each one is slightly different, but the basic process we discuss here will show you how to use them.)

3. The first time you use this routine, WordPerfect will inform you that this template includes an automatic macro routine. Click on **OK** on this dialog to continue the macro.

4. The first time you run this routine, WordPerfect asks you to fill in a screen with your personal information. Type a name in the first field, press **Tab** to enter Title:, and so on until you have filled in the entire form. This information will be included in the return address area of the fax cover sheet. Click on **OK** to close this dialog.

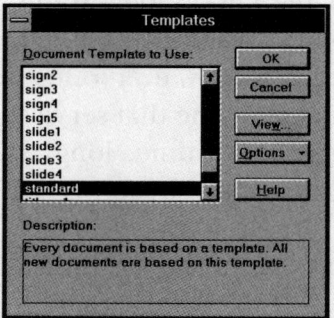

Figure 5.14   Template dialog.

5. When the Template Information dialog is displayed, pro-vide information for your fax in one of these ways:

- Type in the fax recipient information, including Name, FAX number, and Number of pages, then click on **OK** to close this dialog and create the cover sheet.

- Click on **P**ersonal Info if you want to change the infor-mation you entered previously in step 4, above.

- Click on **A**ddress Book to display the dialog shown in Figure 5.15. The address book lets you store name and address information for fax or merge letter use.

- If you're using the address book, complete the follow-ing steps: Click on **A**dd to add a new name and address to the address database. You'll see the dialog in Figure 5.16. (This is similar to your personal information dia-log completed earlier.) Fill in the recipient informa-tion on the Address Book dialog. Click on **OK** when you have the information complete. Then, select a name from the list presented. (The first time you use the address book, there will be only one name, of course.) Click on **S**elect to choose this name and return to the Template Information dialog. The information from the recipient you selected on the previous dialog will appear in the appropriate fields of this dialog.

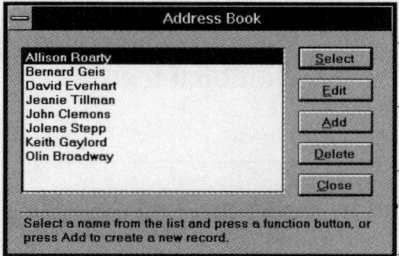

Figure 5.15   FAX1 Address Book dialog.

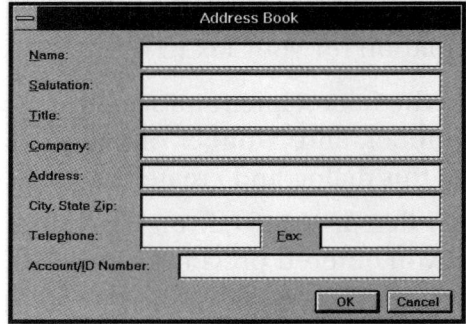

Figure 5.16   Address Book Add dialog.

6. Enter the total number of pages for this fax in the last field of this dialog and click on **OK** to complete the cover sheet.

7. Use **F**ile Save **A**s... if you want to save this cover sheet for future use. (In most cases, however, you will not save this sheet. It is easier to create a new one using the address book and the auto create macro just described.)

What To Do If

• You can easily change information on the cover sheet after the macro ends by using standard WordPerfect editing techniques. The information on the sheet is in standard WordPerfect document format at this point.

• Add text to the completed sheet if you wish simply by typing what you want to add at the location of the insertion point. The macro ends with the insertion point at an appropriate location for additional text.

See Also

• Sending Faxes from Within WordPerfect, p. 187.
• Using Macros, Chapter 8.

Sending Faxes from Within WordPerfect | 83

Like many of today's computer applications, WordPerfect for Windows 6 supports sending faxes from inside the application. All you need is a modem that supports faxes and an appropriate fax driver that runs in Windows. You can't use WordPerfect to send faxes until you have installed a fax program that runs under Windows. When you do, that program's driver should appear in Windows as one of the available printers.

All you need do to send faxes from within WordPerfect is to set up your drivers for use with WordPerfect. After that, you simply choose the fax driver for your printer and print as usual.

Assumptions

- You have installed a Microsoft Windows-based fax program and the appropriate drivers. The driver for that fax program should appear in the list of available printers when you use the **File** **P**rint **S**elect... command sequence.

Exceptions

- None.

Steps

To set up the fax driver for use with WordPerfect:

1. Use **F**ile Select Printer... to display the Select Printer dialog.
2. Select the fax driver from the list of available printers in the Printers: window of this dialog.
3. Click on Setup... to display the Setup dialog.
4. Fill in the appropriate fields on this Setup dialog to specify where the fax is to be sent, and how. (There may be differ-

ent fields for different drivers. Consult the documentation that came with your fax software.)

5. Click on **OK** to return to the Select Printer dialog.

6. Click on **S**elect to make the fax driver your current Word-Perfect printer.

7. Use File **P**rint... as usual to print all or a portion of the current document.

What To Do If

- If you have problems setting up your fax driver or faxing from inside WordPerfect, consult the documentation that came with your fax software. Reinstall the fax software if necessary.

See Also

- Preparing a Fax Cover Sheet, p. 183.
- Printing Letters and Simple Documents, p. 160.

84 Setting Print Defaults

In addition to setting some print characteristics from the Print dialog, you can specify some printing defaults through the Preferences dialog.

Assumptions

- None.

Exceptions

- None.

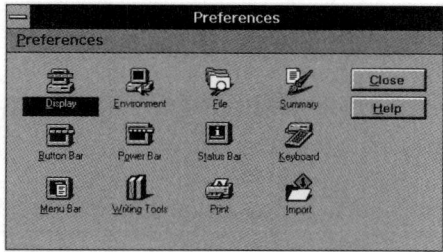

Figure 5.17   Preferences dialog.

_____ **Steps**

1. Use **F**ile **P**references... to display the Preferences dialog shown in Figure 5.17.

2. Double-click on the printer icon to display the Print Preferences dialog shown in Figure 5.18.

3. Change any of the default settings to new values as desired. For example, you can have WordPerfect automatically assume you want to print two copies of every document by entering 2 in the **N**umber of Copies: field on the Print Preferences dialog.

4. Click on **OK** to close the Print Preferences dialog and set the changes you have made.

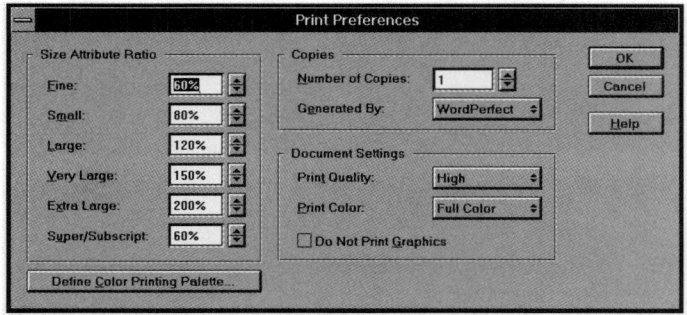

Figure 5.18   Print Preferences dialog.

What To Do If _____

- If you find that some of the changes you made on the Preferences dialog are not what you wanted, simply repeat the process to set the preferences you prefer.

See Also _____

- Printing Letters and Simple Documents, p. 160.
- Installing a New Printer Driver, p. 156.

85 / Starting a Stalled Printer

Printing from WordPerfect is normally an easy task that presents no problems. Occasionally, however, when you send a document to the printer, nothing happens. You can try several things to get the printer started. We'll show you the major steps in this section.

Assumptions _____

- You have used File Print... to print a document or a portion of a document, but nothing is coming out on the printer.
- You have checked the obvious problems: power off, printer off-line, paper out, and so on.

Exceptions _____

- None.

Steps _____

1. Shrink the WordPerfect editing window to an icon by clicking on the minimize arrow at the upper right of the screen (or click on the Control Panel button at the upper left of the screen and choose Minimize).

2. Open the Program Manager, if it is not already maximized.

3. Find the Main application window or open it from an icon if necessary.

4. Double-click on the Print Manager icon to open the Print Manager dialog, shown in Figure 5.19.

5. Note whether the Print Manager displays an error message. If there was a prior print job that did not complete properly (printer turned off, out of paper, etc.), then the latest print job can't complete. Highlight the print job with the error and press **Del** to remove it. Answer **OK** when the Print Manager asks whether you want to delete the print job. The current job should start automatically when the stalled job ahead of it is deleted. If the current print job is the one with the error, check the printer for an out of paper, off-line, or power off condition.

6. Use **P**rinter E**x**it (**Alt+F4**) to exit the Print Manager dialog and return to your document.

What To Do If

• If the Print Manager shows no error condition, then you may have the print destination set to a disk file or to an

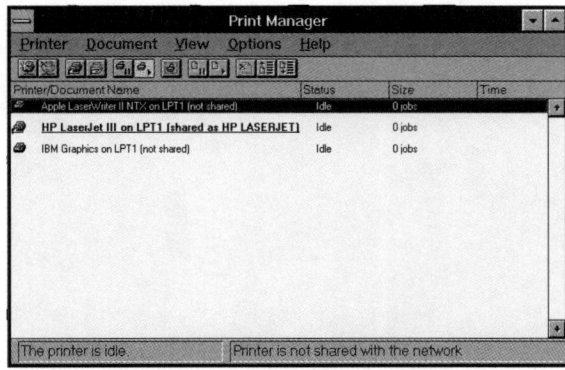

Figure 5.19   Print Manager dialog.

inactive port. Refer to the steps in Printing to a Disk, p. xx, to reset the printer to the proper port.

See Also

- Printing to Disk, p. 175.
- Printing Letters and Simple Documents, p. 160.

Chapter
6

Using Lines (Rules)

USING GRAPHICS WITH WORD-PERFECT 6.0 FOR WINDOWS

WordPerfect handles graphics within documents pretty well. The process is mostly menu-driven, so you can drop a drawing or scanned image or chart or text box into your document quickly and easily. In this chapter, we show you the major WordPerfect graphics features and how to use them.

Using Lines (Rules)

One of the simplest graphics features you can use to enhance your documents is drawing lines. Use horizontal and vertical lines (or rules) to separate columns in a multicolumn document, to emphasize a heading or letterhead, to separate any document segments, and other applications. In this section we show you how to use vertical, horizontal, and custom lines in your Word-Perfect documents.

86 Using Vertical Lines

You will use vertical lines most often (probably) to separate columns in a multicolumn document. However, you can drop in a vertical line almost anywhere in your WordPerfect documents. Once you experiment with how to create these lines, experiment in your documents to see how they can enhance the looks of your text.

Assumptions

• The insertion point is positioned within the column that you want to rule to the left or at a position near where you want the final line to appear.

Exceptions

• None.

Steps

1. Use **G**raphics **V**ertical Line (**Ctrl+Shift+F11**) to insert a vertical line in the margin to the left of the current column. (This is true even if there is only a single column in this portion of the document.)

2. To move the line to a new position in your document, click on the line to select it, then grab the line with the mouse pointer and drag it where you want it.

What To Do If

- If the line is too thin or too thick, select the line and grab one of the handles with the mouse and drag the line wider or narrower.

- Remove an inserted line by selecting the line and pressing **Del**.

See Also

- Using Horizontal Lines, below.
- Using WordPerfect Draw, p. 198.

TIP

You can tell when the line is selected by the small square "handles" that appear at either end of the line. When you move the mouse pointer onto the selected line, the cursor changes to an arrow cross. Press the left mouse button and drag the resulting dotted line to the new line location. Release the mouse button to drop the vertical line.

Using Horizontal Lines   87

Horizontal lines in WordPerfect work similarly to vertical lines.

Assumptions

- The insertion point is located where you want the horizontal line to appear or at least near the final location of the horizontal line.

Exceptions

- Unlike the Vertical Line utility, the Horizontal Line utility places a horizontal line at the location of the insertion point, not at the top or bottom of a paragraph.

Steps

1. Use **Graphics Horizontal** Line (**Ctrl+F11**) to insert a horizontal line at the insertion point location.

2. To move the line to a new position in your document, click on the line to select it, then grab the line with the mouse pointer and drag it where you want it.

What To Do If

- If the line is too thin or too thick, select the line and grab one of the handles with the mouse and drag the line wider or narrower.

- Remove an inserted line by selecting the line and pressing Del.

See Also

- Using Vertical Lines, p. 194.
- Using WordPerfect Draw, p. 198.

TIP

You can tell when the line is selected by the small square "handles" that appear at either end of the line. When you move the mouse pointer onto the selected line, the cursor changes to an arrow cross. Press the left mouse button and drag the resulting dotted line to the new line location. Release the mouse button to drop the horizontal line.

88 ▽   Editing WordPerfect Lines

In addition to editing the size and position of previously placed lines with the mouse, you can use a dialog to change other features of existing lines.

Assumptions

- You have created one or more horizontal or vertical lines and you want to edit one or more of them.

Exceptions

- None.

Steps

1. Select the line you want to edit by clicking on it.
2. Use **G**raphics Edit Li**n**e... to display the Edit Graphics Line dialog shown in Figure 6.1.
3. Use the various fields of this dialog to create your own line characteristics and placement. For example you can set the line style (Single, Double, Thick Single, and so on), Line Color, Thickness, and more.

> **TIP**
>
> You can use the Graphics Custom Line... command sequence to display a version of this dialog to create a line style and placement from scratch. The result is the same as if you inserted a line, then edited it as described here.

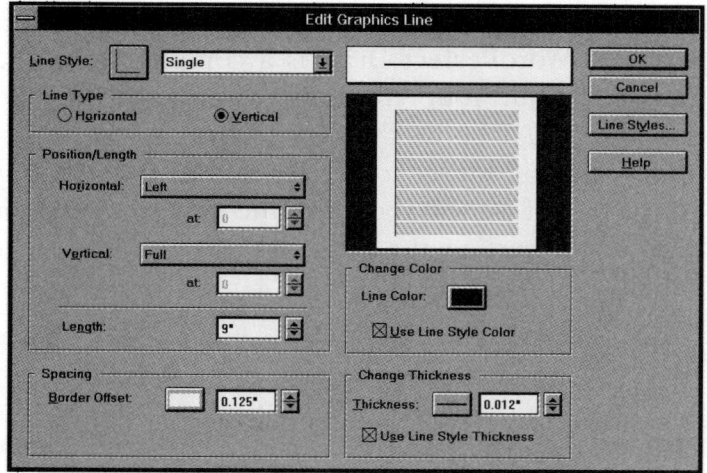

Figure 6.1 Edit Graphics Line dialog.

> **TIP**
>
> You can use the Edit (or Custom) Line dialog to make your lines very wide to add emphasis to areas of your document or to create custom boxes.

What To Do If

- You can fine-tune placement and size of any line by grabbing the line with the mouse and moving it or changing the size.

See Also

- Using Vertical Lines, p. 194.
- Using Horizontal Lines, p. 195.

89 Using WordPerfect Draw

WordPerfect Windows includes a capable draw program that you can use to create images to include in your documents. Although WordPerfect Draw operates like a completely separate application, it is integrated well with WordPerfect itself, and the images you create within it are inserted automatically at the location of the insertion point.

Like Microsoft Paintbrush (included with Windows) and other draw packages, WordPerfect Draw is a complete and relatively complex application. Your WordPerfect package was supplied with a separate 250-page user's guide. Obviously we can't cover all aspects of Draw in this section (refer to your Draw user's guide for full details), but we will show you the basics of accessing the application and inserting the drawings you produce into your WordPerfect documents.

Assumptions

- The current document is the one where you want to insert a WordPerfect Draw image.
- The insertion point is located within the paragraph where you want the WordPerfect Draw image to appear in your document.

_____ **Exceptions**

- None.

_____ **Steps**

1. Use **G**raphics **D**raw... to launch WordPerfect Draw and present the main Draw editing screen shown in Figure 6.2. The drawing tool bar is displayed at the left side of the Draw screen. A Windows-standard menu bar is at the top of the screen.

2. Use **V**iew **B**utton Bar **(F10)** to add the button bar to the Draw menu. This makes it easier to access some of the program's features.

3. Use the tools to create the image you want to insert in your document. This Draw program works similar to other

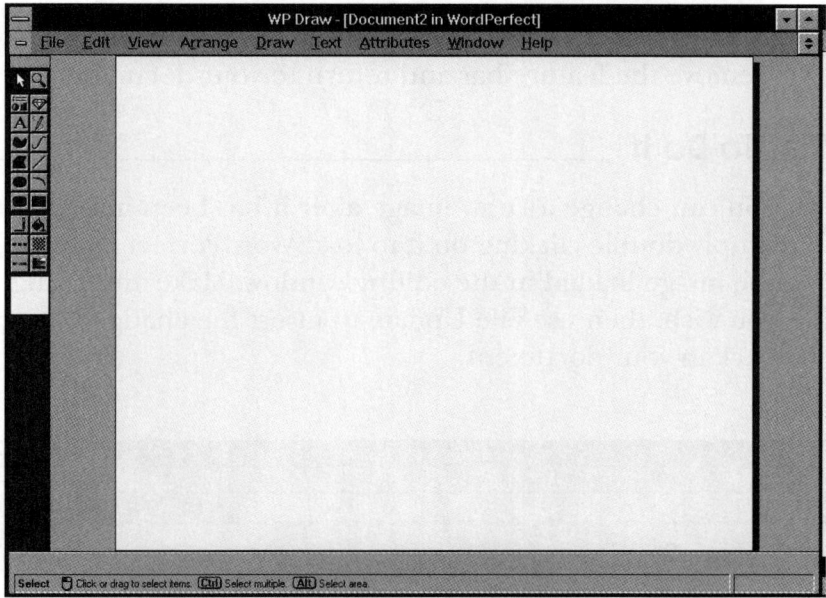

Figure 6.2   Main WordPerfect Draw screen.

low-end drawing packages. A little practice and you will be able to create custom drawings easily to enhance your documents.

4. Use **File Update** to insert the new drawing into the current document. The image will be inserted to the right of the current paragraph.

5. Use **File Exit** to return to your document.

6. Click within the new image to select it. Then you can size it or move it with the mouse, if you need to.

7. With the image selected, use **Graphics Edit Box (Shift+ F11)** to display the Graphics Edit feature bar, shown in Figure 6.3.

8. Click on **Border/Fill** to create a border for the graphics image, if you wish.

9. Click on **Position** to specify how WordPerfect will anchor this image. (As you add text you need a place to "nail down" the image.)

10. Make additional changes as desired, then click on **Close** to remove the feature bar and return to your document.

What To Do If

-   You can change a Draw image after it has been inserted by simply double-clicking on it to load WordPerfect Draw with the image loaded in the editing window. Make any changes you wish, then use File Update to insert the changed image back in your document.

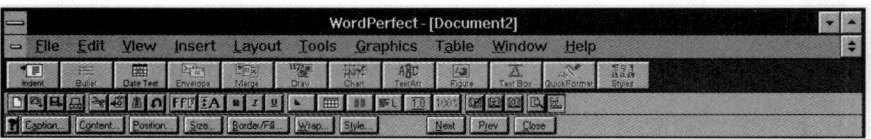

Figure 6.3   Graphics Edit Box feature bar.

See Also

- Using Vertical Lines, p. 194.
- Using Horizontal Lines, p. 195.
- Editing WordPerfect Lines, p. 196.

Using WordPerfect Charts | 90

The WordPerfect charting facility is similar to WordPerfect Draw. It is a separate application that is closely linked to WordPerfect itself. You can use it to transform dry numerical data into graphs and charts that insert right into your documents, making your information more visual and easier to interpret.

Like WordPerfect Draw, Chart is a complete application within itself. We won't cover all aspects of this useful utility here, but we'll get you started and show you the basics of inserting charts into your WordPerfect documents.

Assumptions

- The current document is the one that will receive a chart that results from this process.

Exceptions

- None.

Steps

1. Use **G**raphics Chart... to launch the WordPerfect charting utility and display the main charting screen shown in Figure 6.4. A sample chart—a good starting place for the current chart—is displayed on the screen.

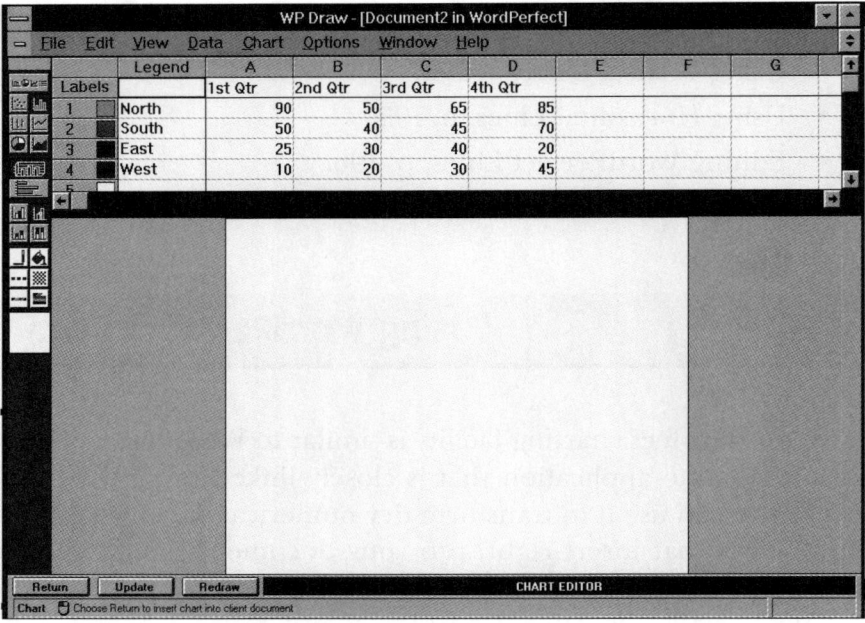

Figure 6.4   WordPerfect Chart main screen.

2. Click in the first field under Legend, beside the number 1, to enter the first legend. The word "North" is in this place by default; put whatever you want for the first data legend.

3. Repeat the preceding process for as many data values (legends) as you require for this chart.

4. Next, click in the first label under "A" (1st Qtr) and enter the description of your first data value.

5. Repeat this process for column "B," "C," "D," and so on until you have all of the data you will be using labeled.

6. Select each data value in turn, changing it to reflect the information you want to display in your document.

7. Use the tool bar to the left of the editing window to select the type of chart you want to use. A three-dimensional bar chart is the default, but you can specify a pie chart, a

stacked bar, line graphics, and more. Experiment with the tools to discover the best format for representing your data.

8. Use **O**ptions **T**itles... to change the default "Title of Chart" to a title that describes the data you are representing in your document. Similarly, add a subtitle and titles for the Y and X axis if you wish.

9. Click on **OK** to close the Titles dialog.

10. Click on Redraw to see how your chart will look with new data.

11. Use **F**ile **U**pdate to place the current chart into your document.

12. Use **F**ile **E**xit to close the Chart utility and return to your document.

_____ **What To Do If**

- If the chart is not placed where you want it, simply select it by clicking on it, then use the mouse to move it anywhere in the document you wish.

- You can also use **G**raphics **E**dit Box to specify position, set a border, create a caption, and more.

_____ **See Also**

- Using WordPerfect Draw, p. 198.
- Importing Graphics Files, below.

| Importing Graphics Files | 91

You can import a variety of graphics images into a WordPerfect document. By default, WordPerfect assumes you will be using WordPerfect graphics format files (*.WPG files), and a number of these files are included with WordPerfect. However, the intrinsic WordPerfect graphics import utility can process a number of file formats: .BMP, .CGM, .EPS, .PIC, .PCX, .TIF and more. These files might come from any number of drawing and graphics programs, including a scanner utility or files converted from another, incompatible format.

Assumptions

- The current document is the one that will receive the imported graphics file.

Exceptions

- None.

Steps

TIP
You can use the features of the WordPerfect File Manager (the same as you use when using File Open...) to locate a graphics file. Use View..., for example, to look at successive graphics files before you insert one into your document (see Figure 6.6).

1. Use **G**raphics **F**igure to display the Insert Image dialog shown in Figure 6.5. By default WordPerfect shows the available .WPG files in the GRAPHICS subdirectory within the directory where WordPerfect was installed.

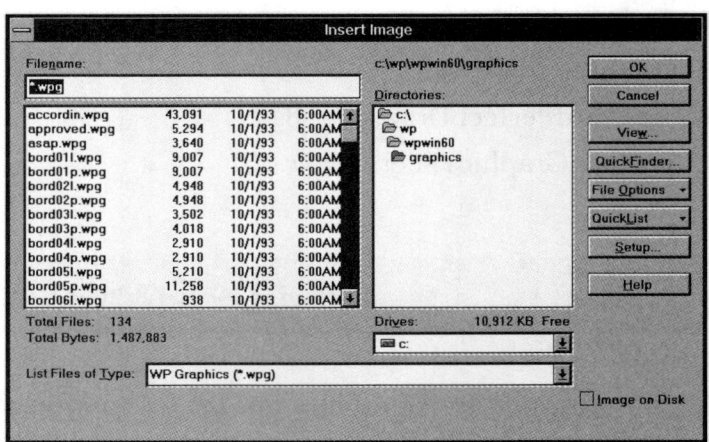

Figure 6.5   Insert Image dialog.

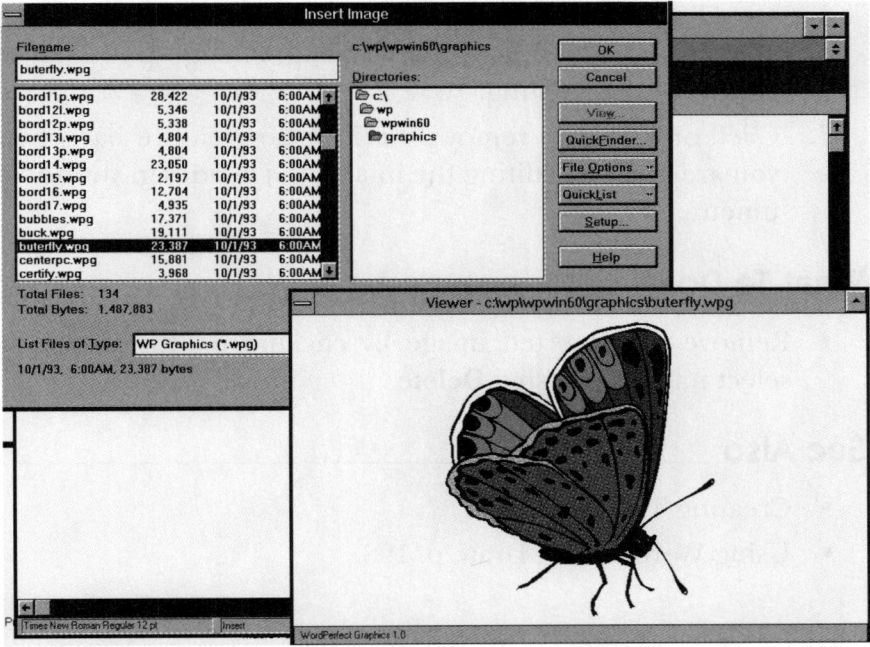

Figure 6.6   Insert Image dialog with view enabled.

2. If you are importing a .WPG file, then use the vertical scroll bar to locate the file you want to use.

3. To display files of other types, click on the down arrow to the right of the List Files of **T**ype: field at the bottom of this dialog. Select the file type you want to use, placing the description in this field.

4. To view other directories, select them in the **D**irectories: window of this dialog. The File**n**ame: list changes as you change file type or view a different directory.

5. When you have found the image file you want to insert, select it and click on **OK,** or double-click on the filename to insert it into your document and close the Insert Image dialog.

6. Use **G**raphics **E**dit Box if you want to add or remove a border around the image, add shading, change position, or conduct other editing.

7. Click on **C**lose to remove the Edit Box feature bar when you are finished editing the image as it resides in your document.

What To Do If

- Remove the inserted image by clicking on the image to select it, then pressing **Delete**.

See Also

- Creating Text Art, p. 207.
- Using WordPerfect Draw, p. 198.

92 ⎔ Creating Text Boxes

When you insert graphics information into a WordPerfect document (see Importing Graphics Files, p. 203), the software actually creates a box, inserts it into the document, and fills the box with the graphics image you select from the Insert Image dialog. You can conduct a similar operation with text material.

Assumptions

- The current document is the one you want to receive the text box.
- The insertion point is positioned near where you want the text box inserted.

Exceptions

- None.

_____ **Steps**

1.   Use **G**raphics **T**ext to insert a text box into your document. By default, WordPerfect inserts a small, thin box with thick top and bottom lines and no lines on the sides. The box is selected and the insertion point is positioned inside the box.

2.   Type the text information you want to appear in this box.

3.   Use conventional editing features (font, attributes and the like) to format the text as you want it.

4.   Use **G**raphics **E**dit Box to display the Edit Box feature bar. Use the buttons on this bar to change the borders of the text box, to move the box, and so on.

5.   Click on **C**lose to remove the feature bar.

_____ **What To Do If**

•   Select the box and press **Delete** to remove the newly inserted box.

•   Select all or a portion of the text inside the box, then use **E**dit **C**opy/**C**ut to place a copy on the Clipboard, then you can use **E**dit **P**aste to put the selected text into your document.

_____ **See Also**

•   Importing Graphics Files, p. 203.

•   Creating Text Art, below.

Creating Text Art | **93**

WordPerfect includes a wide range of fonts and attribute settings for those fonts. Still, there are times when you want to go beyond standard fonts for text. The WordPerfect TextArt Editor lets you do this.

Assumptions

- The current document will receive the text art.
- The insertion point is positioned close to where you want the text art to appear in your document.

Exceptions

- None.

Steps

> **TIP**
>
> Double-click on the TextArt image in your document to relaunch the Text Art Editor to make changes.

1. Use **G**raphics **T**extArt... to display the TextArt Editor dialog, shown in Figure 6.7.
2. Type the text you want to insert into your document in the Enter **T**ext: field of this dialog.
3. Use the pull-down lists beside the Fo**n**t: and **S**tyle: fields to change fonts and attributes, if you wish.

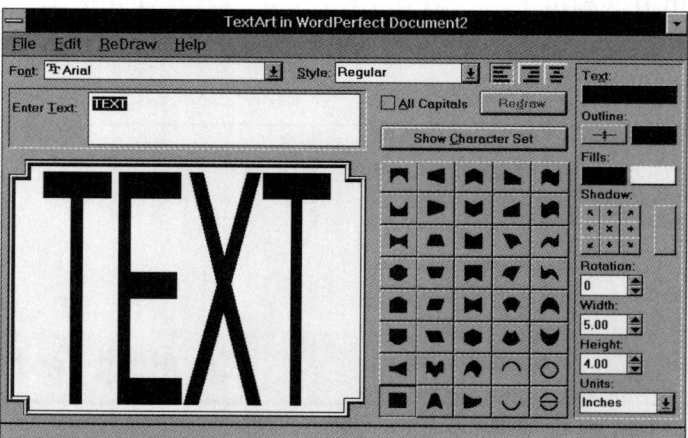

Figure 6.7   WordPerfect TextArt Editor dialog.

4. Click on Show **C**haracter Set to display all of the available characters and symbols within the selected font. This will help you select a font when you want to include special characters in your text art.

5. Click on the Te**x**t: color bar to change the color of the text.

6. Click on Outline: to specify the type of line to use for character outlining, if desired.

7. To change the pattern used to fill in the central part of the characters, click on Fills: to display 16 possible patterns. Click on one of the patterns to select it.

8. Specifying character shadowing by clicking on one of the squares under the Shadow: label on this dialog.

9. Click on one of the text patterns (under the Show Character Set button) to specify how the text will be displayed. Experiment with different selections to achieve the text effect you want in your document.

10. Use **F**ile Save Copy As... if you want to store the text art creation into a separate file. Do this if you want to use the same text art in other documents later.

11. Use **F**ile **U**pdate WordPerfect to insert the text art creation into your document.

12. Use **F**ile E**x**it & Return to WordPerfect to close the TextArt Editor and return to your document.

What To Do If

*   Select the TextArt text by clicking on it, then grab the box to move it wherever you want in your document. You can also resize the box by grabbing one of the handles on an edge of the box.

*   Conduct additional editing with the **G**raphics **E**dit Box feature bar after selecting the text art image.

See Also

- Importing Graphics Files, p. 203.
- Using a Watermark, below.
- Creating Text Boxes, p. 206.

94   ## Using a Watermark

A WordPerfect watermark is a graphics image (including text art) that is printed lightly and positioned beneath the document text. Use a watermark to carry through a company theme, to highlight the idea in your document, or simply to add interest to your reports and other writing. You can use any graphics image supported by WordPerfect as a watermark.

Assumptions

- The current document is the one to receive the watermark.
- The insertion point is positioned near where you want the watermark to appear.

Exceptions

- None.

Steps

1. Use **L**ayout **W**atermark... to load the Watermark dialog.
2. Click on **C**reate to create the "A" watermark for this document and display the Watermark editing screen and feature bar, shown in Figure 6.8.

Figure 6.8 Watermark editing screen and feature bar.

3. To insert a figure (.WPG, .TIF, .PCX etc.) click on the **Fig-ure...** bar to display the Insert Image dialog. This is basi-cally the same dialog you see with **File O**pen... and pro-vides the same file management features.

4. Locate the graphics file you want to insert as a watermark. Double-click on the filename, or select it and click on **OK** to load the image.

5. Once the image is loaded, WordPerfect automatically dis-plays the Edit Box feature bar. Use these tools to fine-tune the watermark image, as required.

6. Click on **C**lose when you are finished editing the image and want to return to the Watermark editing screen.

7. Click on Placement... to select from **O**dd Pages, **E**ven Pages, or **E**very Page, then click on **OK** to set the place-ment of the watermark image.

8. Click on **C**lose to return to your document with the water-mark image in the background.

What To Do If

- If the image is not positioned where you want it, use **L**ayout **W**atermark... **E**dit... to display the Watermark editing screen. Then use **G**raphics **E**dit Box to display the Edit Box feature bar. Use **P**osition... to place the Watermark where you want it.

- Once the watermark image is displayed in the Watermark editing window, double-click on the image if you want to edit it. If the image is compatible with WordPerfect Draw, that application will be launched with the current image in the Draw editing window.

See Also

- Using WordPerfect Draw, p. 198.
- Inserting a Graphic, p. 325.

Using the Equation Editor

Like the frustration of many word processing users who for years wanted to print a simple envelope only to find it was more trouble than it was worth, engineers and other scientific types have railed against the difficulty in getting any but the simplest formula or equation into a word processing document.

Thankfully, word processor designers have addressed both issues in pretty sound fashion. Built-in envelope printing routines make placing a name and address on an envelope nearly painless. And built-in equation editors let you place about any kind of formula into your WordPerfect document.

Assumptions

- The current document is the one to receive the formula.
- The insertion point is positioned near where you want the formula inserted.

Exceptions

- Although WordPerfect's Equation Editor can help you insert about any formula into a document, there are no facilities for solving these formulas. You can only insert the proper symbols and get some help in lining them up properly.

Steps

1. Use **G**raphics **Eq**uation to display the Equation Editor shown in Figure 6.9. This window has three main parts: A command list (on the left of the dialog), the display window that shows the finished formula (on the bottom), and the editing window where you type the formula (on the top).

    The commands window actually displays several types of data that you can access by pulling down a list under the button above this window:

Commands	Keyword commands
Large	Mathematical and scientific symbols in large and small sizes
Symbols	A selection of various symbols that can be used in formulas
Greek	A collection of Greek symbols that can be used in formulas
Arrows	A variety of arrows for use in formulas

2. Type the basic equation in the upper (editing) window of the Equation Editor dialog.

3. Use the command words, symbols, and other tools accessible in the left Commands window as necessary.

4. Click on the **R**edisplay button (or press **Ctrl+F3**) from the button bar to create the formula in graphics form in the

> **TIP**
>
> As you enter commands in the editing window, many are displayed in the editing window as a series of words and symbols. When you click on Redisplay, WordPerfect is smart enough to know how these commands should translate.

Figure 6.9 Equation Editor.

lower window (try simply typing A+B=C in the editing window and see how WordPerfect displays the formula in the lower window when you click on Redisplay).

5. Use **F**ile Save **A**s... to store the formula in a file, if you wish. Later you can use Insert File to recall this formula for reuse if you wish.

6. Use **F**ile **C**lose **(Alt+F4)** to close the Equation Editor, insert the equation into your document and return to the document editing window.

What To Do If

• You can edit an existing equation by double-clicking on the equation in your document, automatically launching the

Equation Editor. Select the text of the formula you want to delete, or position the insertion point within the editing window to add formula information. Then click on **R**edisplay to view the changed formula in the lower window.

- Use **G**raphics **E**dit Box (**Shift+F11**) after selecting the formula in your document to add additional formatting to the formula, including adding a caption, placing a box around the formula, and the like.

See Also

- Inserting a Graphic, p. 325.
- Creating Text Art, p. 207.

Chapter
7

TEMPLATES

217

Whenever you load a new document, you are using a template. Normally, unless you specify something besides the default, you are using a standard template that presents a clean editing screen waiting for your input.

You can enhance your documents with one of the specialty templates (WordPerfect calls them ExpressDocs) supplied with WordPerfect. You can also make document formatting—especially across multiple documents of the same type—by using styles. We'll show you how to use and create templates and styles in this chapter.

96 Using Templates

WordPerfect is supplied with at least 65 interactive templates (ExpressDocs) plus some standard templates, all designed to help you create easily documents with a high level of reader interest. A template is basically a document with some preset formatting that you can use over and over again to create repetitive documents of the same type. An ExpressDoc is a template that includes some macro code to make the document interactive.

Using a template, whether it is a plain template or an interactive template, is as simple as selecting the template you want to use from the Template menu. A template can contain a few simple lines of text, or it can be filled with text, graphics, macro code, or anything else that WordPerfect supports.

Assumptions

- You want to start a new document based on one of WordPerfect's supplied templates.

Exceptions

- When you choose a new WordPerfect template, a new document is opened based on this template. If any other documents already are open, they are not affected by your choice of a template.

_____ **Steps**

1. Use **File Template... (Ctrl+T)** to display the Templates dialog, shown in Figure 7.1.

2. Select the template you want to use from the list. Note that as you highlight individual template names, a short description of this template is shown at the bottom of the dialog.

3. When you have decided on a template to use, highlight it and click on **OK**, or double-click on the template name to launch it into a new document editing window.

4. Fill in any information WordPerfect asks for or that is appropriate for the template.

5. Use **File Save As...** to store the filled-in template as a new document file.

_____ **What To Do If**

• If you discover you have launched the wrong template, exit the running macro (if any) at the first opportunity, then use **File Close** to close the current file and start over with

> **TIP**
>
> Click on **View...** on the Templates dialog to open a view window. Now each time you highlight a new template, the basic format and text for it are shown in a separate viewer window.

> **TIP**
>
> Many of the templates supplied with WordPerfect are "interactive." They ask you questions or fill in information automatically with macros linked to the template file.

Figure 7.1   Templates dialog.

step 1 (see the preceding steps), locating another template to use.

See Also

- Creating Templates, below.
- Creating Interactive Templates, p. 223.
- Sending Faxes from Within WordPerfect, p. 187.

 **97** | **Creating Templates**

Some of the templates supplied with WordPerfect are relatively complex, performing really useful tasks. It is also useful to create relatively simple templates for your own use. Even if you have never programmed a macro (and don't intend to!) you can design and build templates that will help you get through repetitive work... with less work.

Assumptions

- You have previously planned the template you want to create in WordPerfect.

Exceptions

- None.

Steps

1. Use **File Template... (Ctrl+T)** to display the Templates dialog.
2. Click on the **O**ptions button to pull down the Options menu.
3. Choose **C**reate Template... to display the Create Document Template dialog, shown in Figure 7.2.

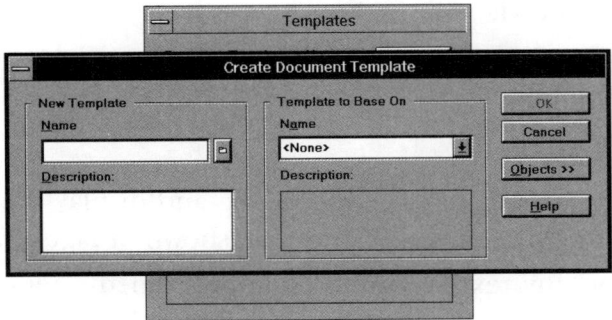

Figure 7.2   Create Document Template dialog.

4. Enter a name for the new template in the **N**ame: field of this dialog. (You can use up to 8 characters for the name, following standard DOS file naming conventions.) You can pull down a list of files and directories to help you select a directory and name for this template by clicking on the file folder icon to the right of the Name: field.

5. Click in the **D**escription: field and enter a brief description for this template. You can use up to 280 characters for the description but, again, shorter is better. Make it easy on yourself and others using this template.

6. If you want to base this new template on an existing template, enter the name of the existing template (including the path) in the Template to Base On **N**ame: field of this dialog. Pull down a list of existing templates by clicking on the down arrow to the right of this field.

7. Click on the **O**bjects>> button to expand the Create Document Template dialog to include individual windows for the objects supported by templates. This will show you the objects already included in the template you are basing this template on. The windows include:

   • Styles
   • Macros

- Abbreviations
- Button Bars
- Menus
- Keyboards

8. Click on **OK** to close the dialog and display the Template editing screen and feature bar, shown in Figure 7.3.

9. Type any text you want to appear on the template (and therefore within your new document).

10. Add any formatting, text attributes, and other features you want to include on the template, just as if you were working with a standard WordPerfect document. Remember, anything you include in the template will be a part of each new document based on the template.

11. Click on **E**xit Template to exit the Template editing screen. Answer **Y**es when WordPerfect asks whether you want to save the changes to the current template.

What To Do If

- You can edit a template to fine-tune it. Use **F**ile **T**emplate... **(Ctrl+T)**, select the template you want to edit, then click on **O**ptions and choose **E**dit Template... . The Template feature bar is displayed and you can make any changes as if you were in the Create mode.

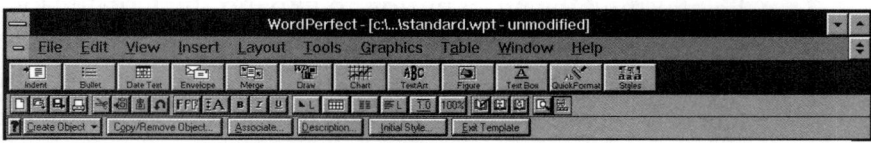

Figure 7.3 Template editing screen and feature bar.

See Also

- Using Macros, Chapter 8.
- Using Templates, p. 218.

Creating Interactive Templates 98

One of the more powerful features of WordPerfect is the preprogrammed macros and templates that provide interactive forms and other WordPerfect documents. These are genuinely useful utilities that are tightly integrated into the WordPerfect software. Also included with WordPerfect are macros designed to help you create your own interactive templates. The best way to learn about these features is to use them, but we'll show you the basics in this section.

Assumptions

- You have created the basic template that includes some areas that require fill-in data.
- The insertion point is positioned where you want the first interactive field inserted.

Exceptions

- None.

Steps

1. Use **F**ile **T**emplate... **(Ctrl+T)** to display the Templates dialog.
2. Click on the **O**ptions button to pull down the Options menu.

TIP

You can grab the dialog and drag it out of the way if you need to place the insertion point under the dialog location.

3. Choose **C**reate Template... to display the Create Document Template dialog.

4. Enter a name for the new template in the **N**ame: field of this dialog.

5. Click in the **D**escription: field and enter a brief description for this template.

6. Select **_autotmp** in the Template to Base On **N**ame window of this dialog. This is a group of template macros that let you build some interesting features in your own templates.

7. Click on **OK** to close the Create Document Template dialog. A WordPerfect editing screen with a Template feature bar is displayed.

8. Use **T**ools **M**acro **P**lay... **(Alt+F10)** to display the Macros List dialog.

9. Click on **L**ocation... to display the Macro Location dialog.

10. Click on the button beside **F**ile on Disk and click on **OK** to close the dialog.

11. Type **Prompts** in the **N**ame: field of the Play Macro dialog.

12. Press **E**nter or click on **P**lay to start the macro. The Prompt Builder dialog is displayed.

13. Click on **A**dd to display the Add a Template Prompt dialog.

14. Type the name of the prompt you want to add in the Template **P**rompt: field of this dialog.

15. Pull down the Link to Address Book Field: list if you want to link this interactive field with any entries in the Address book. This might be helpful in creating an interactive memo form, for example, a fax cover sheet, an envelope macro.

16. Click on **OK** to complete the add process and return to the Prompt Builder dialog.

17. Click on **P**aste to insert the interactive prompt into your template.

18. Click inside your document to deactivate the Prompt Builder dialog temporarily.

19. Move the insertion point to the location of the next interactive field you want to insert.

20. Click inside the Prompt Builder dialog to activate it once again.

21. Repeat steps 13 to 20 for all of the prompts you want to add to your template.

22. Click on **C**lose to remove the Prompt Builder dialog when you have entered all of the interactive fields you want to use. You will be returned to the template editing window.

23. Click on **E**xit Template and choose **Yes** when WordPerfect asks if you want to save the changes to the current template.

24. To use the new template, use **F**ile **T**emplate... **(Ctrl+T)** and choose the name from the Template dialog. The fields you have created cause autofill macros to run, presenting a dialog box that prompts for the specified information.

> **TIP**
> You can insert personal information fields by clicking on Personal... and selecting the fields you want to insert from the Personal Fields dialog. Click on **P**aste to insert the fields.

What To Do If

- You can edit a template to fine-tune it. Use **F**ile **T**emplate... **(Ctrl+T)**, select the template you want to edit, then click on **O**ptions and choose **E**dit Template... . The Template feature bar is displayed and you can make any changes as if you were in the create mode.

See Also

- Using Templates, p. 218.
- Creating Templates, p. 220.

99 Using Styles

Styles are used in WordPerfect to establish repeatable document formatting such as tabs, margins, fonts, line spacing—whatever adjustable WordPerfect document features you wish to set. Styles save you time in formatting documents, and they let you repeat the same settings across many documents, over and over again. There are three steps in using styles:

1. Design the formatting that makes up the style.
2. Save the style document under a name that you can remember later.
3. Load the named style for use within a specific document.

Assumptions

- The insertion point is positioned where you want the style to take effect.

Exceptions

- A style takes effect where it is loaded in your document. If you want it to apply to the entire document, load it at the head of the file or before you start creating the document.
- If you want to use different styles throughout a document, or you want a given style to take effect somewhere other than at the beginning of the file, simply place the insertion point at the location within the document where you want to start the style features.

Steps

1. Use **L**ayout **S**tyles... (**Alt+F8**) to display the Style List dialog shown in Figure 7.4. Unless you have added new styles,

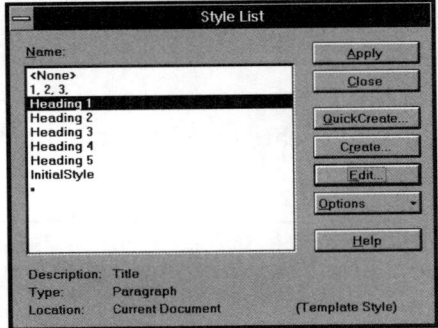

Figure 7.4 Style List dialog.

there are seven entries on this dialog: <none>, five heading styles, and the InitialStyle style.

2. Select the style you want to use by clicking on the style name with the mouse.

3. Click on **A**pply to insert the style code at the location of the insertion point and close the Style List dialog.

What To Do If

- If the style you want to use doesn't appear in the Style List dialog, you'll have to create it. See the description of that process in the next section.

- Remove an inserted style by using Reveal Codes to find it, then use **Backspace** or **Del** to delete it. You can also simply reissue the **L**ayout **S**tyles... command and replace the inserted style with a new one.

See Also

- Creating Styles, p. 228.
- Using Templates, p. 218.
- Creating Templates, p. 220.

Creating Styles

Use the Styles Editor to create or edit a style in WordPerfect.

Assumptions

- The insertion point is positioned where you want the new style to be inserted.

Exceptions

- None.

Steps

1. Use **Layout Styles (Alt+F8)** to display the Style List dialog.
2. Click on **Create...** to display the Styles Editor dialog, shown in Figure 7.5.

> **TIP**
> You can create a style from existing text easily. Once you have a block of text formatted as you want it, select the text, then use **Layout Styles...** (**Alt+F8**) to display the Style List dialog. Click on **Quick-Create...** and fill in the information asked for on the Styles QuickCreate dialog (Style Name, Description, and Type).

```
┌─────────────────────────────────────────────────────┐
│ ─                  Styles Editor                      │
│  Edit  Insert  Layout  Tools  Graphics  Table        │
│                                                       │
│  Style Name:   [Heading 1            ]      ┌──────┐  │
│                                             │  OK  │  │
│  Description:  [Title                ]      └──────┘  │
│                                             ┌──────┐  │
│  Type:              ⊠ Enter Key will Chain to:│Cancel│ │
│  [Paragraph (paired) ⬍] [<None>          ⬍] └──────┘  │
│                                             ┌──────┐  │
│  Contents                                   │ Help │  │
│  ┌─────────────────────────────────────┐   └──────┘  │
│  │ Bold)(Very Large)(Hd Center on Marg)(Mrk Txt ToC)(HPg)│  │
│  │ Mrk Txt ToC                          │              │
│  │                                      │              │
│  │                                      │              │
│  └─────────────────────────────────────┘              │
│  ⊠ Reveal Codes        ⊠ Show 'Off Codes'             │
└─────────────────────────────────────────────────────┘
```

Figure 7.5   Styles Editor dialog.

3. Enter a name for the style in the **S**tyle Name: field of this dialog.

4. Type a description in the **D**escription: field.

5. Select the type of style you want to create. You can choose from **D**ocument, **P**aragraph, or **C**haracter style.

6. To have the Enter key function normally by entering a hard return and carriage return without turning off the style, deselect the E**n**ter Key Will Chain To: box.

7. Enter the style information in the Contents area of this dialog. You can select WordPerfect document, paragraph, or character features from the pull-down menus on the menu bar, press keystrokes, or enter text as part of the style.

8. Click on **OK** to return to the Style List dialog. The new style you just created should be in the Name: window of this dialog.

What To Do If

- You can add or remove document features from a style you create by selecting the style in the Style List dialog, then clicking on **E**dit...

See Also

- Using Styles, p. 226.
- Using Templates, p. 218.

Chapter 8

USING MACROS

Although relatively few WordPerfect users apply the program's macro facility, it provides powerful features that nearly everyone would find useful. Many users probably shy away from macros on the mistaken assumption that they are difficult or complicated to design and use. Users sometimes say, "I don't use macros because I'm doing just simple stuff with WordPerfect." So do people avoid WordPerfect macros because they think their tasks are too simple to warrant macros? Or, perhaps the majority of WordPerfect users simply haven't learned to *think* about using macros.

Whatever the reason, WordPerfect's macro facility is underused, compared to the number of installed programs and the size of the program's user base. But if you take even a few minutes to learn about macros and how to use them, then practice a little thinking about how macros can be used for your particular applications, you'll probably find this another useful WordPerfect tool.

A *macro* is a data file of keystrokes and mouse movements, a series of WordPerfect commands, screen movements, and text that can be replayed whenever necessary. Macros are extremely useful when you have to type the same information repeatedly in a document, for example. As you prepare your company's annual report you can assign the company name to a simple Ctrl+ key combination; then anytime you need to place the company name in the document, you just hold the **Ctrl** key and press, say, the **A** key.

In addition to repetitive text, you can store a series of WordPerfect menu selections or dialog interactions. You could create a macro to change the default printer on your system, for example, or to load a file, merge the contents of another file with it, and print the combination. This could be useful if you regularly combine monthly reports from two or more divisions before printing them, for example.

And, the WordPerfect macro language is a powerful programming language that can be used to create custom documents, interactive documents, and other custom program features.

| Recording Macros | **101**

The easiest way to create a macro in WordPerfect is to record it. You turn on a macro recording routine, conduct the menu operations and keystrokes you want to store in the macro, then turn off the recorder. The macro facility converts your keystrokes into macro language commands.

Assumptions

- The insertion point is located where you want the macro you are about to record to execute.

Exceptions

- When recording a macro, WordPerfect doesn't blindly record every keystroke or mouse movement you use during the recording session. All that is recorded is the ultimate result of the operation. Several keystrokes or menu selections may be involved in accomplishing a given task, but all that is recorded is the macro language command that accomplishes the same thing. The result is a more efficient macro that is easier to edit, but that requires you to learn a little about the macro language if you plan to write macros or edit recorded macros.

Steps

1. Use **Tools Macro Record...** (**Ctrl+F10**) to display the Record Macro dialog shown in Figure 8.1.

2. Enter a name for the macro in the **Name:** field of this dialog. Use conventional DOS-compatible names, but use names that are easy for you to interpret. You can pull down a list of existing macros and a directory list by clicking on

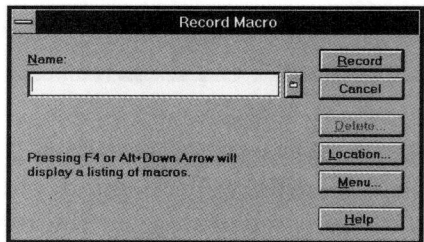

Figure 8.1   Record Macro dialog.

the file folder icon to the right of the Name: field on this dialog. The directory display gives you access to the WordPerfect File Manager.

3. Click on **R**ecord to start macro recording. A memo on the status bar indicates *Macro Record* to tell you that macro recording is taking place.

4. Enter any text, formatting, graphics, or menu choices you want to include in this macro.

5. Use **T**ools **M**acro **R**ecord... **(Ctrl+F10)** to turn off macro recording and store the program you just created to disk under the filename you gave earlier.

What To Do If

*   Don't worry too much about making mistakes while recording macros. For the most part, only the last setting you enter will be recorded as a macro. Again, the WordPerfect macro facility is a command-oriented utility, not a keystroke-oriented utility, so if you make a mistake and correct it, the latest setting overrides the earlier one, in many cases.

*   If you need to change something in a macro, you need not redo the whole process. Simply use **T**ools **M**acro **E**dit... to display the Edit Macro dialog. Specify the name of the macro you want to edit, and use the Macro editing window and feature bar to make your changes.

See Also

- Using WordPerfect Macros, p. 248.
- Creating (Writing) Macros, p. 238.
- Editing a WordPerfect Macro, below.
- Assigning Macros to the Keyboard, p. 241.
- Assigning Macros to the Button Bar, p. 241.

Editing a WordPerfect Macro | 102

In many ways, recording a macro is easier than editing it. If you are trying to make changes to a relatively simple macro that you recorded earlier, the easiest way to accomplish this task is probably to record it over again. By re-recording the macro you don't have to worry about understanding WordPerfect's macro language or interpreting how WordPerfect places your keystrokes and mouse movements into a macro.

For complex macros, however, if you only want to change a search-for item, the measurements of a margin, the placement of a box, or other relatively simple modification, then you can use the Macro Editor to good advantage.

And, finally, the WordPerfect macro language—much of it, at least—is straightforward and relatively easy to understand. Most command words are obvious in function and you can learn quickly how to interpret WordPerfect macro code.

Assumptions

- You have previously created or recorded a macro that you want to change.

Exceptions

- None.

TIP

Because you will
be dealing with
this macro at a
basic level, it is a
good idea to make
a backup copy of
your macro be-
fore editing it.
Use **Tools Macro
Edit...** and click on
the file folder icon
to launch the
WordPerfect File
Manager. Use **Op-
tions Copy...** to
make a copy of the
macro you are
going to edit.

Steps

1. Use **Tools Macro Edit...** to display the Macro Edit dialog.

2. Enter the name of the macro you want to edit in the **Name:** field of this dialog. You can get a list of current macros by clicking on the file folder icon to the right of the **Name:** field on this dialog.

3. Click on **OK** to close this dialog and load the macro instructions into a WordPerfect editing screen like the one shown in Figure 8.2.

4. Use conventional WordPerfect editing procedures to change any text or formatting within the macro.

5. If you need to add a macro command, click on the Command Inserter button to display the WordPerfect Macro Command Inserter dialog, shown in Figure 8.3.

6. Use the vertical scroll bar to locate the command you want to use. Note the description of each command beside the Description: label at the bottom of this dialog.

7. Click on **Edit** to copy the command into the Command Edit window of this dialog if you want to add parameters or change defaults.

8. Click on **Insert** to place the selected command in the current macro program at the location of the insertion point.

9. Click on **Save & Compile** to save the code and compile it into an executable form.

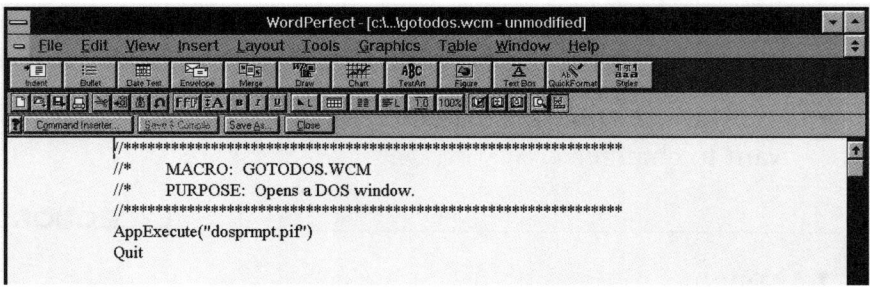

Figure 8.2   Macro loaded in Editor with feature bar.

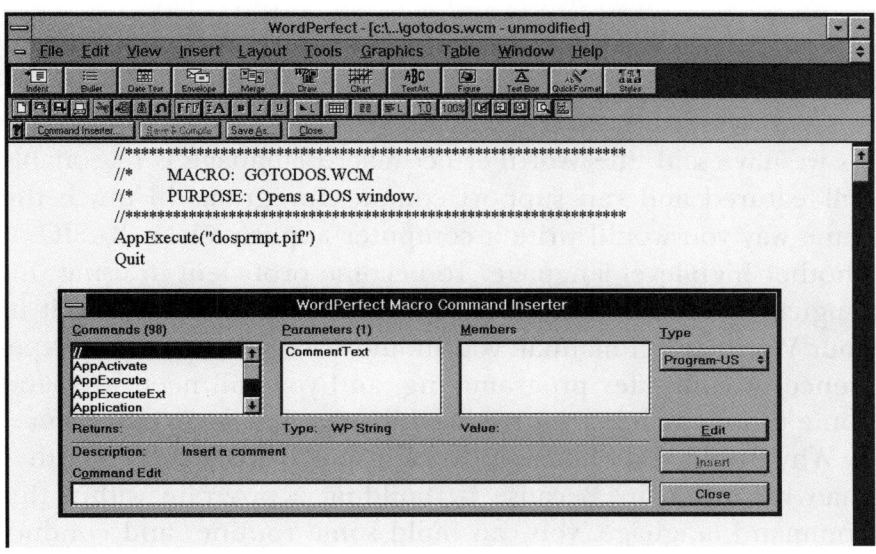

Figure 8.3   WordPerfect Macro Command Inserter dialog.

10.   Click on Close on the Command Inserter dialog to exit the Command Inserter when you have added the last command.

11.   Click on **C**lose on the Macro Editor feature bar to close the editor and return to your document.

What To Do If

• If you think that you may have damaged the macro or entered commands or text you hadn't intended, simply click on **C**lose and choose **No** when you are asked if you want to save the changes. This will let you start over with a clean copy of the macro on disk.

See Also

• Recording Macros, p. 233.
• Creating (Writing) Macros, p. 238.
• Assigning Macros to the Button Bar, p. 244.
• Assigning Macros to the Keyboard, p. 241.

Creating (Writing) Macros

As we have said, the WordPerfect macro language is reasonably full-featured and can support complex programs in much the same way you would write a computer application in BASIC or another high-level language. To become proficient in using this language you will need to read the information on using it in your WordPerfect manual, you should have some previous experience in computer programming, and you will need to spend some time practicing your skill with some hands-on experience.

Why would you choose to write a macro from scratch rather than recording it? Because by building a program within this command language, you can build some routines and conduct some tasks you can't really do by recording a macro. Nevertheless, a good place to start writing a WordPerfect macro is to record as much of it as you can, then use the edit routine to modify that basic code.

Teaching you how to program in a complex language such as WordPerfect macro language is beyond the scope of this book. However, we can show you how to access the macro editing facilities and offer some suggestions on how to learn.

Assumptions

- You have planned the basic macro so that you understand what you want it to do before you start writing the code on the computer.

Exceptions

- For most end-user macro applications the recording process is easier to use and does all that you need to do. Before you try to write a macro from scratch, consider recording the macro instead, or certainly consider recording the basic macro and then using the macro editing facilities to add to it.

_____ **Steps**

1. If you have previously recorded a portion of the macro you want to create, use **T**ools **M**acro **E**dit..., type the name of the macro you recorded previously, and click on **OK** to load the existing code in the macro editing window and to display the Macro Editor feature bar.

2. If you are writing a macro from scratch, use **T**ools **M**acro **M**acro Bar to open a blank editing screen and present the Macro feature bar.

3. Click on Command Inserter... to display the WordPerfect Macro Command Inserter dialog at the bottom of your screen (see Figure 8.4).

4. Begin the macro with one or more comment lines to identify the macro. At the least enter the filename, a description

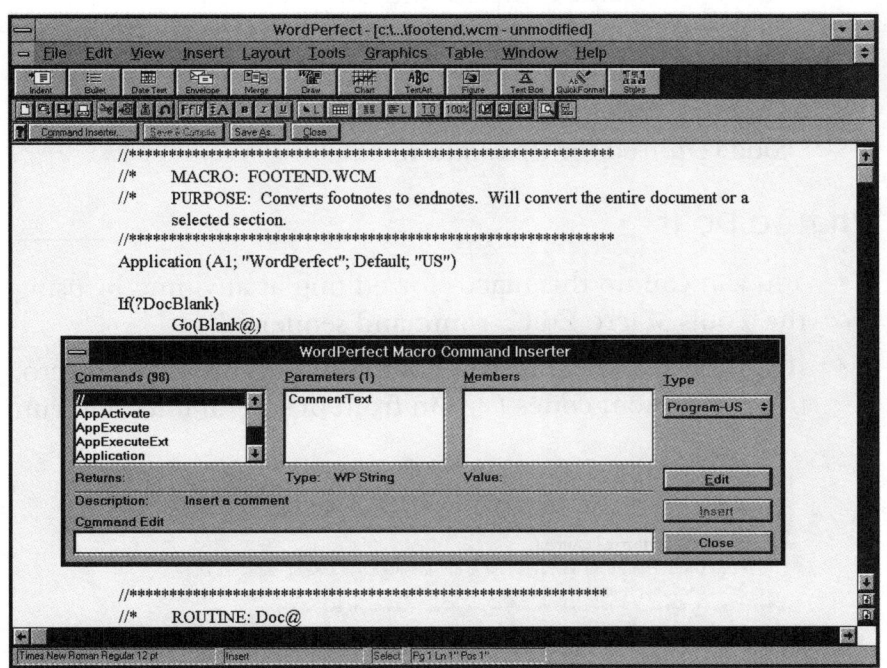

Figure 8.4   WordPerfect Macro Command Inserter dialog.

of what it does, your name or initials, and the date. Comments in WordPerfect macros are preceded by the double-slash symbol, the first command in the list of **C**ommands in the Command Inserter dialog. Figure 8.5 shows a typical macro "header" from one of those supplied with the program.

5. Place the insertion point one or two lines below the header information, and insert the first command, which should be an environment statement such as

    Application (A1;"WordPerfect";Default;"US")

6. Continue entering commands as required to complete the macro.

7. Use **S**ave & Compile to save the macro for the first time (this loads the Save As... dialog the first time you use it) and to test what you have written so far for errors. If the macro saves and compiles without errors, then your code is correct, though that is no guarantee the code does what you intended!

8. Click on **C**lose when you have entered all of the macro code required for this routine.

What To Do If

- You can call up this macro for editing at any time by using the **T**ools **M**acro **E**dit... command sequence.

- If you have problems with compiling or running a macro, place comment codes (//) in front of several lines and run

```
//****************************************************************
//*    MACRO: EXPNDALL.WCM
//*    PURPOSE: Expand all abbreviations in the document that are defined in the current,
            default and supplemental templates.
//****************************************************************
```

Figure 8.5 Typical Macro comment header from WordPerfect Macro.

it again. Repeat this process until you have a macro that will compile successfully. Now, remove the lines a few at a time until you locate the problem.

- Note the error messages provided by WordPerfect during the macro compile. They will show you the line where an error exists and point to the word or character that seems to be causing problems.

See Also

- Recording Macros, p. 233.
- Using WordPerfect Macros, p. 248.
- Editing a WordPerfect Macro, p. 235.

Assigning Macros to the Keyboard | 104

Unfortunately, when you create a WordPerfect macro, either by recording it or by writing lines of code (as described in Task 103), you don't automatically assign the macro program to a keystroke combination. You can run the macro with the **Tools Macro Play... (Alt+F10)** command sequence, but you can't simply press a couple of keys and have the macro play back for you. It is fairly easy to assign an existing macro to a keystroke combination, as we'll show in this section.

Assumptions

- You have previously recorded or written a macro that you want to assign to a keyboard key combination.

Exceptions

- None.

Steps

1. Use **F**ile P**r**eferences... to display the Preferences dialog shown in Figure 8.6.

2. Double-click on **K**eyboard to load the Keyboard Preferences dialog.

3. Select the keyboard you want to edit from the list displayed in the **K**eyboards: window of this dialog. The **WPWIN 6.0 Keyboard** is the default.

4. Click on C**r**eate to display the Create Keyboard dialog.

5. Enter the name of the new keyboard definition in the **N**ew Keyboard Name: field of this dialog.

6. Click on **OK** to exit this dialog and display the Keyboard Editor, shown in Figure 8.7.

7. Click on the button beside Play a **M**acro in the Assign Key To section of this dialog.

8. Click on the keyboard sequence you want to use for this macro. WordPerfect shows you what the current assignment of this keystroke combination is, if any.

9. Click on **A**ssign Macro... to display the Select Macro dialog. Type in the name of the macro you want to use, or click on the file folder icon to display a list of available macros. Select the one you want to assign to the keyboard and click on **OK.**

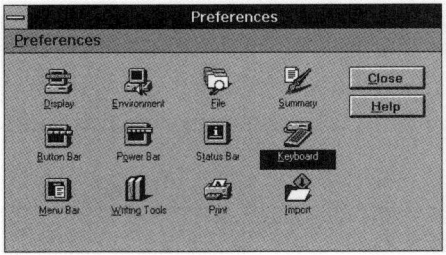

Figure 8.6   Preferences dialog.

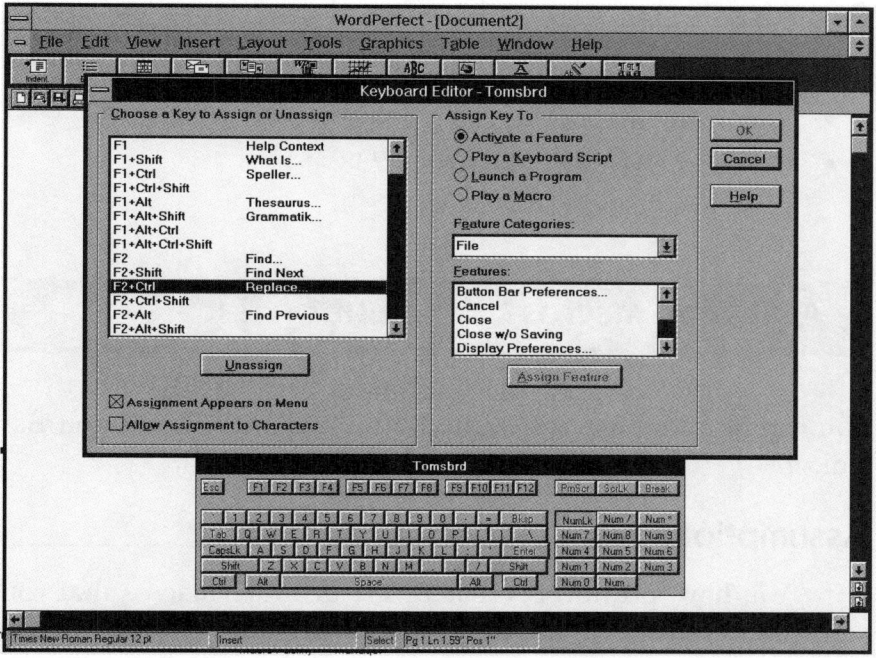

Figure 8.7   Keyboard Editor with new keyboard definition displayed.

10. Click on **S**elect on the Select Macro dialog.

11. Answer **Yes** when WordPerfect asks if you want to save the macro with full path. The new macro name should appear in the keystroke assignment list beside the keystroke combination you specified earlier.

12. Click on **OK** to complete the keyboard assignment. Now when you press the combination of keys you specified, the selected macro should execute.

What To Do If

- If the keyboard combination you select already has a command or macro assigned to it, simply select another keystroke combination, or ignore the current assignment, replacing the existing assignment with the new one.

See Also

- Assigning Macros to the Button Bar, below.
- Recording Macros, p. 233.
- Creating (Writing) Macros, p. 238.

105 ▼ Assigning Macros to the Button Bar

You can also add macros to the button bar with the Button Bar Editor.

Assumptions

- You have previously created one or more macros that you want to install on the button bar.

Exceptions

- None.

Steps

1. Place the mouse pointer anywhere on the button bar and click the right button to display the Button Bar command list.

2. Choose **E**dit... to display the Button Bar Editor, shown in Figure 8.8.

3. Click on the button beside Play a **M**acro to activate that feature.

4. Click on the **A**dd Macro... button to display the Select Macro dialog.

5. If the macro you are adding to the button bar is not located in a file on disk (if it is part of the current template, for example), click on **L**ocation... to display the Macro

---

TIP

Use the **V**iew... option at the bottom of the Select File dialog. This opens another window that shows the contents of each macro file as it is selected. Even if you didn't create the macro, the information in this window should be enough for you to understand generally what the macro does before you assign it to the button bar.

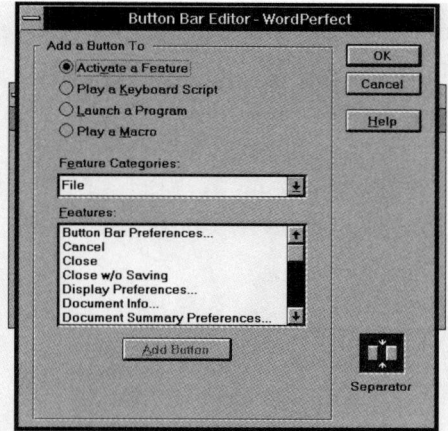

Figure 8.8 Button Bar Editor dialog.

Location dialog. Select the proper location button for your macro and click on **OK** to return to the Select Macro dialog.

6. Enter the name of the macro you want to add to the button bar in the **N**ame: field of this dialog. You can pull down a list of macro files and directories by clicking on the file folder icon to the right of this field.

7. Click on **S**elect to close the Select Macro dialog.

8. Answer **Yes** when WordPerfect asks whether to save the macro with full path (if you are using a macro on disk) and return to the Button Bar Editor dialog and place a new button on the button bar.

9. Double-click on the new button just inserted on the button bar to display the Customize Button dialog shown in Figure 8.9.

10. Enter a short name for the new button. (WordPerfect has placed "Macro" on the button. Enter a name that reflects what the macro does.)

11. Enter text for the Help **P**rompt:, the text that appears when you point to the button with the mouse.

TIP

If the new macro button isn't visible on the button bar, click on the up or down arrows at the right of the button bar to display the next line of the button bar.

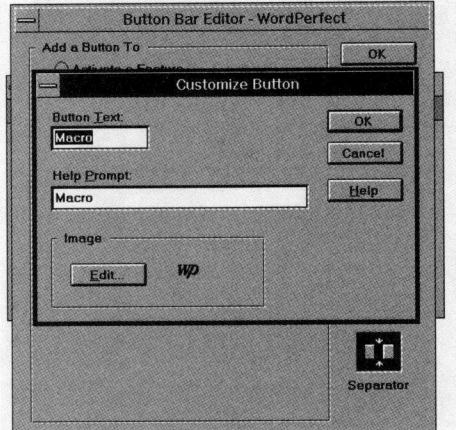

Figure 8.9   Customize Button dialog.

12. Click on **Edit...** to change the icon used on the new button, if you wish. This will display the Button Bar Image Editor, which lets you manually draw a new image for the button or edit the WordPerfect-generated image.

13. Click on **OK** to close the Customize Button dialog and effect the changes to the new button.

What To Do If

- If you assign macros to the button bar and exit the Edit Button Bar dialog by clicking on Cancel, the macros you have added will be removed. Be sure you click on **OK** to exit the Button Bar Editor.

- Remove the newly installed button by pointing to the button bar and pressing the right mouse button to display the Button Bar menu. Click on **Edit...** to display the Button Bar Editor. Point to the new button and press the right button again. You are given two menu choices: Customize and Delete. Click on **Delete** to remove the button.

_____ **See Also**

- Using WordPerfect Macros, p. 248.
- Assigning Macros to the Keyboard, p. 241.

Adding WordPerfect Macros to the Menu   106

If you wish, you can have WordPerfect macros appear on the
Macro menu. With macro names installed on the Macro menu,
when you use Tools Macro you can pick off a macro to run from
the menu, bypassing the Play... and selection process.

_____ **Assumptions**

- You have previously created one or more macros that you
  want to install on a WordPerfect menu.

_____ **Exceptions**

- None.

_____ **Steps**

1. Use **T**ools **M**acro **E**dit... to display the Edit Macro dialog.

2. Click on **M**enu... on this dialog to display the Assign Macro
    to Menu dialog. The first time you use this dialog the Avail-
    able Macros window will be blank.

3. Click on **I**nsert to display the Select Macro dialog. Enter a
    macro name in the **N**ame: field, or click on the file folder
    icon to display a list of available macros and directories.
    When you have the macro you want to add to the menu in
    the **N**ame: field of the Select Macro dialog, click on **S**elect
    to return to the Assign Macro to Menu dialog. The name

of the macro you just selected should appear in the Available Macros window of this dialog.

4. Click on **OK** to close this dialog and return to the Edit Macro dialog.

5. Click on **Cancel** to close this dialog and return to your document.

What To Do If

- To remove a macro from the menu, use **T**ools **M**acro **E**dit... **M**enu to display the Assign Macro to Menu dialog. Select the macro you want to remove from the menu and click on **D**elete.

See Also

- Assigning Macros to the Keyboard, p. 241.
- Assigning Macros to the Button Bar, p. 244.
- Using WordPerfect Macros, below.

Using WordPerfect Macros

Designing and creating WordPerfect macros is the hard part of using macros. Once you have designed what you want macros to do and have recorded them or written the code necessary to carry out the desired actions, using the macros is as simple as selecting the one you want to use from a list or the button bar.

Assumptions

- The insertion point is positioned where you want the next macro to begin execution.

Exceptions

- None.

Steps

1. Use **T**ools **M**acro **P**lay... **(Alt+F10)** to display the Play Macro dialog.
2. Enter the name of a macro in the **N**ame: field of this dialog, or use the File Manager by clicking on the file folder to the right of this field.
3. Click on **OK** to close the dialog and begin macro execution.

What To Do If

- If you can't locate the macro you want to use, use the WordPerfect File Manager, which you can access from the Play Macro dialog by clicking on the file folder icon to the right of the **N**ame: field.

See Also

- Assigning Macros to the Button Bar, p. 244.
- Adding WordPerfect Macros to the Menu, p. 247.
- Assigning Macros to the Keyboard, p. 241.
- Creating (Writing) Macros, p. 238.
- Recording Macros, p. 233.

> **TIP**
>
> You can also install selected macros on the button bar, on the Macro menu, or assign macros to keyboard key combinations. These are quicker ways to access macros than going through the process described here.

Chapter
9

WORKING
WITH LINKED
DATA

Applications in today's computer environment stand alone less and less. Word processors can link with data in spreadsheet programs and databases. They can load files from numerous foreign word processing programs, and they can import and link with graphics images. We'll show you the basics of working with linked data in WordPerfect in this chapter.

108 ▾ Using Hypertext

Hypertext is a process for linking multiple portions of a document, of linking one WordPerfect document to another document, and of linking a word in a WordPerfect document to a macro.

Once a hypertext link is established, you can jump directly from one place in a document to another or from one document to another. In addition, you can click on a hypertext link, a word or phrase in a document specially configured as a link, and execute the linked macro.

This feature is useful in building interactive documents for education or training, for designing forms that help you fill them out, and more.

Assumptions

- You have prepared a document or documents for which you want to create hypertext links.
- The document that will hold the hypertext link is open and is the current document.

Exceptions

- None.

Steps

1. To create a link to another location within the same document, create a bookmark.

    • Select a word to serve as the anchor for the bookmark, or place the insertion point where you want the bookmark inserted.

    • Use Insert **B**ookmark... to display the Bookmark dialog shown in Figure 9.1.

    • Click on C**r**eate... to display the Create Bookmark dialog.

    • Enter a unique name for the bookmark in the **B**ookmark Name: field of this dialog.

    • Click on **OK** to close this dialog. Then click on **C**lose to return to your document.

2. Use **T**ools **H**ypertext to display the Hypertext feature bar, shown in Figure 9.2.

3. Select the word, phrase, or symbol you want to use as the link.

> **TIP**
>
> The process is the same when you want to link to another document, only you must specify the name of the document as well as the name of the bookmark within that document that will serve as the target of the link. You can also link to an existing WordPerfect macro by selecting the macro button at the bottom of this dialog.

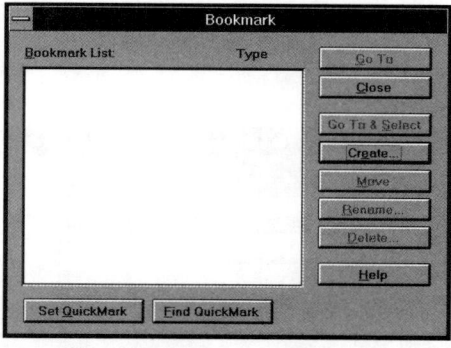

Figure 9.1   Bookmark dialog.

Figure 9.2   Hypertext feature bar.

4. Click on Create... on the feature bar to display the Create Hypertext Link dialog, shown in Figure 9.3. WordPerfect automatically selects Go To Bookmark: and inserts the name of the first bookmark in your document in the field.

5. Click on the down arrow to the right of the Go To Bookmark: field to view a list of the bookmarks in the current document.

6. Select the bookmark you want to use as the target of the current hypertext link.

7. Click on Button under the Appearance title if you want the hypertext link to appear as a button instead of straight text.

8. Click on OK to close the Create Hypertext Link dialog and return to your document.

9. Click on Close to remove the Hypertext feature bar.

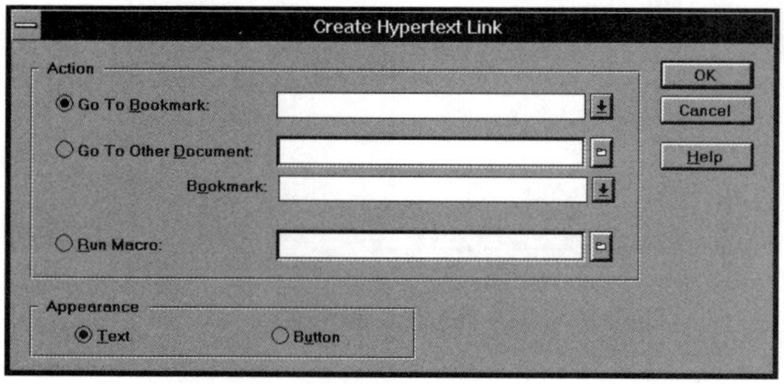

Figure 9.3   Create Hypertext Link dialog.

10. To use the link, simply click on the word or button that you specified as the source, and you are jumped immediately to the target of the link—bookmark within the same document, a bookmark within another document, or a WordPerfect macro.

What To Do If

- Delete (remove) a hypertext link by displaying the Hypertext feature bar (Tools Hypertext), then selecting the link you want to remove and clicking on **Delete**.

See Also

- Linking Spreadsheet Data, below.
- Linking Database Data, p. 259.

Linking Spreadsheet Data   109

A spreadsheet is an excellent tool for comparing data and for presenting financial projections and other numerical data. A word processor is an excellent tool for writing reports and describing the data a spreadsheet holds. With the spreadsheet links in WordPerfect you can have the best of both worlds.

You can tie data from a spreadsheet into a WordPerfect document in two ways: import and link. When you import data, the information is copied from the spreadsheet into the WordPerfect document. When you use a link, WordPerfect knows when the information in the spreadsheet changes and updates the document containing the linked data.

Assumptions

- You have previously created a spreadsheet that you want to use in a WordPerfect document. To make the job of linking the two applications easier, you should also name the range in the spreadsheet that you want to use within WordPerfect.

- The insertion point is positioned where you want the linked or imported data to appear in your WordPerfect document.

Exceptions

- WordPerfect can import or link data with the following formats only: PlanPerfect, Lotus 1-2-3, Microsoft Excel, Quattro Pro, Spreadsheet DIF.

Steps

To import spreadsheet data:

1. Use Insert Spreadsheet/Database to display the Import/ Link menu.

2. Click on Import... to display the Import dialog shown in Figure 9.4.

3. If Spreadsheet is not displayed in the Data Type: field of this dialog, click on the up and down arrows to the right of this field and choose Spreadsheet.

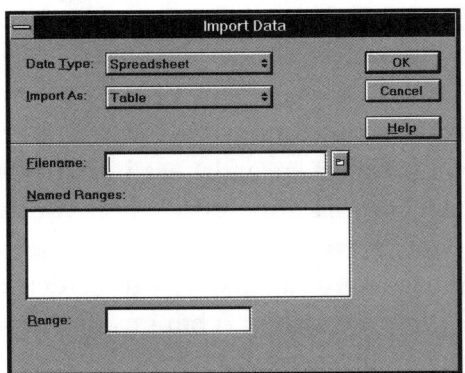

Figure 9.4   Spreadsheet/Database Import dialog.

4. Click on the up and down arrows to the right of the **I**mport As: field to select the type of import to perform. The options are:

Table Information is imported from the spreadsheet into a WordPerfect table that is structured to match as closely as possible the original spreadsheet information format. This is the default format and probably the one you will use with imports most of the time.

Merge Data File Information is imported as a WordPerfect Merge data. In this form you can create links with multiple documents during a merge operation. Use this option when you want to include spreadsheet data in a merged form letter, for example.

Text Import a file in delimited text format. You must save your spreadsheet in delimited format before using this format.

5. Enter the name of the file you want to import in the Filename: field. Include the full path. Use the File Manager to help you find the file by clicking on the file folder icon to the right of this field.

6. Specify the name of the range you want to import. Choose the range from the list WordPerfect automatically provides in the Named Ranges: window of this dialog.

7. Click on **OK** to close this dialog and complete the import operation. WordPerfect inserts the specified data right into your document at the location of the insertion point.

8. Use table editing procedures to fine-tune the data presentation, if necessary.

To link spreadsheet data:

1. Use Insert Spreadsheet/Database to display the Import/ Link menu.

2. Click on **C**reate Link... to display the Create Link dialog shown in Figure 9.5.

3. If Spreadsheet is not displayed in the Data **T**ype: field of this dialog, click on the up and down arrows to the right of this field and choose Spreadsheet.

4. Click on the up and down arrows to the right of the **L**ink As: field to select the type of link to perform. The options are:

Table Information is linked from the spreadsheet into a WordPerfect table that is structured to match as closely as possible the original spreadsheet information format. This is the default format and probably the one you will use with links most of the time.

Merge Data File Information is imported as a WordPerfect Merge data. In this form you can create links with multiple documents during a merge operation. Use this option when you want to include spreadsheet data in a merged form letter, for example.

Text Import a file in delimited text format. You must save your spreadsheet in delimited format before using this format.

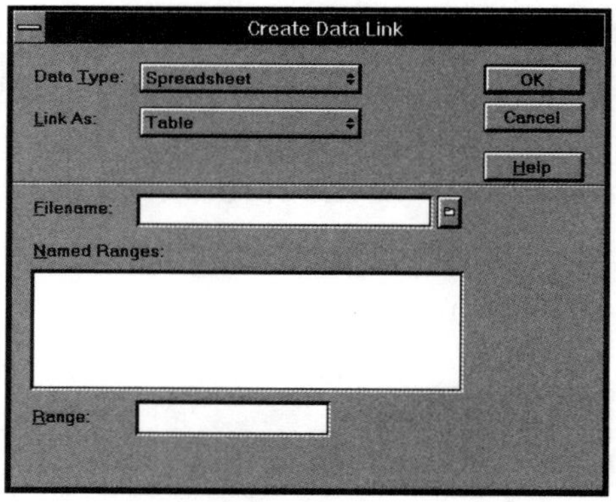

Figure 9.5 **Spreadsheet/Database Create Link dialog.**

5. Enter the name of the file you want to link in the **Filename:** field. Include the full path. Use the File Manager to help you find the file by clicking on the file folder icon to the right of this field.

6. Specify the name of the range you want to link. Choose the range from the list WordPerfect automatically provides in the Named Ranges: window of this dialog.

7. Click on **OK** to close this dialog and complete the link operation. WordPerfect inserts the specified data right into your document at the location of the insertion point.

8. Use table editing procedures to fine-tune the data presentation, if necessary.

_____ **What To Do If**

- If some of the information in your spreadsheet range doesn't appear in your document, it may mean that the range resulted in a table with more than 64 columns. WordPerfect will link and import only 64 columns of information.

_____ **See Also**

- Linking Database Data, below.
- Using Hypertext, p. 252.

Linking Database Data **110**

As with spreadsheets, database files also can be linked or imported into a WordPerfect document. The procedure is essentially the same as working with spreadsheets (see the preceding discussion of importing/linking spreadsheet data).

Assumptions

- The database file you want to import or link has been created.
- The WordPerfect document you want to receive the database information is loaded and current, and the insertion point is positioned where you want the database information to appear.

Exceptions

- WordPerfect can import or link data with the following formats only: Clipper, Fox Pro, DataPerfect, dBase, Paradox, DB2, Informix, Netware SQL, Oracle, SQL Base Server, SQL Server, Sybase, XDB.

Steps

To import database information:

1. Use **I**nsert Spreadsheet/Database to display the Import/ Link menu.
2. Click on **I**mport... to display the Import dialog.
3. Pull down the list of available formats in the Data **T**ype: field of this dialog (see Figure 9.6).
4. Choose the database type you want to use. All database imports are conducted as tables.
5. Enter the name of the file you want to import in the Filename: field. Include the full path. Use the File Manager to help you find the file by clicking on the file folder icon to the right of this field.
6. Choose the fields you want to include in the import. WordPerfect selects all fields by default. Click on each field you *do not* want to use to deselect it.
7. Click on the box beside Use field names as headings if you do not want the imported table to use existing field names as headings.

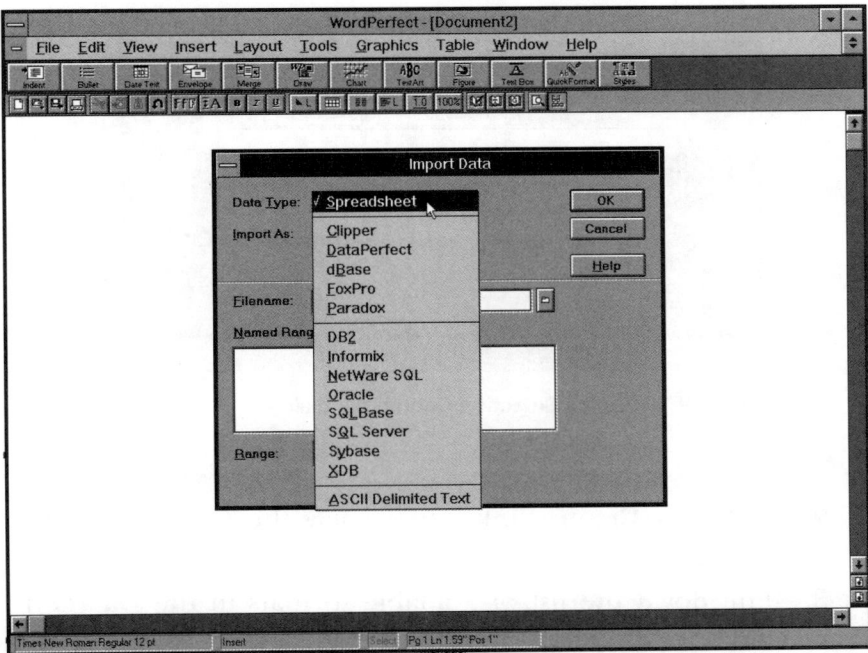

Figure 9.6 Import Data dialog with Data Type list displayed.

8. Click on **Query...** if you want to extract a portion of the database. WordPerfect displays the Define Selection Conditions dialog shown in Figure 9.7. You can specify up to four conditions for up to three fields in the database.

9. Click on **OK** when you have entered the search criteria. WordPerfect searches the database for the records you have specified.

10. Click on **OK** to close this dialog and complete the import operation. WordPerfect inserts the specified data right into your document at the location of the insertion point.

11. Use table editing procedures to fine-tune the data presentation, if necessary.

To link database information:

1. Use **Insert Spreadsheet/Database** to display the Import/Link menu.

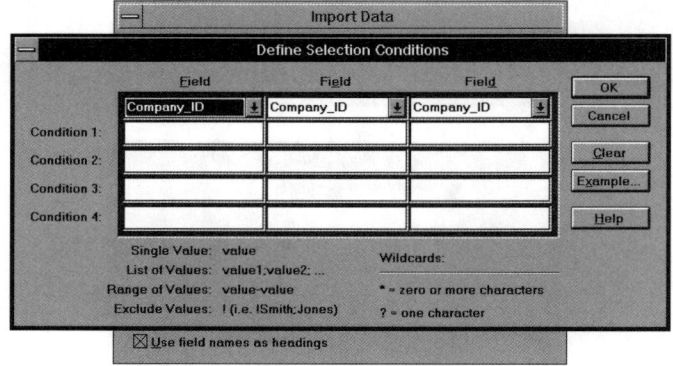

Figure 9.7   Define Selection Conditions dialog.

2. Click on **C**reate Link... to display the Create Data Link dialog.

3. Pull down the list of available formats in the Data **T**ype: field of this dialog (see Figure 9.8).

4. Choose the database type you want to use. All database information is linked as a table.

5. Enter the name of the file you want to import in the File-name: field. Include the full path. Use the File Manager to help you find the file by clicking on the file folder icon to the right of this field.

6. Choose the fields you want to include in the link. Word-Perfect selects all fields by default. Click on each field you *do not* want to use to deselect it.

7. Click on the box beside Use field names as headings if you do not want the imported table to use existing field names as headings.

8. Click on **Q**uery... if you want to extract a portion of the database. WordPerfect displays the Define Selection Conditions dialog shown in Figure 9.9. You can specify up to four conditions for up to three fields in the database.

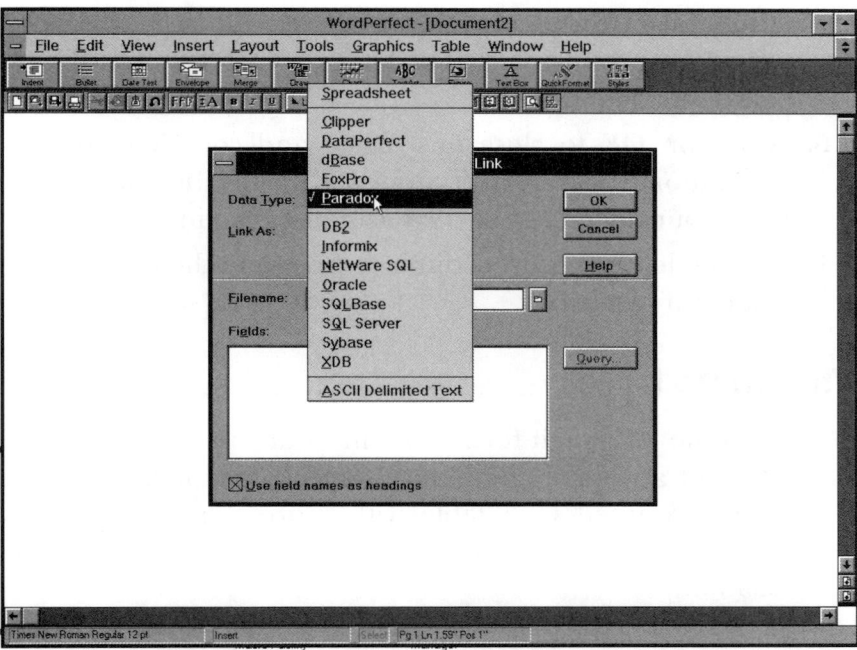

Figure 9.8   Import Data dialog with Data Type list displayed.

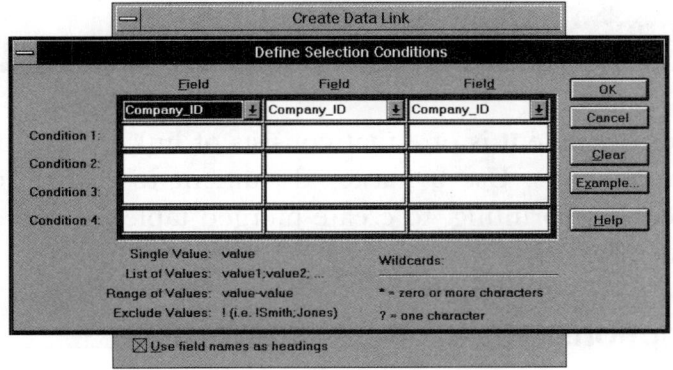

Figure 9.9   Define Selection Conditions dialog.

9. Click on **OK** when you have entered the search criteria. WordPerfect searches the database for the records you have specified.

10. Click on **OK** to close this dialog and complete the link operation. WordPerfect inserts the specified data right into your document at the location of the insertion point.

11. Use table editing procedures to fine-tune the data presentation, if necessary.

What To Do If

• If some of the information in your spreadsheet range doesn't appear in your document, it may mean that the range resulted in a table with more than 64 columns. WordPerfect will link and import only 64 columns of information.

See Also

• Linking Spreadsheet Data, p. 255.
• Using Hypertext, p. 252.

111 ▼ Creating a Master Document

A master document is one that consists of links to two or more other documents. Use a master document to gather multiple documents for printing, to create merged tables of contents, or to create other lists.

Assumptions

• You have previously created two or more documents that you want to combine in a master document.

- You have scanned each individual document, removing separate headers, footers, or other special codes that might disrupt printing or cause inconsistent document formatting.

Exceptions

- Building a master document from multiple individual documents doesn't change the originals unless you select to save each individual file when the master document is compressed.

- To print an expanded master document you must have enough disk space to store the expanded document twice: once for the master document and once for the print spooler. That makes three copies of the information, including the individual smaller documents.

Steps

1. Use **F**ile Master **D**ocument **S**ubdocument... to display the Include Subdocument dialog shown in Figure 9.10.

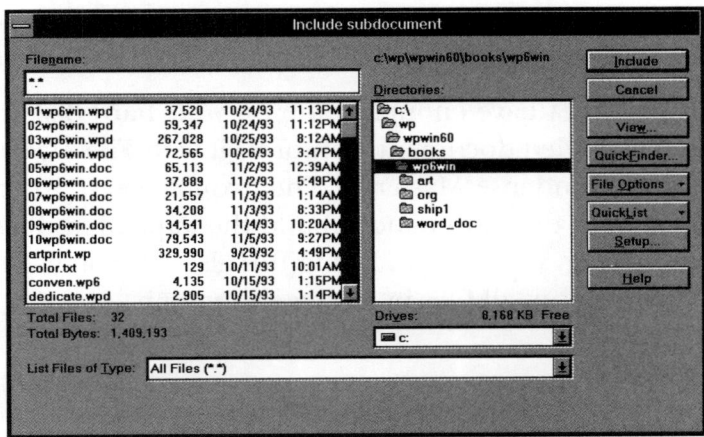

Figure 9.10   Include Subdocument dialog.

> **TIP**
>
> Although you can create headers and footers and build indexes and tables of contents without expanding the master document, you must expand it to print it.

2. Choose a directory from the **D**irectories: list in this dialog.

3. Choose a filename from the File**n**ame: list, or type the name of a file in the File**n**ame: field.

4. Click on **I**nclude to place a code for the specified document into the open WordPerfect editing window.

5. Press **Shift+Enter** to place a hard page code after the subdocument code. This starts each new chapter or document segment at the top of a new page.

6. Repeat steps 1 to 5 for each document you want to include in the master document.

7. Insert any define codes you need for tables of contents or other lists.

8. Generate the document.

9. Create any headers or footers you want at the top of the file so they will apply to all documents.

10. Use **F**ile Save **A**s... to store the new master document.

11. If you want to print the entire document, use the **T**ools **M**aster Document **E**xpand sequence to pull all of the subdocuments into the current document. Then use **F**ile **P**rint... to print the combined document.

What To Do If

- If you don't have enough room on your hard disk to store the expanded document, compress it with **F**ile Master **D**ocument **C**ondense Master.... Then you can save the master document definition and rebuild the expanded document again when you need it. Doing this also lets you use the latest versions of all files in master documents.

See Also

- Printing Long Documents (Master Document Feature), p. 168.

| Using Merge Documents | `112` |

Document merge—sometimes called Mail merge—lets you pull information from a secondary data file into a primary file to print continuous letters, invoices, statements, forms, and the like. Creating a merge document takes three steps:

1. Create a data file (a name and address file, for example).
2. Create a form file (the letter that will go to each person in the name and address data file, for example).
3. Create a merge file (combine the name and address information with the form file, creating a large document that contains multiple copies of the form document).

Assumptions

- None.

Exceptions

- None.

Steps

1. Use **T**ools **M**erge... to display the Merge dialog shown in Figure 9.11.
2. Click on the **D**ata... button to display the Create Merge File dialog.
3. Click on one of the buttons according to whether you want to use the file in the active window or to use a new document window.
4. Click on **OK** to close this dialog and display the Merge feature bar and the Create Data File dialog shown in Figure 9.12. This dialog makes creating a data file in WordPerfect

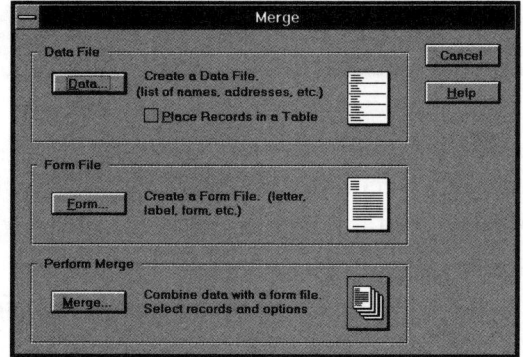

Figure 9.11   Merge dialog.

extremely easy. The process is similar to creating a data file in a database application.

5. Enter the first field name in the **N**ame a Field: field of this dialog. Click on **A**dd and the new field label should appear in the Field Name List: window of this dialog.

6. Continue adding fields until you have defined the structure of the data file. A simple data structure is shown in Figure 9.13.

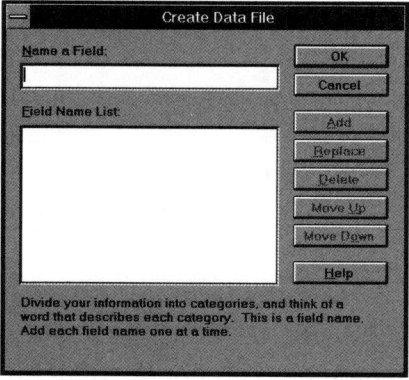

Figure 9.12   Create Data File dialog.

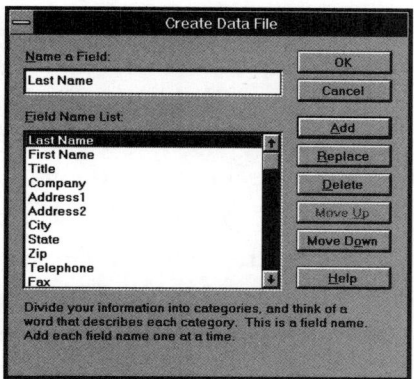

Figure 9.13   Create Data File dialog with
sample database structure.

7. Click on **OK** to close this dialog and display the Quick Data Entry dialog shown in Figure 9.14.

8. Enter as many records as you wish on this dialog. Click on New **R**ecord each time you complete the information for one record to go on to the next blank record.

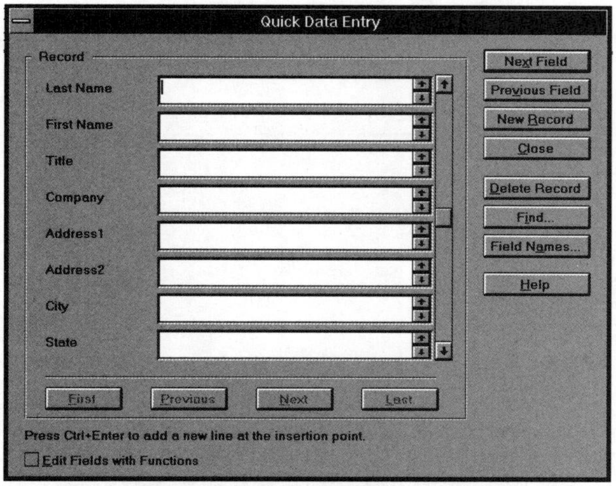

Figure 9.14   Quick Data Entry dialog.

9. Click on **C**lose when you have entered all of the records you wish. Answer **Yes** when WordPerfect asks whether you want to save the data to disk. WordPerfect enters the re- cords into a document file, one record to a page. Each line ends with an ENDFIELD code and each record ends with an ENDRECORD code (see Figure 9.15).

10. Click on **G**o to Form, then choose **C**reate from the Associ- ate dialog that is displayed next. A blank editing screen is displayed with a Form feature bar displayed at the top.

11. Type the information you want to include in the form file.

12. Position the insertion point where you want information from the data file to appear and click on **I**nsert Field... to display the Insert Field Name or Number dialog, shown in Figure 9.16.

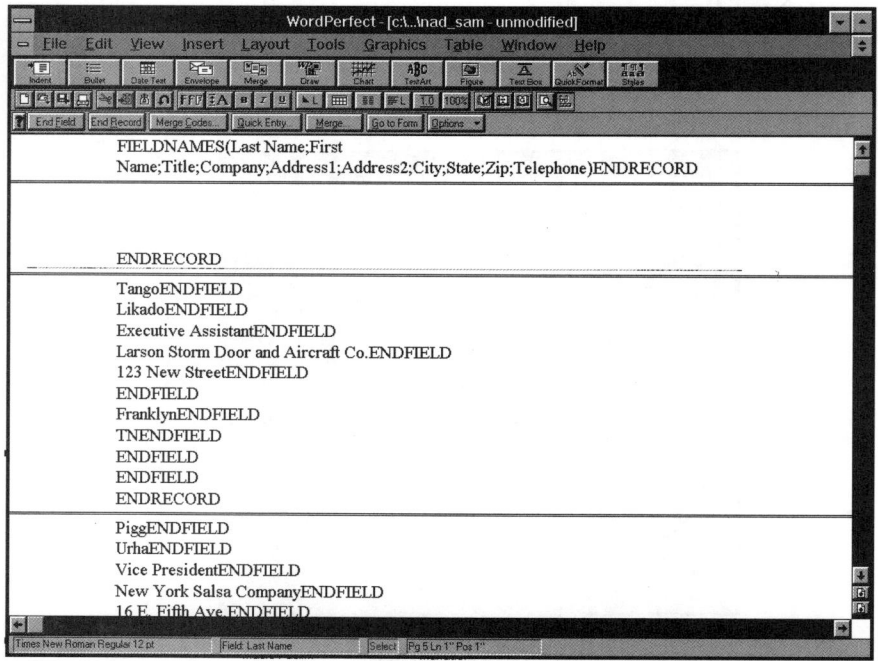

Figure 9.15   Sample data document.

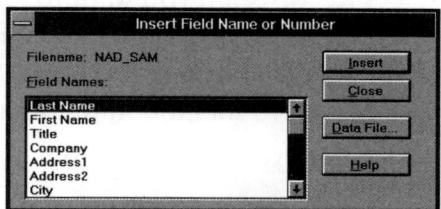

**Figure 9.16   Insert Field Name or Number
dialog.**

13. Double-click on the field data you want to insert into the form at the insertion point.

14. Reposition the insertion point where you want the next data record field to appear. Double-click on the next field in the Insert Field Name or Number dialog.

15. Repeat the previous step until all of the field data is placed where you want it in the form document.

16. Click on **C**lose to return to the form.

17. Click on **M**erge... to display to display the Merge dialog again.

18. Click on **M**erge... to display the Perform Merge dialog shown in Figure 9.17.

19. Enter the form file, data file, and output file information. You can probably accept WordPerfect defaults.

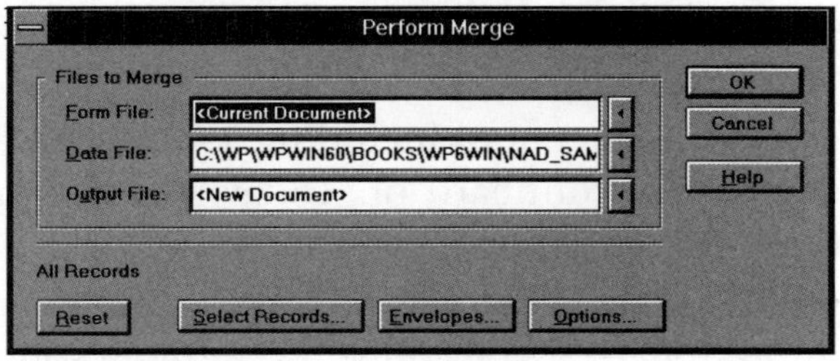

Figure 9.17   Perform Merge dialog.

20. Click on **S**elect Records... if you want to use only a portion of the records stored in the database. You can specify up to four pieces of information for up to three fields to select the records you want to include in the merge.

21. Click on **OK** when you have finished the specifications entry.

22. Click on **O**ptions on the Perform Merge dialog to show the Perform Merge Options dialog. Accept the defaults or make any changes required on this dialog. Click on **OK** to close this dialog.

23. Click on **OK** on the Perform Merge dialog. WordPerfect performs the merge, creating a new document with the merged information.

24. Use **F**ile Save **A**s... to store the merged document on disk. Print the file with **F**ile **P**rint when you are ready.

What To Do If

*   You can add more records to the data file at any time by repeating the preceding process, specifying the previous file instead of a new file.

See Also

*   None.

113 Inserting Sound in WordPerfect Documents

A few years ago the concept of including sound with a word processing document was unheard of. Today sound is becoming a natural part of the word processing environment. You can use sound to document portions of your file, to carry the majority of the information in it, or as a novelty. By coupling sound files and macros you can create a multimedia presentation that could, for example, present a self-running instructional presentation that includes sound and graphics.

Assumptions

- The document in which you want to include sound is loaded and is the current document.
- The insertion point is positioned where you want the sound clip to appear.

Exceptions

- Sound in WordPerfect must be in digital audio (*.WAV) or MIDI (*.MID) format. Digital files can be recorded on your computer with the proper hardware. These files are similar to recording sound on tape, except that the sounds are digitized and placed on disk. MIDI (Musical Instrument Digital Interface) records program instructions for reproducing sound in firmware and hardware.
- To use sound in WordPerfect you need a sound output device, either an internal bus card or an external sound device that attaches to a serial or parallel port.

Steps

1. Use **I**nsert **S**ound... to display the Sound Clips dialog, shown in Figure 9.18.
2. Click on **I**nsert... to display the Insert Sound Clip into Document dialog (see Figure 9.19).
3. Enter the name of the sound file you want to insert into your document. Include a full path to the sound file. You can use the File Manager by clicking on the file folder icon to the right of the File: field on this dialog.
4. Click on the button beside **S**tore in Document at the bottom of the dialog. If you accept WordPerfect's default, the document is linked to the sound file on disk so that if you

TIP

If you have more than one sound clip at nearly the same location, WordPerfect displays a small insert icon in the left margin. If you click on this icon, then multiple speaker icons are displayed, pointing to the precise location of the sound clip.

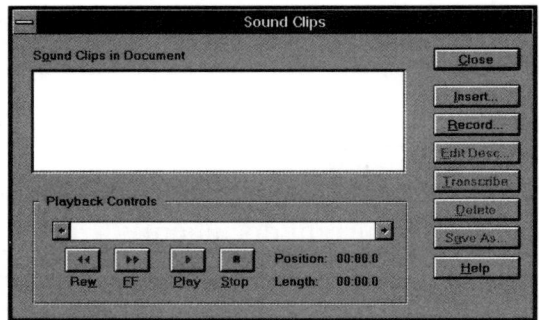

Figure 9.18 Sound Clips dialog.

change the sound file the new version will show up in your document automatically.

5. Click on **OK** to close all dialogs and return to your document. A speaker icon is displayed in the margin of your document beside the location of the insertion point.

6. To play the sound file, simply click on the speaker icon.

What To Do If

- If you are creating files that will be telecommunicated or carried to other machines, make sure to select **S**tore in Document on the Insert Sound Clip into Document dialog.

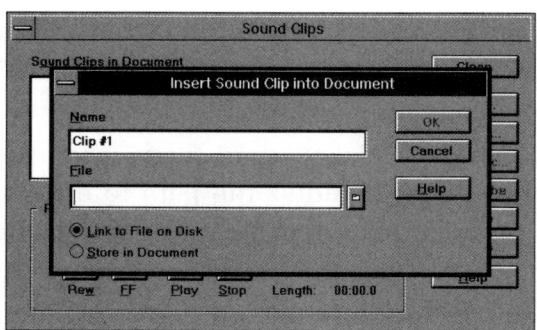

Figure 9.19 Insert Sound Clip into Document dialog.

- You can launch the Windows Sound Recorder from inside WordPerfect. Use **I**nsert **S**ound **R**ecord... to launch the Windows Sound Recorder. After recording the sound, use the procedure described here to insert the sound into a WordPerfect document.

_____ **See Also**

- Using Hypertext, p. 252.

Chapter
10

Preferences

Practical WordPerfect Macros

Other Practical Projects

PRACTICAL
PROJECTS

You've seen in the rest of this book the basics of how to use Word-Perfect. We can't cover every single aspect of using this complex and capable program, of course, but throughout the previous chapters we have shown you the major features.

In this chapter, we'll show you some practical applications that will explain some of the features already covered in previous chapters, and we'll introduce a few new concepts as well. Scan the major headings here, and use the project samples as a starting point for your own WordPerfect applications.

Preferences

We've shown you earlier how to use some of the Preferences utilities. This is how you tell WordPerfect how to behave by default, how to handle data, how to display information on the screen, and more. We'll show you in this section how to use some of these Preference features to customize the look and feel of Word-Perfect.

Of course you may not agree with our settings or our approach, but if you step through the samples here, you'll get a hands-on feeling for how these features work so that you can design your own Preferences. Any changes you make in the Preferences windows remain in effect as the WordPerfect defaults until you change them.

There are 12 preference settings, all accessible from the Preferences dialog (**F**ile P**r**eferences...) shown in Figure 10.1.

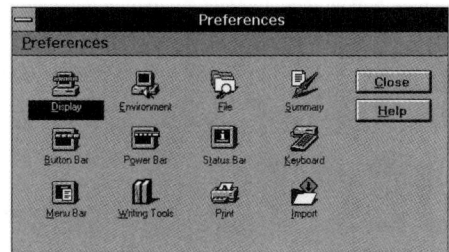

Figure 10.1   Preferences dialog.

The first step in making any changes is to display this dialog. From there you can access the various areas that can be set.

Altering the Display Preferences

The display preferences let you decide how WordPerfect displays certain items on the screen. The preset values give WordPerfect its default appearance. We will show you how to change just two of these preset values to change ever so slightly the default appearance of your WordPerfect documents.

Assumptions

- You have displayed the Preferences dialog with File Preferences... .

Exceptions

- None.

Steps

1. Double-click on the display icon to show the Display Preferences dialog shown in Figure 10.2.

2. Click on the box beside the Windows System Colors entry in the Show section of this dialog. That forces WordPerfect to display Windows system colors for text and dialog boxes.

3. Click on View/**Z**oom to enable the view choices of this dialog. Notice that WordPerfect is set to display documents in Page mode.

4. Click on **Dr**aft under the Default View heading. This "cleans up" the display for normal, day-to-day data entry, removing the large lines on page breaks, for example, and in general providing a less-cluttered data entry screen.

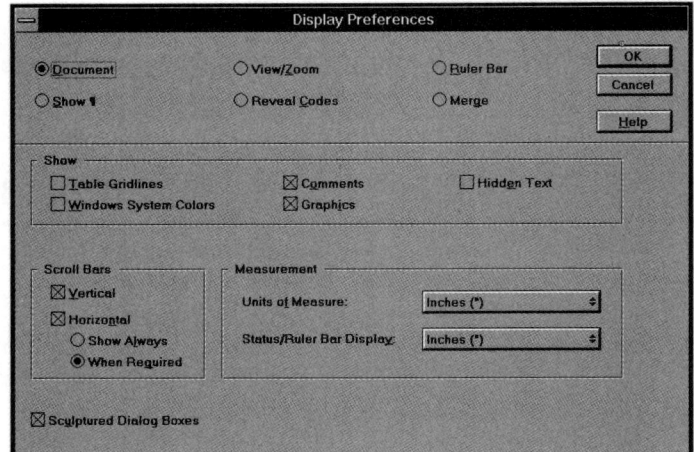

Figure 10.2   Display Preferences dialog.

5. You can display additional menu choices by clicking on other areas at the top of the screen.

6. When you have made all of the display changes you wish, click on **OK** to close this dialog and return to the Preferences dialog.

7. Select another Preferences icon, or click on **C**lose if you are finished with the Preferences utilities.

What To Do If

- You can make changes to the Display settings at any time. Simply redisplay the Display Preferences dialog and make changes as desired.

See Also

- Altering the Environment Preferences, p. 281.
- Altering the Button Bar Preferences, p. 285.
- Setting the Power Bar Preferences, p. 287.

Altering the Environment Preferences **115**

WordPerfect's environment settings establish how several features operate. For the most part, you can accept the defaults and get along very well. There are two settings on this dialog that we like to change, however, making WordPerfect operate more like we do business.

In this section we'll show you how to have WordPerfect save your workspace when you exit the program so that when you start up WordPerfect again, the same files you were working with before will be loaded. In addition, we will turn on QuickMark on Exit so that there is a bookmark at the last location of your insertion point when the files load. These are two useful features when you work on the same project over a rather long time, such as when you work on a couple of book chapters over several days, or you keep the current company annual report in your workspace, fine-tuning it over a period of time before going on to another project.

_____ **Assumptions**

- You have previously displayed the Preferences dialog with File Preferences... .

_____ **Exceptions**

- None.

_____ **Steps**

1. Double-click on the environment icon to display the Environment Preferences dialog, shown in Figure 10.3.

2. Click on the button beside **A**lways or Prompt on **E**xit under the Save Workspace title at the bottom of the

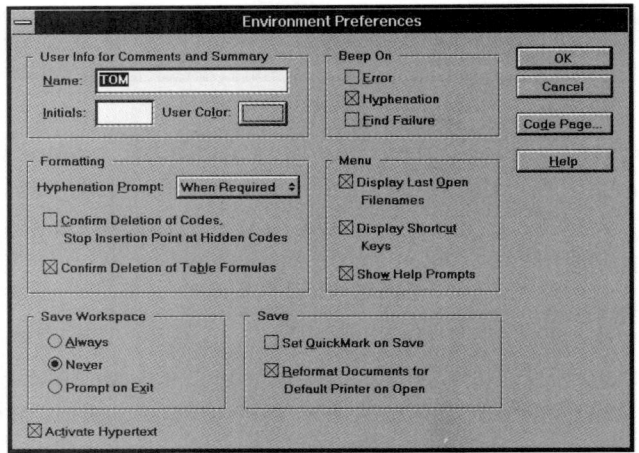

Figure 10.3   Environment Preferences dialog.

screen. This tells WordPerfect to save information about which files you were working on when you exited Word-Perfect. When the program starts again, those same files will be open and available for editing.

3. Click on Set **Q**uickMark on Save. This causes a special bookmark (a QuickMark) to be inserted at the location of the insertion point each time you save a document. That way, when you open that document again, you can jump directly to the last place you viewed or edited easily.

4. Click on **OK** to return to the Preferences dialog.

What To Do If

- If your work habits change, you may no longer want to save the workspace on exit or even have WordPerfect ask you if you want to save the workspace. Reverse the process by repeating the preceding steps 1 and 2. These settings are toggles, so if you click on these entries after they are enabled, they will be turned off.

> **TIP**
>
> Use **I**nsert **B**ook-mark **F**ind Quick-Mark to return to the QuickMark location.

_____ **See Also**

- Altering the File Preferences, below.
- Altering the Display Preferences, p. 279.

| **Altering the File Preferences** | 116 |

During installation you—or the WordPerfect install routine—decided where to locate certain files used by and generated by the programs that make up the WordPerfect system. In addition, other features such as whether you want to make a backup copy of the original document file every time you save a document and whether to enable a timed backup of your current files also were set.

The File Preferences dialog lets you review these settings and make changes if you wish. Study this dialog to see where all the various files that make up the WordPerfect system are stored. We'll show you here how to change the backup options.

_____ **Assumptions**

- You have displayed the Preferences dialog (File Preferences...).

_____ **Exceptions**

- None.

_____ **Steps**

1. Double-click on the file icon on the Preferences dialog to display the File Preferences dialog, shown in Figure 10.4.
2. Click on Timed Document Backup to disable this feature. We have a long-standing habit of saving the current

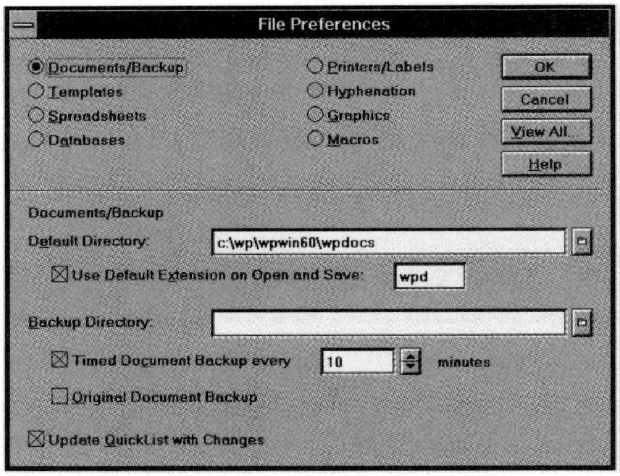

Figure 10.4 File Preferences dialog.

> **TIP**
>
> One change you might want to make for special projects is the default file extension, normally set at WPD (WordPerfect Document). As you work on long documents with different writers, you could use each writer's initials as the file extension, or you could use a departmental code or other special file extension to help you track information. To make this change, click in the field that holds the default .WPD file extension and type a new one.

document every 5 or 10 minutes (or after any significant changes) anyway, so the timed backup becomes somewhat of a nuisance. If you want to retain the automatic timed backup, skip this step.

3. Click on **O**riginal Document Backup if you want to enable another type of backup. With this box checked, WordPerfect makes a backup copy of the current document whenever it is saved, rather than writing over the previous version on disk.
4. You can make other changes to this screen if you wish, but they probably aren't necessary unless you have rearranged your hard disk and you want to modify how WordPerfect uses files.
5. Click on **OK** to close this dialog and return to the Preferences dialog.

What To Do If

- If you need to see an overall view of the WordPerfect directory and file structure, click on **V**iew All... to display a dialog with all the directory information in it.

See Also

- Altering the Display Preferences, p. 279.
- Altering the Environment Preferences, p. 281.

Altering the Button Bar Preferences

The button bar (or tool bar, as some applications call it) is a relatively recent addition to mainstream applications such as WordPerfect, but it is an addition that makes using the program a whole lot easier. By representing major tasks as icons on a button bar, the program becomes easier to interpret and more tasks—even those that may be buried under several menu levels—are available for all users.

This feature is made even more powerful by the fact that you can customize the button bar by moving the buttons to different locations, by adding buttons for your own functions, and by creating multiple button bars so that you have a separate bar for each type of task.

Assumptions

- You have displayed the Preferences dialog with the File Preferences... command sequence.

Exceptions

- None.

Steps

1. Double-click on the button bar icon to load the Button Bar Preferences dialog shown in Figure 10.5. This dialog shows you which button bar configurations are available. The default is WordPerfect, but as you work on different tasks

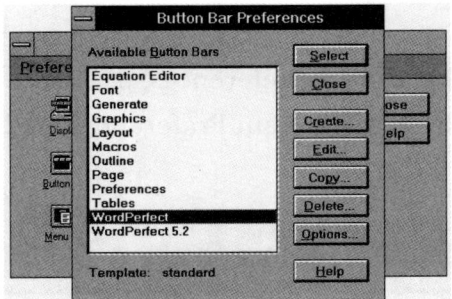

Figure 10.5   Button Bar Preferences dialog.

you may want to enable another button bar.

2.   Select the button bar you want to customize.

3.   Click on **O**ptions to display the Button Bar Options dialog.

4.   Select the font face you want to use from the **F**ont Face: list on this dialog and choose a new font size if you wish.

5.   The WordPerfect button bar default displays both picture and text. You can reduce the size of the button bar a little by selecting only pictures or only text. Do this, if you wish, in the Appearance section of the dialog.

6.   The default position for the button bar is at the top of the screen. You can move it to another location in the Location area of this dialog. Click on the position you prefer.

7.   WordPerfect normally displays only a single button bar row, letting you display additional buttons by rotating other rows onto the screen. You can specify up to three rows by entering a value in the **M**aximum number of Rows/Columns to Show: field on this dialog.

8.   Click on **OK** when you have made all the changes you want to the fields on the Button Bar Options dialog.

9.   Click on **S**elect on the Button Bar Preferences dialog to make the edited button bar the current one and to return to the Preferences dialog.

What To Do If

- If you want to remove buttons from any of the button bars listed in the Button Bar Preferences dialog, select the button bar name, and click on **E**dit to display the Button Bar Editor. Now use the mouse pointer to grab the button you want to delete and drag it off of the bar. When you drag the button off of the bar, WordPerfect turns the button into a trashcan to let you know that you are about to delete the button.

- To start from scratch with a new button bar, click on **C**reate on the Button Bar Preferences dialog. Give the new button bar a name and click on **OK** to display the Button Bar Editor. A blank button bar is displayed and you can add macros or other features listed on the Button Bar Editor.

See Also

- Setting the Power Bar Preferences, below.
- Assigning Macros to the Button Bar, p. 244.

Setting the Power Bar Preferences | 118

The power bar offers another range of WordPerfect commands and functions. The default commands offer a good selection of commands, but you may want to change the list for your own preferences.

Assumptions

- You are using the default WordPerfect power bar.
- You have displayed the Preferences dialog (File Preferences...).

Exceptions

- None.

TIP

You can adjust the available fonts on the Font Power Bar button by clicking on Fonts... on the Power Bar Preferences.

Steps

1. Double-click on the power bar icon to display the Power Bar Preferences dialog. A list of the WordPerfect commands and features you can place on the power bar is shown in the Items: window of this dialog. The items with the checked boxes are the ones already on the power bar.

2. Click on any checked item to remove it from the power bar.

3. Click on any unchecked item to add it to the power bar.

4. Click on **OK** to make the changes effective and return to the Preferences dialog.

What To Do If

- If you remove an item from the power bar, then add it back, it is placed at the end of the power bar. Put it back in its old position by grabbing the icon and dragging it to its original position.

- If, after adding and deleting power bar items, you decide you'd really rather put it back the way it was, click on **Default** on the Power Bar Preferences dialog.

See Also

- Altering the Button Bar Preferences, p. 285.

119 Setting the Status Bar Preferences

The WordPerfect status bar provides continuous feedback on certain document and program conditions. You can use the Preferences dialog to customize the status bar.

Assumptions

- You have displayed the Preferences dialog (File Preferences...).

Exceptions

- None.

Steps

1. Click on the status bar icon on the Preferences dialog to display the Status Bar Preferences dialog. The Status Bar Items window on this dialog shows all of the items you can put on the status bar. The items with a check mark are on the bar; items without a check mark can be displayed but aren't right now.

2. Click on any item with a check mark to remove it from the status bar.

3. Click on any item without a check mark to place it on the status bar.

4. Grab any displayed item on the status bar to resize it.

5. Click on **OK** when you have configured the status bar the way you want it.

What To Do If

- You can return to the WordPerfect default status bar at any time by clicking on **D**efault on the Status Bar Preferences dialog.

See Also

- Setting the Power Bar Preferences, p. 287.
- Altering the Button Bar Preferences, p. 285.

120 Setting the Keyboard Preferences

WordPerfect is supplied with three keyboard definitions, but you can customize any or all of those to meet your own needs.

Assumptions

- You have displayed the Preferences dialog (File Preferences...).
- You are working with the WordPerfect default keyboard definitions and you want to customize one of those.

Exceptions

- None.

Steps

1. Double-click on the keyboard icon on the Preferences dialog to display the Keyboard Preferences dialog.
2. Select the keyboard definition you want to customize from the list in the Keyboards: window.
3. Click on Create... to display the Create Keyboard dialog.
4. Enter a name for the new keyboard definition, which will be based on the keyboard you selected previously.
5. Click on **OK** to close this dialog and present the Keyboard Editor dialog, shown in Figure 10.6.
6. Click on key combinations you want to check or change. If you click on **Ctrl,** then click on **B,** for example, the **B+Ctrl Attribute Bold** line is displayed in the Choose a Key to Assign or Unassign window of this dialog.
7. Click on **Assign** or **Unassign** to change this key combination function.
8. Select from the Assign Key To list to change the display in the Assign or Unassign window.

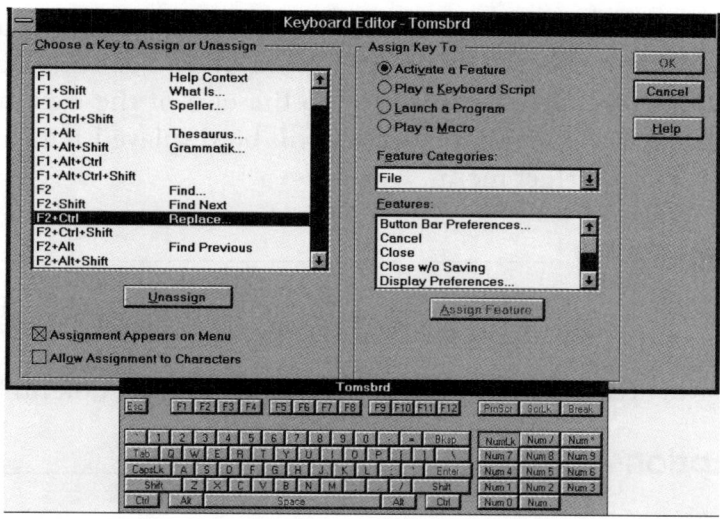

Figure 10.6   Keyboard Editor dialog.

9. Click on **OK** to create the new keyboard.

_____ **What To Do If**

• Once a new keyboard has been created, you can use Edit from the Keyboard Preferences dialog to make changes to it.

_____ **See Also**

• Assigning Macros to the Keyboard, p. 241.

Setting the Menu Bar Preferences 121

The basic WordPerfect menu bar (the second row on the Word-Perfect screen) gives you access to nearly all WordPerfect features. Some menu items are redundant offerings that also are available on the power bar or the button bar.

With the Menu Bar Preferences feature you can add your own items to the menu bar. If there is room on the existing bar, any new items you add will be added to the end of the existing bar. When that line fills up, new items will be displayed beneath the default WordPerfect menu.

Assumptions

- You have displayed the Preferences dialog (File Preferences...).
- You are working with the default WordPerfect menu bar.

Exceptions

- None.

Steps

TIP
You can double-click on any menu item while the Menu Bar Editor is displayed to edit the text of the menu entry. When you add a macro, for example, the menu item says simply "macro." Double-click on this menu item and add your own, more descriptive text for it.

1. Double-click on the menu bar icon to display the Menu Bar Preferences dialog.

2. Click on Create... to display a Create Menu Bar dialog.

3. Enter a name for the new menu bar in the Name: field of this dialog.

4. Click on **OK** to display the Menu Bar Editor, shown in Figure 10.7.

5. Use the scroll bar to view available features in the Features: window of this dialog.

6. Select each item you want to appear on your custom menu and click on **Add Menu Item** to add it to the menu.

7. Click on **OK** to close the Menu Bar Editor.

What To Do If

- Remove any menu items, including the default entries supplied with WordPerfect, by grabbing the item with the mouse and dragging it off of the menu bar.

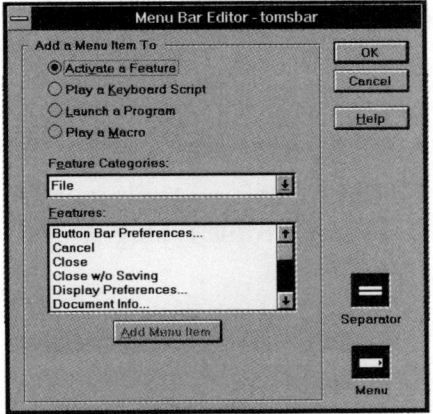

Figure 10.7   Menu Bar Editor.

_____ **See Also**

- Altering the Button Bar Preferences, p. 285.
- Setting the Power Bar Preferences, p. 287.
- Adding WordPerfect Macros to the Menu, p. 247.

Setting the Writing Tools Preferences   122

WordPerfect writing tools are the speller, thesaurus, and grammar checker. They appear on the Tools menu in that order. You can remove some or all of these items from the menu and change the order or the list on the Tools menu.

_____ **Assumptions**

- You have displayed the Preferences dialog (File Preferences...).

Exceptions

- None.

Steps

1. Double-click on the writing tools icon on the Preferences dialog. The Writing Tools dialog shown in Figure 10.8 is displayed.

2. Click on any of the listed tools to remove them from the Tools menu.

3. Click on Move **U**p or Move **D**own to change the position of these items on the Tools menu.

4. Click on **OK** to close this dialog.

What To Do If

- If you change your mind about reconfiguring the Writing Tools display, click on Cancel on the Writing Tools dialog to close this dialog without making any changes.

See Also

- Setting the Menu Bar Preferences, p. 291.
- Setting the Power Bar Preferences, p. 287.
- Altering the Button Bar Preferences, p. 285.

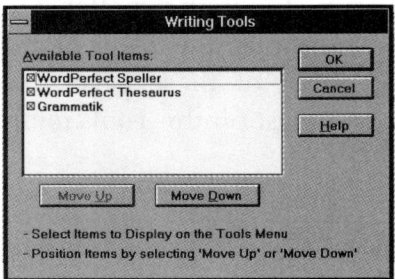

Figure 10.8   Writing Tools dialog.

Setting Print Preferences | 123

You have some control over how WordPerfect prints your documents through the Preferences dialog.

Assumptions

- You have displayed the Preferences dialog (File Preferences...).

Exceptions

- None.

Steps

1. Double-click on the print icon to display the Print Preferences dialog shown in Figure 10.9. On the left side of this dialog are fields to set the size attribute ratios; the right side of the dialog lets you specify the number of copies to print by default and other settings.

2. If you normally print multiple copies of your documents, set the default **N**umber of Copies: to what you need.

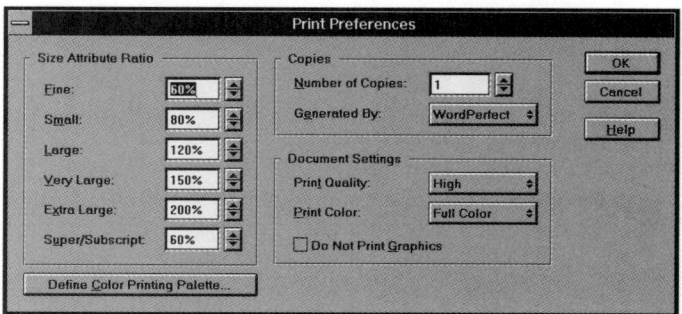

Figure 10.9   Print Preferences dialog.

3. Click on the Generated By: button and select Printer to have the printer generate multiple copies. This will speed up printing in most cases.
4. Make other changes on this dialog as necessary.
5. Click on **OK** to set the changes and close this dialog.

What To Do If

- Although the settings you make on this dialog will appear as the default when you print a document, you can always override them on the Print dialog before your current document is printed.

See Also

- Using Color Output Devices, p. 182.
- Printing Multiple Copies of a Document, p. 171.

Setting Import Preferences

WordPerfect can import files from a number of other application formats, but the bottom line for interoperability is the ASCII delimited file and .WPG graphics files. You can make changes to the default import formats through the Preferences utility.

Assumptions

- You have displayed the Preferences dialog (File Preferences...).

Exceptions

- None.

_____ **Steps**

1. Double-click on the import icon on the Preferences dialog to display the Import Preferences dialog, shown in Figure 10.10.

2. Change field, record, and character delimiters if necessary to import the files you need to import.

3. You can tell WordPerfect to convert graphics files in place, instead of the default of retaining both formats. Click on these buttons to toggle changes, if you wish.

4. Click on **OK** to close this dialog and make the changes effective.

_____ **What To Do If**

• The WordPerfect defaults are pretty functional. Change these defaults only if you know that the files you will be working with need other settings.

_____ **See Also**

• Importing Graphics Files, p. 203.

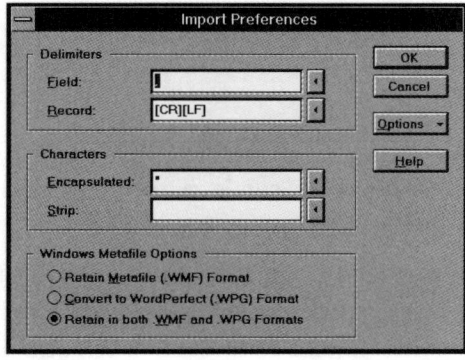

Figure 10.10   Import Preferences dialog.

Designing Business Cards

Remember Jim Rockford of "Rockford Files"? This unorthodox TV detective carried a small printing press in his car to turn out custom business cards. He'd pull up to a home or business to do a little gumshoe work, slip a blank business card into the little press, dial in a new name, and suddenly he was someone else.

Business cards are reasonably priced today. You can buy 250 cards for around $10 at some print shops—nothing special, you understand, but serviceable business cards nevertheless.

So, why would you want to make your own business cards?

We make business cards with WordPerfect occasionally when we run out of cards and have to leave for a show or for a research trip before we can get new ones back from the local printer. We use this technique anytime we need "quick and dirty" cards in small quantity, or when we want to lay out our own cards for the local printer. Ask around, and you'll probably find that the low-priced printers have one rate for their design and another price for your design. If you supply them the layout in WordPerfect format, however, you can frequently get your design at their price.

Assumptions

- None.

Exceptions

- Unless you have your cards printed at a print shop, you can't produce "raised" print on your cards.
- Unless you are using the card design as a template or sample, you'll need card stock paper for printing your cards. Most laser printers can feed card stock successfully (ask for Hammermill Cover #10913-2 or equivalent paper).
- Standard business cards measure 2" × 3.5". That's what we show you how to design here, but you can create your own

card size (a fold-over design, for example) with a little experimentation.

• This procedure requires a sheet-feed printer.

Steps

1. Use **L**ayout **L**abels... **C**reate... to display the Create Labels dialog shown in Figure 10.11.

2. Enter "Business Cards" in the **L**abel Description: field of this dialog.

3. Change the **W**idth: under Label Size to 3.5".

4. Change **H**eight: under Label Size to 2".

5. Change the Le**f**t Edge: measurement to 0.500".

6. Change **R**ows: under Labels Per Page to 5.

7. Click on **OK** to close the Create Labels dialog and return to the Labels dialog. The label format you just created should be selected.

8. Click on **S**elect on the Labels dialog to close the dialog and open a WordPerfect editing screen with the business card label format on the screen.

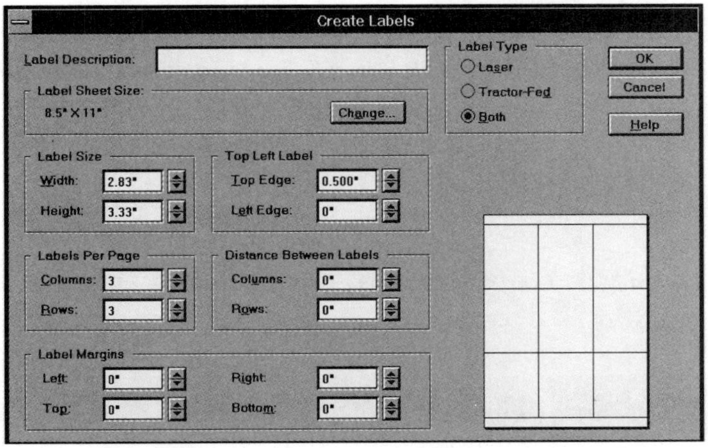

Figure 10.11   Create Labels dialog.

TIP

Once you have a copy of the business card information on the Clipboard you don't have to use Edit Copy again. Simply position the insertion point on the next card and press **Shift+Ins** or use **E**dit **P**aste to fill the next blank card with information.

9. Type the information you want to include on your business card. We created the basic card shown in Figure 10.12. Remember, you can use any WordPerfect characters, graphics, and attributes as part of your card design. We used a WordPerfect-supplied figure file as a watermark on our sample card.

10. Use **F**ile Save **A**s... to store the file with the first card.

11. Position the insertion point at the end of the first card and press **Enter**. WordPerfect displays a second blank business card.

12. Select the entire text on the first business card. Use **E**dit **C**opy to place a copy of the business card copy on the Clipboard.

13. Position the insertion point at the upper left corner of the second blank card.

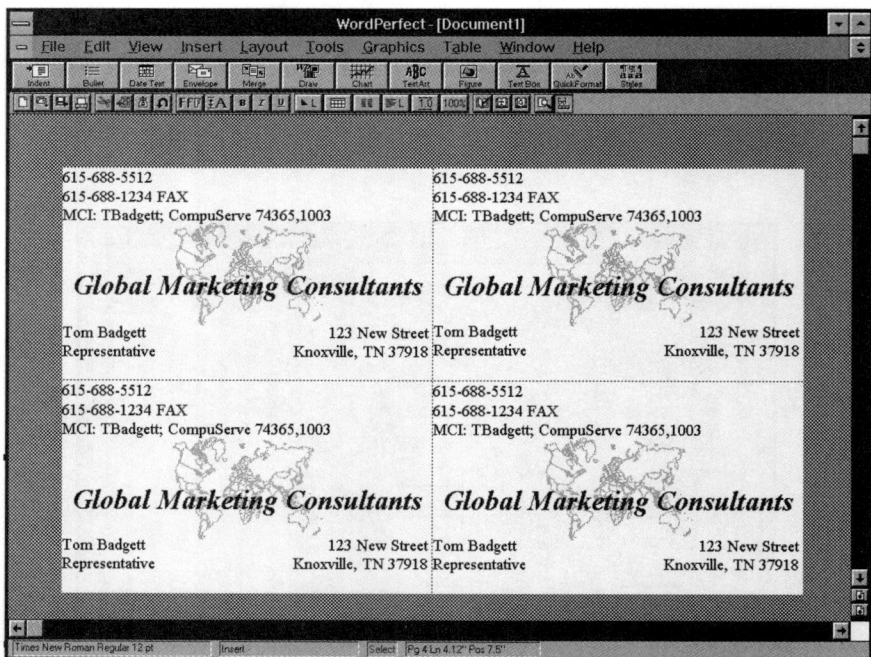

Figure 10.12   Basic business card format on business card label stock.

14. Use **E**dit **P**aste to put business card text (and graphics if you are using any) on the second card.

15. Repeat steps 11 to 14 until you have filled the page with cards. (Our design places ten cards to a page.)

16. Use **F**ile **S**ave to store your completed business card label sheet.

17. Use **F**ile **P**rint to print your sheet of business cards.

What To Do If

• The hard part about printing your own business cards is cutting them after they are printed. For a few dollars you can usually get a print shop to cut a stack of cards for you. They can do this while you wait, whereas they usually have to send off a card printing request.

See Also

• Designing Invitations, below.
• Designing a Letterhead, p. 305.

Designing Invitations | 126

You can use WordPerfect to design any number of documents. But once you have learned the basic techniques, many different documents can be designed with the same technique. Here's another practical application that uses WordPerfect's built-in label page design, just as we did with the preceding business card application.

We'll show you here a basic card design creatively based on the label utility. Use this idea as a starting point to incorporate creative graphics, text art, or whatever to make invitations, signs, announcements, and other documents.

Assumptions

- This project assumes you have a page printer such as a laser or ink-jet sheet-fed printer.

Exceptions

- For best results with this project you should have card stock paper. Many companies offer colored stock for this type of application.

Steps

1. Use **La**yout La**b**els... to display the Labels dialog.
2. Click on **C**reate... to launch the Create Labels routine.
3. Enter a description in the **L**abel Description: field of the Create Label dialog.
4. Change the label width to 4" in the **W**idth: field of this dialog.
5. Change the label Height to 8" in the **Hei**ght: field of this dialog.
6. Change **C**olumns: to 2 and **R**ows: to 1 under the Labels Per Page heading on this dialog.
7. Change the **L**eft Edge: measurement to 0.200".
8. Click on **OK** to return to the Labels dialog. The label you just defined should be selected in the Labels: window of this dialog.
9. Click on **S**elect to load this label definition into an editing window like the one in Figure 10.13.
10. To reproduce the label we used in this example, use **G**raphics **F**igure to display the Insert Figure dialog.
11. Choose **Board02p.wpg** from the list of files in the File-name: window of this dialog.
12. Select the graphic after it is pasted onto your label stock.

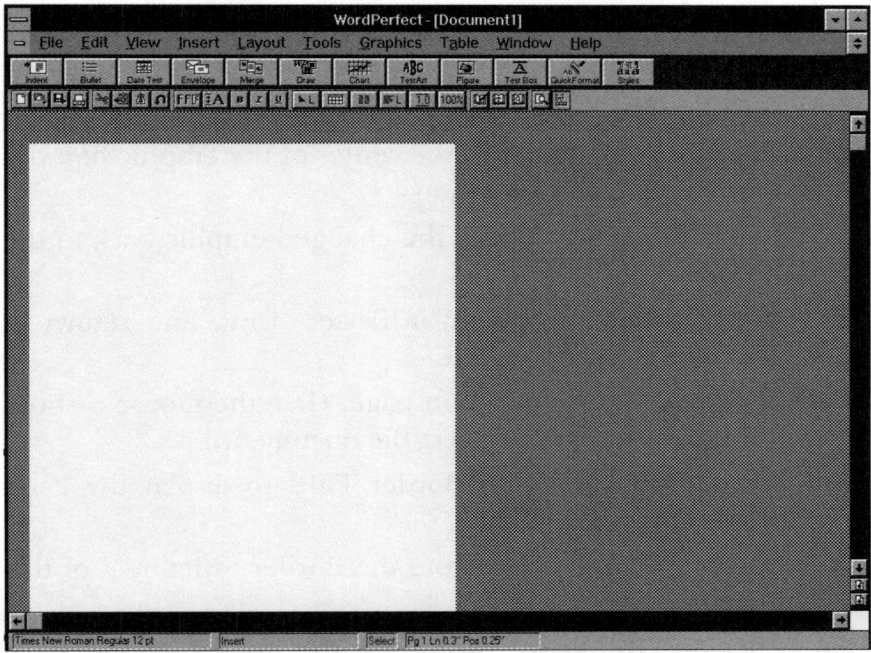

Figure 10.13   Invitation blank label in Edit window.

Grab the lower border and drag it about halfway down the
label.

13. Use **G**raphics **E**dit Box **(Shift+F11)** to display the Edit Box
feature bar.

14. Select **B**order/Fill... and choose Thick from the **B**order
Style: field of the Box Border/Fill Styles dialog.

15. Click on **OK** to set the border around the top part of the
invitation.

16. Double-click on the board graphic at the top of the invitation to launch WordPerfect Draw.

17. Select the text icon from the Draw tool bar.

18. Use **Text Font... (F9)** to display the Font selection dialog.

19. Choose Times New Roman, 36 point, bold italic text, and click on **OK.**

20. Type the word **Party!** in the center of the graphic box you loaded from your invitation.

21. Use **File Update** to copy the changed graphic back to the invitation.

22. Use **File Exit** to close WordPerfect Draw and return to your invitation document.

23. Select the entire invitation page. (Use the mouse or hold down the Shift key to select the document.)

24. Use **Layout Paragraph Border/Fill...** to display the Paragraph Border dialog.

25. Choose Thick Shadow from the Border Style: field of this dialog.

26. Click on **OK** to close this dialog and place a thick shadow border around the invitation.

27. Enter the text of the invitation in the lower half of the document. Use a large font for the name at the top and a relatively smaller font for the rest of the text. Use whatever wording you like, just make sure it fits into the lower 4" × 4" portion of the invitation.

28. Select the entire invitation and use **Edit Copy** to place a copy of the invitation on the Clipboard.

29. Use **Ctrl+End** to go to the bottom of the page and press **Enter** once or twice to force WordPerfect to display the second invitation page beside this one.

30. Click at the top of this new page and use **Edit Paste** to fill the page with the finished invitation.

31. Use **File Save As...** to store the invitation and **File Print** to print it.

What To Do If

- If, after printing the invitations, you need to make changes, simply use standard WordPerfect editing procedures to fine-tune the document.

See Also

- Designing Business Cards, p. 298.
- Designing a Letterhead, below.

Designing a Letterhead   127

Just as you may find it convenient to print an occasional run of business cards with WordPerfect, you may want to roll your own letterhead. In fact, with the new, low-priced 600 dpi printers, many of them in color, it almost doesn't make sense for a small business to pay someone else to design and print a small order of letterhead. Large companies always will need the services of a high-speed press to turn out enough letterhead for their needs, but at the small end of the scale, some careful design and a high-resolution printer will give you a creative business image at a reasonable cost.

You can approach the design of a letterhead in WordPerfect in various ways. If you already have a letterhead design, of course, simply use this as a basis on which to build your new one. Or, you can study your files looking for letterhead examples from other companies to give you a place to start. And, of course, you can just start with a blank page and use the flexibility afforded by word processing to manipulate text and graphics until you come up with what you want.

Assumptions

- This procedure assumes you are using a page printer, such as a laser or ink-jet device.

Exceptions

- We will design a letterhead around a WordPerfect template. That will make it easier to reuse the design later.
- For a quick letter or to use a simple design with interactive addressing, use one of the letter templates supplied with WordPerfect. Use **F**ile **T**emplate... **(Ctrl+T)** to display the Templates dialog and choose **Letter1** through **Letter5** for your letter.

Steps

1. Use **F**ile **T**emplate **(Ctrl+T)** to display the Templates dialog.
2. Select **O**ptions and choose **C**reate Template... to display the Create Document Template dialog, shown in Figure 10.14.
3. Enter a name for the template in the **N**ame: field of this dialog. We used **ltrhead**.
4. Click on **OK** to close the Create Document Template dialog and present a WordPerfect editing window topped by a Template feature bar.
5. Use **G**raphics Tex**t**Art to display the text art in WordPerfect dialog.

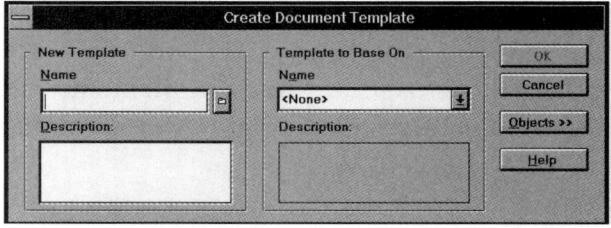

Figure 10.14   Create Document Template dialog.

6. Choose **Brooklyn** from the Font: window of this dialog.

7. Select **Bold** from the Style: field of this dialog. (These settings are pretty arbitrary. Experiment with different fonts and attributes to fit your business and personal preference.)

8. Type the name of your company in the Enter Text: window of this dialog.

9. Select the wrap around pattern from the group in the center of this dialog (the first icon in the upper left corner of this section of the dialog).

10. Change the Height: field in this dialog to 2 inches.

11. Use File Save Copy As... to give this file a name, and save it to disk. Who knows, you might want to use this creation again somewhere else.

12. Use File **U**pdate WordPerfect to copy the company name to your letterhead template.

13. Click on **OK** to close this dialog and return to the Template Editor.

14. Grab the text art box and drag it to about the center of the page, toward the top margin.

15. Use Graphics Text to launch the Text Box Editor.

16. Use Layout Font... **(F9)** to display the Font dialog.

17. Choose **Brooklyn, 14 point, bold** from this dialog.

18. Click on **OK** to return to the Text Box Editor.

19. Type a company motto, underline text, or promotional text (e.g., Serving Whoville since 1952).

20. Click on **C**lose to copy the text box to your template and close the Text Box Editor. The text box won't be correctly placed at this point. Don't worry. Leave it where it is.

21. Select the text box. Use **Graphics Edit Box (Shift+F11)** to display the Edit Box feature bar.

22. Click on **B**order/Fill and choose **None** to remove WordPerfect's default top and bottom thick border.

23. Click on **OK** to close the Box Border/Fill Styles dialog.

24. Grab the text box and drag it into position beneath the company name, within the semicircle (if you have chosen a different text art design, place the text box in the appropriate position).

25. Click on **C**lose on the Edit Box feature bar to close the bar.

26. Use **G**raphics Text to launch the Text Box Editor again.

27. Once again use Layout Font... **(F9)** to choose the Brooklyn typeface. This time specify **12-point regular** text. Click on **OK** to close the Font dialog.

28. Use Layout Line **C**enter to place the insertion point in the center of the text box.

29. Type the company address and telephone number as the text box entry.

30. Click on **C**lose to copy the box to the letterhead template and close the Text Box Editor.

31. Select the text box and use **G**raphics **E**dit Box to display the Edit Box feature bar.

32. Click on **B**order/Fill and specify "Single" in the **B**order Style: field of this dialog. Click on **OK** to return to the letterhead template.

30. Grab the text box and drag it toward the bottom of the page so it is clear of the company name. Now grab a handle and enlarge the box so that the full name and address fits into a single, thin box.

34. Click on **P**osition to display the Box Position dialog.

35. Click on the button beside **P**ut Box on Current Page to establish a page anchor.

36. Select bottom margin in the from button under the Vertical placement title.

37. Enter 0.3" in the Place: field under the Vertical placement title.

TIP
You can use View Zoom to view the page at 50 percent of normal so you can see how the various elements you have installed fit together.

38. Click on **OK** to close this dialog.

39. Click on **C**lose to remove the Edit Box feature bar.

40. Press **Enter** several times until the insertion point is positioned in the left margin beneath the company name.

41. Use **L**ayout **F**ont... **(F9)** to select the font you want to use for your letters. A 12-point, regular Times Roman or Times New Roman is a good general choice.

42. Click on **E**xit Template to close the Template Editor.

43. Answer **Yes** when WordPerfect asks if you want to save the changes to the template.

What To Do If

- If you need to adjust the text position within the text box (either the underline or the company address), select the box and use **G**raphics **E**dit Box to display the Edit Box feature bar. Now click in the box again and you can enter new text, adjust placement of text, add attributes, and the like.

- To use the new template to type a letter, use **F**ile **T**emplate **(Ctrl+T)** and choose **Ltrhead** from the list of available templates. Type your letter as usual, and use **F**ile Save **A**s... to store it under a different filename.

See Also

- Designing Business Cards, p. 298.
- Designing a Newsletter, below.

Designing a Newsletter 128

You can use generally the same technique for newsletters as we used for the letterhead in the last section. Simply open the Templates dialog and choose **C**reate, then experiment until you achieve the design you want.

With WordPerfect 6 for Windows, however, you have some supplied templates to start with. Use these to learn about newsletter design, then use **F**ile **T**emplate... **E**dit to customize one of the designs, or use one of these designs as a basis to create your own newsletter template.

Assumptions

- None.

Exceptions

- None.

Steps

1. Use **F**ile **T**emplate... **(Ctrl+T)** to display the **T**emplates dialog.

2. Choose one of the newsletter formats from the list. Newsltr1 is a three-column design with a cursive title, making it less formal than Newsltr2.

3. Click on **OK** to open a new document based on the Newsletter template.

4. Enter the issue number and date in the appropriate fields when WordPerfect prompts you for them. Click on **OK** when these fields are complete.

5. Either type the text for the newsletter, or use **I**nsert **F**ile to load an existing WordPerfect text file into the newsletter format. Position the insertion point under the **HEADER** prompt in the left column, then issue the **I**nsert **F**ile command and choose a file. The straight text will automatically load into the newsletter format.

6. Use **F**ile **S**ave **A**s... to store the template-based newsletter under a unique filename.

_____ **What To Do If**

- Use **G**raphics **F**igure to insert a graphics image into the newsletter, if you wish. You also can use other WordPerfect features—Watermark, TextArt, and so on—to enhance this basic newsletter design.

- To create a second page for the newsletter, define a document with three columns that uses Times New Roman, 12-point, regular type.

_____ **See Also**

- Using Columns, p. 94.
- Importing Graphics Files, p. 203.
- Designing a Letterhead, p. 305.

Using KickOff | 129

One more way to customize the operation of WordPerfect is through the use of KickOff, a utility that keeps track of the date and time and lets you launch a variety of applications or tasks automatically. This may not fit at the top of your list of things to use every day, but like setting a VCR to record a TV program you can't be present to view, KickOff will serve you well when you need it.

_____ **Assumptions**

- None.

_____ **Exceptions**

- None.

TIP

You can minimize
KickOff if you wish,
but you can't close
it or the applica-
tions you added
won't be launched
on time.

Steps

1. Exit WordPerfect or minimize the WordPerfect window by clicking on the Minimize button at the upper right of the screen.

2. Locate the WordPerfect application window in the Program Manager. Double-click on the KickOff icon in this window. The KickOff dialog shown in Figure 10.15 is displayed. Unless you have used KickOff before, the Events: window should be blank.

3. Click on **A**dd... to display the Edit/Add dialog shown in Figure 10.16.

4. Enter a command on the **C**ommand Line: of this dialog. Include a full path to the program you want to launch. Use **B**rowse... if you want KickOff to present the path and enter the path and file information on this line for you.

5. Enter the date and time when you want the application to launch.

6. Enter a repeat interval, if you want the application to launch every so many days, hours, or minutes.

7. Click on **OK** to close the Edit/Add dialog and return to the KickOff dialog. The task you just added should appear in the Events: window of the KickOff dialog.

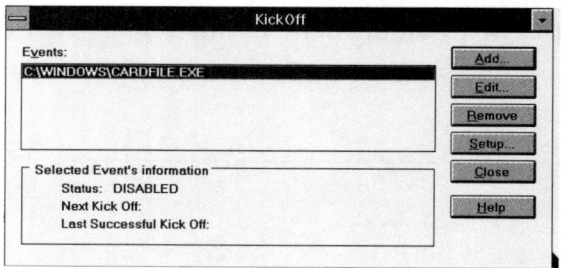

Figure 10.15   KickOff dialog.

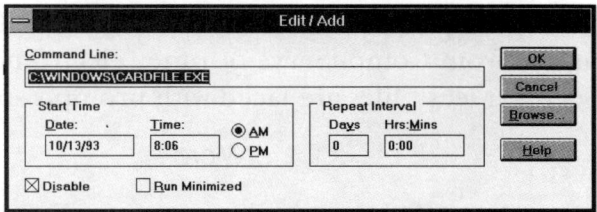

Figure 10.16   Edit/Add KickOff dialog.

_____ **What To Do If**

- If you change your mind about the starting time of an event, select the event in the Events: window and click on Edit to change the entry.

_____ **See Also**

- None.

Practical WordPerfect Macros

In this section we'll offer you some suggested applications for macros. We won't spend much time on how to build and use these macros here. You can learn about that in Chapter 8. However, by giving you some ideas about how macros can be used, perhaps we'll set the stage for you to exercise your own creativity and set you on the right track for making more use of macros.

| Conducting Document "Cleanup" | 130 |

Sometimes, when you import a text document from another application, it is full of unwanted and unnecessary information.

For example, we frequently load into WordPerfect information captured on-line from CompuServe or other electronic services. In CompuServe, at least, files are laced with prompts such as

Press <CR> for More...

Most on-line services give you similar prompts. To make these files more useful and less cluttered in WordPerfect, you want to scan the document and delete this information. A macro is the logical way to do this, because once you have the routine recorded correctly, you can step through a document deleting unwanted lines with a few keystrokes.

Assumptions

- You have studied a portion of the document you want to clean up to determine that the text you want to remove is consistent.

- The text you want to remove is contained on an entire line. You will not be removing text on a portion of a line.

Exceptions

- You should make a backup copy of any file you will manipulate with a macro. That way if the file format changes at some point and information is lost, you can return to the original to recover.

Steps

TIP
You also can remove a portion of a line. Simply press **Backspace** or **Del** as often as necessary to remove the proper text, or hold Shift and use the arrow keys to mark the text you want to erase, then press **Del**.

1. Use **T**ools **M**acro **R**ecord... **(Ctrl+F10)** to display the Record Macro dialog.

2. Enter a name for the macro in the **N**ame: field of this dialog. We call our version of this macro "ZAP" because it zaps unwanted material from a document.

3. Click on **OK** to return to your document and start recording the macro.

4. Use **Edit F**ind to display the Find dialog.

5. In the **F**ind: field of this dialog, enter a portion of the text you want to find and remove. This should be a distinctive entry that would be unlikely to show up outside of the line you are removing.

6. Click on **F**ind Next to locate the first occurrence of the search text.

7. Press **Esc** to clear the Find dialog and place the insertion point at the end of the text you searched for.

8. Press **Home** to place the insertion point at the beginning of the current line.

9. Press **Shift+End** to mark the entire line of text.

10. Press **Del** to erase the line.

11. Press **Ctrl+F10** or use **T**ools **M**acro **R**ecord... to stop macro recording.

_____ **What To Do If**

- If you accidentally erase more text than you intended, try using Undelete, or load your backup version of this document and copy the removed information from the backup document to the original.

- To use the macro, assign it to a keystroke combination (see Chapter 8 for information) and press the keys to launch the macro. Notice how it functions each time so that you don't remove the wrong text.

_____ **See Also**

- Assigning Macros to the Keyboard, p. 241.
- Creating (Writing) Macros, p. 238.

131 ▼ Converting the Case of Text

In formatting a document, you sometimes have sections of a document that you want to appear in all uppercase. Sometimes you decide to do this after the document is completed. Here's a macro that lets you assign case conversion to an easy keystroke combination.

Assumptions

- You have some text you want to change from lowercase to all uppercase.
- The block of text you want to convert is selected.

Exceptions

- None.

Steps

1. Use **Tools Macro Record...** (**Ctrl+F10**) to display the Record Macro dialog.
2. Enter a name for the macro in the **Name:** field of this dialog.
3. Click on **OK** to return to your document and start recording the macro.
4. Use **Edit Convert Case Uppercase** to convert the selected block.
5. Use **Ctrl+F10** or **Tools Macro Record...** to stop recording.

What To Do If

- To reverse the process, create another macro or edit this one to select Lowercase under Convert Case instead of Uppercase. To convert from uppercase to words with initial caps, choose Initial capitals from this menu.

_____ **See Also**

- Creating (Writing) Macros, p. 238.

| Moving (Extracting) Text to Build a List | **132** |

If you are like many WordPerfect users, there are times when you need to extract information from an existing document and add it to a new document. We use this technique to extract interview notes or downloaded information, for example, from an original document and store it in a new document. We also use this macro to pull selected paragraphs from an original document and place them in a new document, which we then use as a reference for new work.

_____ **Assumptions**

- You have one or more existing documents from which you want to extract selected data and place it in a new document.
- The original document is open and is the current document.
- You have a secondary document open to receive the data and those are the only two documents open.
- The first block of data you want to extract is selected.

_____ **Exceptions**

- None.

_____ **Steps**

1. Use **T**ools **M**acro **R**ecord... **(Ctrl+F10)** to display the Record Macro dialog.
2. Enter a name for the macro in the **N**ame: field of this dialog.

3. Click on **OK** to return to your document and start recording the macro.

4. Use **E**dit **C**opy (or **E**dit **C**ut if you want to permanently remove the selected data from the original document) to place the selected data on the Clipboard.

5. Press **Ctrl+F6** to switch to the secondary document.

6. Press **Shift+Ins** or use **E**dit **P**aste to copy the data from the Clipboard into the secondary document.

7. Press **Ctrl+End** to move the insertion point to the end of the block of text you just copied from the original document.

8. If you want to separate the portions of text you move into the secondary document, enter separating data now. Use a dotted line, a series of equal signs, or another method of showing where one block of text stops and another starts.

9. Press **Ctrl+F6** to return to the original document.

10. Press **Ctrl+F10** or use **T**ools **M**acro **R**ecord... to stop macro recording.

What To Do If

- Use **T**ools **M**acro **E**dit... to change the segment separator or make other changes to this macro, if necessary.

See Also

- Creating (Writing) Macros, p. 238.
- Assigning Macros to the Button Bar, p. 244.
- Assigning Macros to the Keyboard, p. 241.

133 ▽ Printing a Single Page

The WordPerfect power bar includes an icon to launch the print routine, but it stops on the Print dialog. This is the same as pressing F5 from the keyboard. We use this macro regularly when we want to print the current page to get a quick look at something in hard copy. Once you have completed the macro, you can assign it to the button bar, install it on the power bar, or give it a keyboard keystroke combination.

Obviously, it would be easy to modify this macro so that it prints the entire document without stopping on the Print dialog to wait for you to press Enter or click on OK.

Assumptions

- The document you want to print is the current document and the insertion point is positioned anywhere on the page you want to print.

Exceptions

- None.

Steps

1. Use **Tools Macro Record...** (**Ctrl+F10**) to display the Record Macro dialog.

2. Enter a name for the macro in the **Name:** field of this dialog.

3. Click on **OK** to return to your document and start recording the macro.

4. Use **File Print...** (**F5**) to display the Print dialog.

5. Click on the button beside **Current Page** to turn on that feature.

6. Click on **Print** to print the current page.

7. Press **Ctrl+F10** or use **Tools Macro Record...** to stop recording and return to your document.

What To Do If

- To modify this macro to print the entire document, bypass step 6, accepting WordPerfect's default setting.

See Also

- Recording Macros, p. 233.
- Printing from WordPerfect 6.0 for Windows, Chapter 5.

134 ► Printing Current File to Disk

You don't always want to send word processor output to a printer. Sometimes it is very convenient to create a printer-format disk file instead. This lets you carry or transmit the printed file to another machine for remote printing. Perhaps you need to print a file on a printer that is not physically attached to your machine, or maybe you need to transmit a file to someone to print, but they don't have WordPerfect or another word processor that will accept WordPerfect files. Besides, most conversion programs don't do a perfect job of conversion, so you're better off to send a printer-format file and let someone at the remote printer simply copy the file to a printer.

Assumptions

- The file you want to print is loaded and is the current document.
- You have previously created a printer definition to print to file. If you are using an HP LaserJet, for example, you should have two printer definitions for that printer, one that outputs to LPT1 and one that outputs to file. See Chapter 5 for more information on how to create this printer definition.

- You are using a Microsoft Windows printer driver (the Word-Perfect default).

_____ **Exceptions**

- The procedure described here writes a macro for printing to disk with an HP LaserJet printer or another device that requires you to go to the Microsoft Windows printer routines. Refer to the description in Chapter 5 on how to print to a disk file with a PostScript printer.

- When you use this routine, the resulting file is in native printer format, PCL in the case of our HP LaserJet example. The file will have a different format with each printer type that you use.

_____ **Steps**

1. Use **Tools Macro Record... (Ctrl+F10)** to display the Record Macro dialog.

2. Enter a name for the macro in the **Name:** field of this dialog.

3. Click on **OK** to return to your document and start recording the macro.

4. Use **File Print... (F5)** to display the Print dialog.

5. Click on **S**elect... to display the Select Printer dialog.

6. Choose the previously defined HP LaserJet on FILE definition from the **Printers:** window of this dialog.

7. Click on **S**elect to return to the Print dialog.

8. Click on **P**rint to display the Print To File dialog.

9. Enter the path and filename where you want the output to be stored. (We use PRINTFI.PCL in the WordPerfect subdirectory. Use whatever filename you can remember easily.)

10. Click on **OK** to start printing to disk.

11. When the print process is finished, use **File Select Printer...** to display the Select Printer dialog.

12. Choose HP LaserJet on LPT1 from the Select Printer dialog.

13. Click on **S**elect to close this dialog and return to your document.

14. Use **Ctrl+F10** or **T**ools **M**acro **R**ecord... to turn off macro recording.

What To Do If

- For quick access to this routine, assign the macro to the menu bar where you can access it with an Alt+keystroke combination.

  If you use a WordPerfect printer driver, you can specify the filename once on the Printer Setup dialog (**F**ile Select Printer... **S**etup...). Then every time you run this macro, the output will go to the same file.

See Also

- Printing Letters and Simple Documents, p. 160.
- Printing to Disk, p. 175.
- Creating (Writing) Macros, p. 238.

135 ⏷ Sorting a Selected Block of Text

Sorting information is one of the strengths of WordPerfect. You can sort almost any block of text in a variety of ways.

Assumptions

- The block of text you want to sort is selected.
- You want to conduct a paragraph sort.

Exceptions

- This macro assumes you will be conducting an ascending sort based on the first field of each line.

Steps

1. Use **Tools Macro Record... (Ctrl+F10)** to display the Record Macro dialog.
2. Enter a name for the macro in the **Name:** field of this dialog.
3. Click on **OK** to return to your document and start recording the macro.
4. Click on **Tools Sort... (Alt+F9)** to display the Sort dialog.
5. Accept the WordPerfect defaults by clicking on **OK**. (If you want to customize the search, make any necessary changes on the Sort dialog before clicking on OK.)
6. Use **Ctrl+F10** or **Tools Macro Record...** to stop macro recording.

What To Do If

- If you need to automate a line sort instead of a paragraph sort, repeat these steps but specify **Line** sort on the Sort dialog.

See Also

- Creating (Writing) Macros, p. 238.
- Sorting a List, p. 84.

Bolding a Single Character   136

This macro routine does a simple little job, but if you need to set in boldface a single character within a word on a regular basis (as when writing WordPerfect commands in the form we have shown them in this book), then it is a useful routine. Besides, this little program shows you how to use seemingly simple macros to save a lot of time. Study this macro and think about ways to use the idea of simple routines in your daily WordPerfect life.

Assumptions

- The insertion point is positioned to the right of the character you want to set in boldface.

Exceptions

- None.

Steps

1. Use **Tools Macro Record... (Ctrl+F10)** to display the Record Macro dialog.
2. Enter a name for the macro in the **Name:** field of this dialog.
3. Click on **OK** to return to your document and start recording the macro.
4. Press **Shift+Left Arrow.**
5. Press **Ctrl+B**.
6. Press **right arrow**.
7. Use **Ctrl+F10** or **Tools Macro Record...** to turn off recording.

What To Do If

- This macro isn't all that useful if you have to use the Tools menu to launch the macro. If you assign the macro to a keyboard combination, on the other hand, you save a couple of keystrokes every time you use it.

_____ **See Also**

- Assigning Macros to the Keyboard, p. 241.
- Creating (Writing) Macros, p. 238.

| Inserting a Graphic | **137** |

You can use this macro whenever you need to insert a graphic image into the current document. This routine is particularly useful when you are using a graphic for a company logo, or when you repeatedly use a graphics image as part of a report or other document. We use it to drop in a small company logo, for example, and sometimes to help illustrate a manuscript with small icons that denote certain features. For example, you may want to use one icon for a comment or note, another for a technical reference, another for financial information, and so on. In these examples, the same (or several) graphics images will be inserted repeatedly throughout a document. This is a classic application for a macro. If you need to insert more than one image you will need a separate macro for each image you want to use.

_____ **Assumptions**

- You have previously created, or at least have available, the graphic you want to use.

_____ **Exceptions**

- None.

_____ **Steps**

1. Use **T**ools **M**acro **R**ecord... **(Ctrl+F10)** to display the Record Macro dialog.

TIP

If the file you want isn't displayed in the current graphics directory, select the directory you want from the **Di-rectories:** window of this dialog, or simply enter the entire path and file-name in the File-**n**ame: field.

2. Enter a name for the macro in the **Name:** field of this dialog.

3. Click on **OK** to return to your document and start recording the macro.

4. Use **G**raphics **F**igure to display the Insert Image dialog box.

5. Select the name of the graphics file you want to insert.

6. Click on **OK** to close the dialog and return to your document. WordPerfect displays the Graphics power bar as part of the process. We're assuming you don't want to manipulate or edit the image at this point, so we will close this power bar.

7. Click on **C**lose on the power bar to remove it and deselect the inserted image.

8. Press **Ctrl+F10** or use **T**ools **M**acro **R**ecord... to turn off macro recording.

What To Do If

• If the image is not in the right location or if it is not the right size for this application, click anywhere inside the image to select it, then grab a corner to drag it to a new location or grab a sizing handle to resize the box.

See Also

• Importing Graphics Files, p. 203.

138   Inserting a Document Component

As we wrote this book, and frequently in preparing other documents that use repetitive document components, we used macros to insert titles and other document information. You can build several macros of this type to help you place any repetitive components into your document.

_____ **Assumptions**

- None.

_____ **Exceptions**

- None.

_____ **Steps**

1. Use **File New** to start a new document.

2. Type the text, insert graphics, and add formatting for the document portion you want to insert with this macro. Remember, you are creating a standard WordPerfect document, so you can use any of WordPerfect features to create this document fragment. A document that we used in preparing this book is shown in Figure 10.17.

3. Use **File Save** to store the document fragment you want to insert into other documents.

4. Use **Tools Macro Record...** (**Ctrl+F10**) to display the Record Macro dialog.

5. Enter a name for the macro in the **Name:** field of this dialog.

6. Click on **OK** to return to your document and start recording the macro.

7. Use **Insert File...** to display the Insert File dialog, shown in Figure 10.18.

8. Type the path and filename in the **Filename:** field, or select a directory and locate the file you created earlier and that will be inserted when this macro is run.

9. Click on **Insert** to close this dialog and present the query dialog shown in Figure 10.19.

> **TIP**
> You will now write a macro that will insert this document fragment into a separate WordPerfect document. For the purposes of the macro creation, it doesn't matter what document is current.

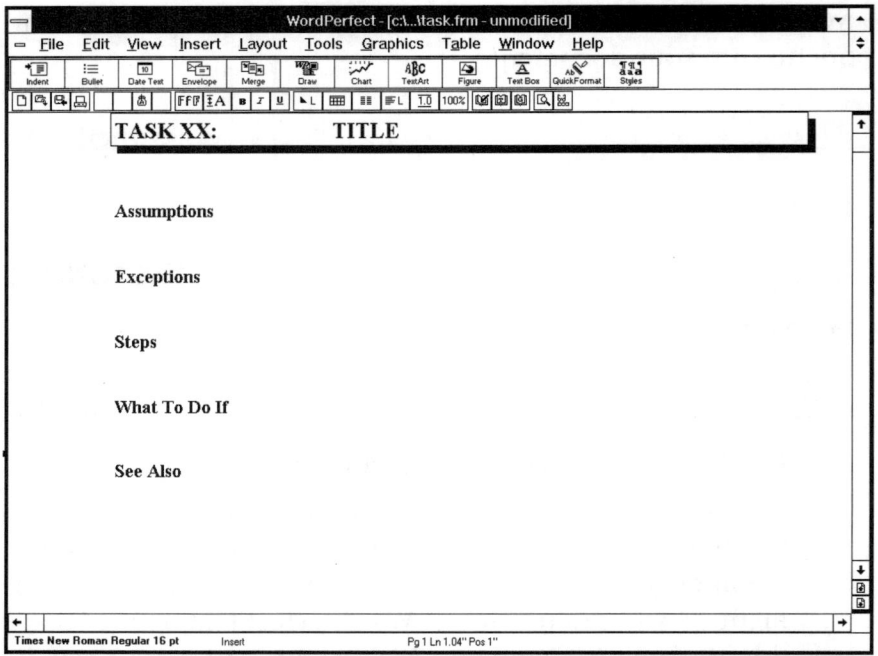

Figure 10.17   TaskFrm Document for WordPerfect book.

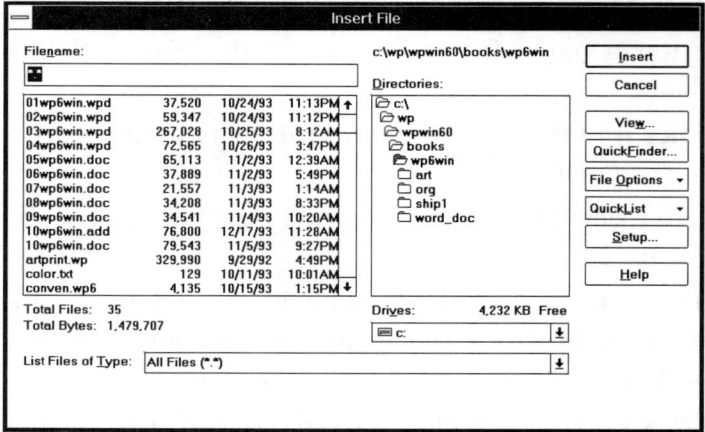

Figure 10.18   Insert Figure dialog box (Insert File... command).

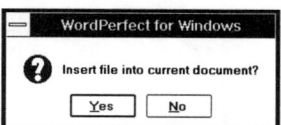

**Figure 10.19 Yes/No dialog
after Insert File
dialog.**

10. Click on **Yes**. The specified file is inserted into the current document at the location of the insertion point.

11. Use **T**ools **M**acro **R**ecord... **(Ctrl+F10)** to turn off macro recording.

What To Do If

- If, after inserting the new file fragment you discover an error or something you want to change, simply use **F**ile **O**pen to load the document fragment, make any necessary changes, then use **F**ile **S**ave to store the modified version. You don't need to make any changes to the macro. The next time the macro runs, the new version of the file will be inserted.

See Also

- Inserting Files into Existing Documents, p. 38.
- Assigning Macros to the Keyboard, p. 241.

Inserting Header and Footer ⟩139⟩

If you are preparing multiple documents or if you regularly produce documents that use a header or footer, this simple macro will help you make them consistent. You can insert the same header and/or footer, complete with any formatting you wish.

Assumptions

- None.

Exceptions

- None.

Steps

1. Use **Tools Macro Record... (Ctrl+F10)** to display the Record Macro dialog.

2. Enter a name for the macro in the **N**ame: field of this dialog.

3. Click on **OK** to return to your document and start recording the macro.

4. Use **Layout Header/Footer...** to display the Headers/ Footers dialog shown in Figure 10.20.

5. Click on **C**reate to open an editing window with the Header/Footer power bar shown in Figure 10.21.

6. Enter the text you want for the Header or Footer.

7. Change the attributes for the text if you want to use other than the current document default. Do this by selecting the text, then using the tool bar or the **Layout Font...** dialog to change attributes.

8. Click on **C**lose on the power bar when the header or footer is entered and formatted as you want.

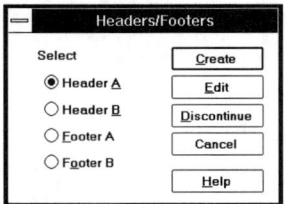

Figure 10.20 Headers/Footers dialog.

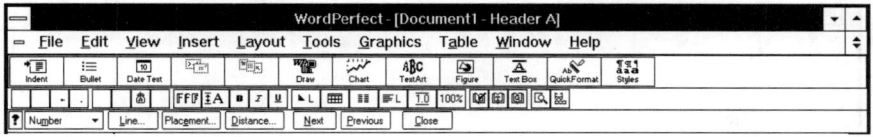

Figure 10.21   Header/Footer power bar.

TIP

Usually you want to use header and footer text that is a couple of points smaller than the body text. If your document is printed in 12-point type, for example, it is a good idea to specify 10-point type for the header and footer. Also, a bold header or footer adds emphasis. And, don't forget the power bar that lets you draw a graphics line, specify placement of the header or footer, and select distance between the text and the header or footer.

9. Use **T**ools **M**acro **R**ecord... **(Ctrl+F10)** to turn off macro recording.

What To Do If

- If you decide to change the header or footer text, use **T**ools **M**acro **E**dit... to display the Macro Editor. Although Word-Perfect inserts commands and other macro features that you may not recognize, you should be able to locate the text for your macro. Simply use standard document editing techniques to change it.

See Also

- Assigning Macros to the Keyboard, p. 241.

Inserting Paragraph Border and Shading   140

You may find that with some types of documents you regularly use paragraph borders and shading. We frequently set off paragraphs that include tips or other "aside" material by adding a border and shading the text, like the sample in Figure 10.22.

The keystroke sequence to add shading and borders to a paragraph isn't difficult, but when you need to add these attributes regularly during document creation, a simple macro makes the task even easier.

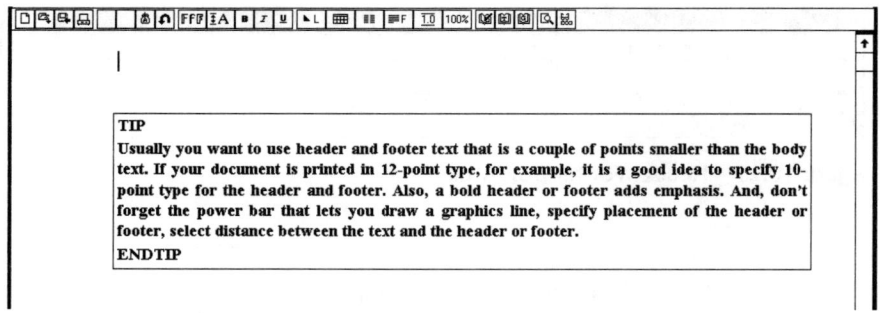

Figure 10.22   Sample paragraph with a border and shading.

Assumptions

- When you run the macro you create in this section, the insertion point must be located anywhere within the paragraph to which you wish to add a border and shading.

Exceptions

- None.

Steps

1. Use **T**ools **M**acro **R**ecord... **(Ctrl+F10)** to display the Record Macro dialog.

2. Enter a name for the macro in the **N**ame: field of this dialog.

3. Click on **OK** to return to your document and start recording the macro.

4. Use **L**ayout **P**aragraph **B**order/Fill... to display the Paragraph Border dialog shown in Figure 10.23.

5. Select the border style you want from the pull-down list beside the **B**order Style: prompt under Border Options in this dialog.

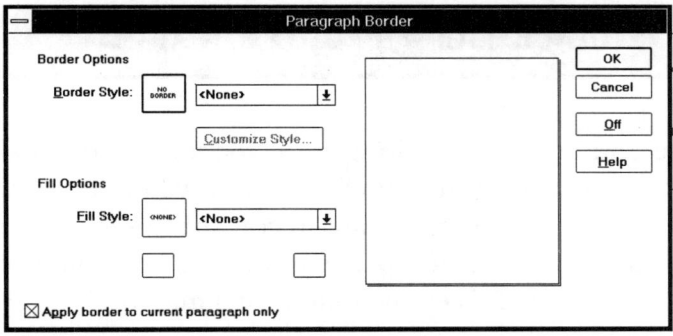

Figure 10.23   Paragraph Border dialog.

6. Select the fill style you want from the pull-down list beside the **F**ill Style: prompt under Fill Options in this dialog.

7. Click on **OK** to close this dialog and apply the specified paragraph attributes.

8. Use **T**ools **M**acro **R**ecord... **(Ctrl+F10)** to turn off macro recording.

What To Do If

- If you decide after recording this macro that you want to change the shading percentage or switch to a different type of border, the easiest way to do it is to repeat these steps. When you enter the name of the macro in step 2 and then click on OK on step 4, WordPerfect will ask if you want to replace the existing macro with this name. Answer Yes and continue with steps 4 to 8.

See Also

- Assigning Macros to the Keyboard, p. 241.
- Setting Column Borders and Fill, p. 99.

Converting Existing Text to a Text Box

Suppose you are writing along in a document and realize that something you have just written would serve better as a note or an aside comment. You may want to convert this existing text to a text box that you can then place as a callout or note box within your document. This is easily done with a macro.

Assumptions

- The text you want to convert to a text box has been entered and has been selected.

Exceptions

- The default text box formatting in WordPerfect is with a broad line at the top and bottom of the box and with no shading. You can change this default after a box is created by selecting the box (click in the box) and then using the **G**raphics **E**dit Box **(Shift+F11)** command sequence.

Steps

1. Use **T**ools **M**acro **R**ecord... **(Ctrl+F10)** to display the Record Macro dialog.
2. Enter a name for the macro in the **N**ame: field of this dialog.
3. Click on **OK** to return to your document and start recording the macro.
4. Use **E**dit **C**ut to remove the text from the body of your document and place a copy on the Clipboard.
5. Use **G**raphics **T**ext to display the Text Box Editor.
6. Use **E**dit **P**aste to copy the text from the Clipboard into the Text Box Editor.

7. Add any text formatting you want to this text. We prefer text boxes with bold text. To set bold text, for example, select the text, then press **Ctrl+B** or click on the bold icon on the tool bar.

8. Click on **C**lose to close the Text Box Editor and insert the box into your document at the location of the insertion point.

9. Use **T**ools **M**acro **R**ecord... **(Ctrl+F10)** to turn off macro recording.

_____ **What To Do If**

• If the text box isn't located where you want it, simply grab it with the mouse and move it to the proper location in your document.

_____ **See Also**

• Assigning Macros to the Keyboard, p. 241.
• Creating Text Boxes, p. 206.

Finding Text Macro   142

WordPerfect supports powerful text find features with the **E**dit **F**ind... **(F2)** command sequence. For a casual search, you don't need a macro; simply issue the command. There are times, however, when you may find it useful to have a macro to conduct a repetitive search. For example, during document preparation (especially as we write books), we frequently insert "dummy" figure references such as

Fig. 10.xx: Screen Shot of WP Screen.

With long documents you may want to show that some illustration belongs at a specific location, but you may not actually insert the image. Moreover, you may not even be sure what the number of the figure will be because the document is still being edited. Obviously, if you specify a figure number, then rearrange the document or add new figures before an existing figure, then all the figure numbers after the new one will change.

Once the document is finished, however, you need to scan the document and add numbers to the figure captions. With the preceding example, you would search for **10.xx**, change the **xx** to a number, then search for the next occurrance of **10.xx**. That's where this macro is useful, and it is a simple matter to edit it to search for new text.

Assumptions

- None.

Exceptions

- None.

Steps

1. Use **Tools Macro Record...** (**Ctrl+F10**) to display the Record Macro dialog.

2. Enter a name for the macro in the **Name:** field of this dialog.

3. Click on **OK** to return to your document and start recording the macro.

4. Use **Edit Find...** (**F2**) to display the Find Text dialog shown in Figure 10.24.

5. Type the repetitive text you want to find (such as 10.xx, for example).

6. Click on **OK** to initiate the search. WordPerfect locates the specified text, but keeps the Find Text dialog active.

7. Click on **C**lose to remove the Find Text dialog. The insertion point will be placed at the end of the specified search text.

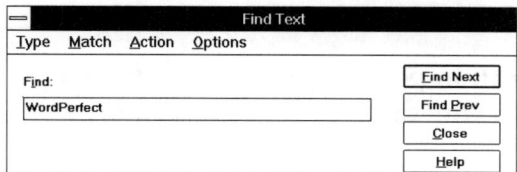

Figure 10.24   Edit Find Text dialog.

8. Conduct any edits you may want to include as part of the macro. In our example we press Backspace twice to remove the "xx" so we can type in a number for the figure.

9. Use **T**ools **M**acro **R**ecord... **(Ctrl+F10)** to turn off macro recording.

_____ **What To Do If**

• To change the text you search for, use **T**ools **M**acro **E**dit... and choose the macro you just created from the list. When WordPerfect displays the macro in the editing window it will be easy to locate the specific search text, set off by quotes, and change it to something else.

_____ **See Also**

• Assigning Macros to the Keyboard, p. 241.

Formatting a Single Word | 143

We showed you earlier how to format a single character for emphasis. Sometimes you will want to add attributes to an entire word. If you find yourself doing it regularly—setting a word in bold or italics, for example—then use this simple macro instead.

Assumptions _____

- The insertion point is positioned anywhere inside the word for which you want to change attributes.

Exceptions _____

- None.

Steps _____

1. Use **Tools Macro Record... (Ctrl+F10)** to display the Record Macro dialog.

2. Enter a name for the macro in the **Name:** field of this dialog.

3. Click on **OK** to return to your document and start recording the macro.

4. Press **Ctrl+Right Arrow** to move the insertion point to the beginning of the next word.

5. Press **Left Arrow** once to move the insertion point to the end of the word you want to change.

6. Press **Shift+Ctrl+Left Arrow** to select the word.

7. Issue the attribute command you want to use (Ctrl+B to set the word in boldface, for example, or Ctrl+I to make it italicized).

8. Press **Left Arrow** once to deselect the word.

9. Use **Tools Macro Record... (Ctrl+F10)** to turn off macro recording.

What To Do If _____

- To change the macro for another attribute, re-record it using the same name or use **Tools Macro Edit...** to display the macro in an editor and change the attribute statement to something else. If you specified bold, for example, you will find {bold!} after an AttributeAppearanceToggle command. Change to italic attribute by replacing bold! with

Italics!, for example, or change to underline by changing to Underline!.

See Also

- Setting Text Attributes, p. 16.
- Assigning Macros to the Keyboard, p. 241.

Creating a Text (ASCII) Document

WordPerfect does an excellent job of converting files from other word processor formats, and it can save your WordPerfect document into many other formats. However, there are times, such as when transmitting files across a telephone line to a host or to another user who does not use WordPerfect, when you need a straight text (ASCII) document. WordPerfect will convert your documents to ASCII so you can load the text into any text editor or another program that supports text files. If you do this frequently, use this macro to make the job easier.

Assumptions

- You will use a single file for all your ASCII file conversions. This is a temporary file that you will copy to another file or directory or that you will transmit to another user, after which it will no longer be needed. The next time you use this routine, WordPerfect will replace the previous text file with the new one.
- The document you want to convert from WordPerfect format is the current document.

Exceptions

- If you don't use text files but do find that you frequently need to convert WordPerfect documents to another word processing format, simply substitute the format you want for the text format we specify in this macro.

Steps

1. Use **F**ile Save **A**s... **(F3)** to display the Save As dialog shown in Figure 10.25.

2. Type **C:\ASCIIDOC.TXT** in the Filename: field of this dialog (substitute another path for the C:\ if you have another directory you want to use for the text file storage).

3. Click on **OK**.

4. Use **T**ools **M**acro **R**ecord... **(Ctrl+F10)** to display the Record Macro dialog.

5. Enter a name for the macro in the **N**ame: field of this dialog.

6. Click on **OK** to return to your document and start recording the macro.

7. Use **F**ile Save **A**s... to display the Save As... dialog.

8. Type **C:\ASCIIDOC.TXT** in the Filename: field of this dialog (substitute another path for the C:\ we used if you used a different path above).

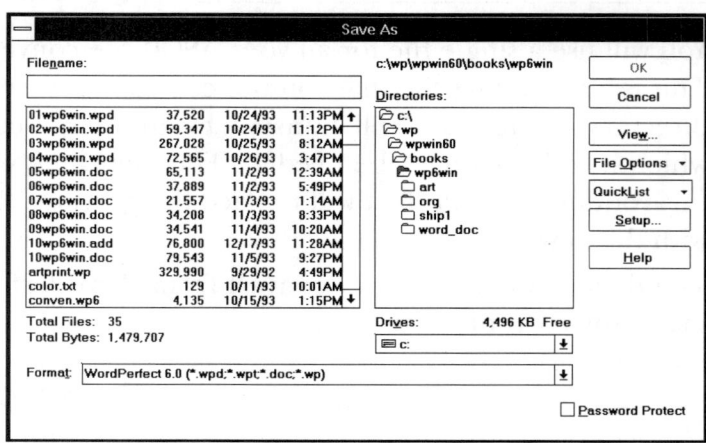

Figure 10.25   Save As dialog.

9. Click on the down arrow at the right of the Format: field to pull down the Format menu.

10. Select **ASCII Text (DOS) (*.*)** from this list (choose another format if you want to create a macro that converts to a format other than text).

11. Click on **OK** to close this dialog.

12. Click on **Yes** when WordPerfect asks whether you want to replace the existing file.

13. Use **T**ools **M**acro **R**ecord... **(Ctrl+F10)** to turn off macro recording.

What To Do If

- You can easily change the filename you use either by re-recording the macro or with the Macro Editor (**T**ools **M**acro **E**dit...). In the editor you can find the path and file-name easily. Use standard document editing methods to change the name.

See Also

- Using the WordPerfect File Manager, p. 48.
- Storing a Document, p. 7.
- Assigning Macros to the Keyboard, p. 241.

Other Practical Projects

We showed you earlier in this chapter some of the most common things you may want to do. In this section we will expand on that idea, providing another handful of projects that you can use as we present them here or modify them to fit your individual needs. Even if you don't think you need a particular project, it might be a good idea to study it or at least read through the steps. We will show you how to do a number of useful things in this sections, steps you can use with your own projects.

145 ▾ Creating a Memo

Memos are an integral part of any office environment. By using a form at the top of the memo you provide the recipient a lot of information about the subject and source of the communication and you avoid the need for preparing a full-fledged business letter.

Luckily WordPerfect includes a lot of built-in support for preparing memos through the interactive templates. We'll show you here how to prepare a memo with one of the templates; you can use the same technique to customize your own memos with any of the supplied template forms.

Assumptions

- Your personal information should be up to date. The memo templates use this information to place the return address on the memo form.

Exceptions

- None.

Steps

TIP
You can also click on Personal Info to update your personal information file, or use Address Book to place the current entry in the address book or to use an existing entry as the addressee for this memo.

1. Use **File Template...** (**Ctrl+T**) to display the Templates dialog shown in Figure 10.26.

2. Use the scroll bars to locate the macro templates. We chose Memo5 for this exercise.

3. Double-click on the memo template you want to use, or select the memo template and click on **OK** to close the Templates dialog and initiate the Autofill macro that is part of the template.

4. Enter the template information when the macro prompts for it.

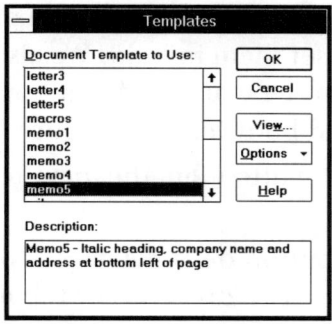

Figure 10.26   Templates dialog.

5. Click on **OK** when you have completed the Name:, CC:, and Subject: fields of the Template Information dialog. The associated macro will fill in the blank information on the Memo sheet. If you selected Memo5 from the Template dialog, your screen should look similar to the one in Figure 10.27. Notice that this routine inserts a new tool bar to make it easier for you to enhance the memo.

6. Type the text for the memo.

7. Make any changes you want to text attributes, and add other enhancements such as watermark, lines, and the

> **TIP**
> To view the entire memo use View Zoom . . . Full Page.

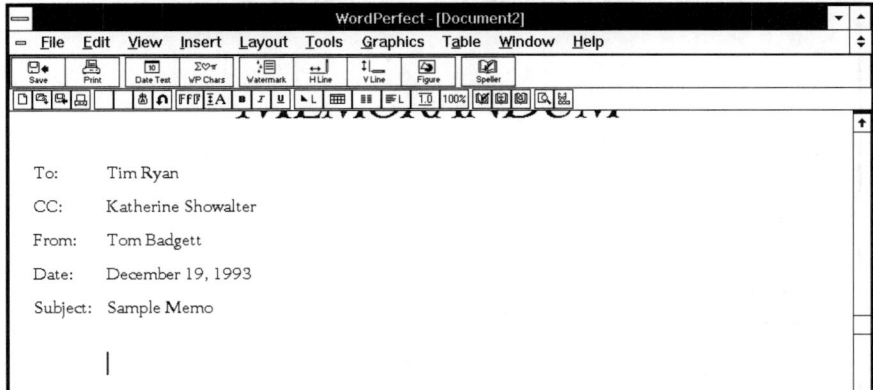

Figure 10.27   Sample memo form using MEMO5 template.

TIP

If you send regular memos it is a good idea to create a separate subdirectory to hold them, and you might want to keep separate memo subdirectories under the main one to separate your memos by topic, date, subject, department, and so on. Unless you frequently need to reprint your memos or send them via electronic mail, the best choice is to make two or more copies when you print each memo, then don't save a disk-based copy. If you do save your memos to disk, get in the habit of regularly reviewing what you have stored and copying them off to floppy or deleting them.

like. We decided to increase the size of the title fonts to 18 points and to set them in bold. We also increased the body text to 14-point type and added a horizontal line between the header and body text. See Figure 10.28.

8. Use the Print button on the new tool bar to print the memo.

9. Use the Save button on the new tool bar to save the memo if you need to save a disk copy of the message.

10. Use **F**ile **C**lose to remove the memo and its associated tool bar from the screen.

What To Do If

- You can make font and other changes to the template permanent. Use **F**ile **T**emplate... **O**ptions and choose **E**dit

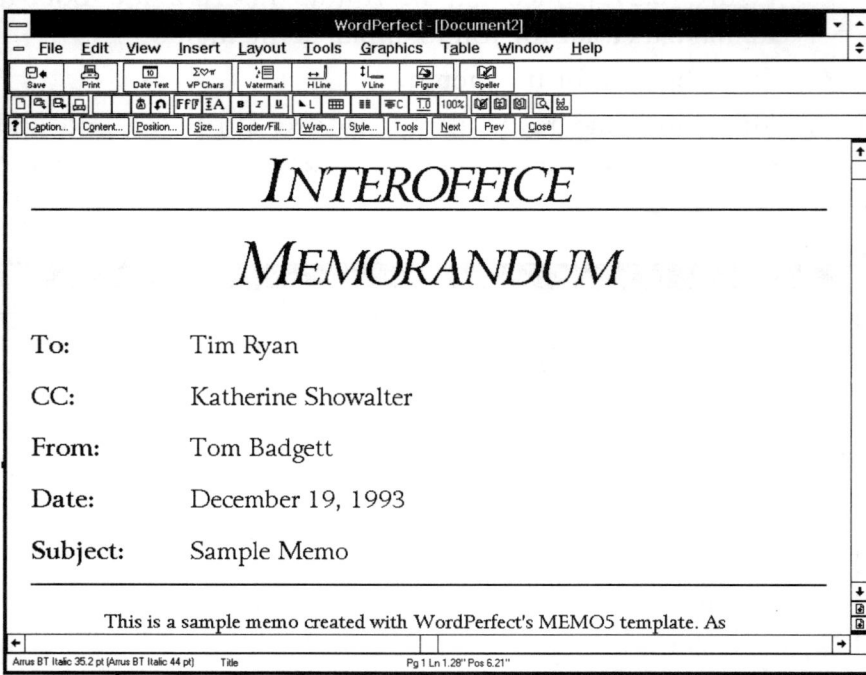

Figure 10.28 Sample enhanced memo based on MEMO5.

Template.... WordPerfect will dislplay the template on the screen along with its special tool bar. Make any changes you wish and click on the **S**ave button on the tool bar. Notice that the return address information is included in a text box. To change the format of this area, double-click on the text to open the Text Box Editor.

_____ **See Also**

- Preparing a Fax Cover Sheet, p. 183.

Creating a Monthly Calendar	**146**

Within Windows you have an excellent calendar facility and you may have other calendar programs to help you track your schedule. However, we find that sometimes it is convenient to print a custom calendar to take to meetings, to send to coworkers with major events premarked, and the like. WordPerfect includes a template to help you do this. And, as usual, you can customize the "canned" version for your own use.

_____ **Assumptions**

- None.

_____ **Exceptions**

- None.

_____ **Steps**

1. Use **File Template...** (**Ctrl+T**) to display the Templates dialog.
2. Use the scroll bars to locate the **Cal_Side** template (this will print a calendar with a landscape orientation. Choose **Cal_Up** if you prefer a portrait orientation).

TIP

If you selected the landscape format, you won't be able to see all of the calendar side-to-side on the screen. Use the horizontal scroll bars at the bottom of your screen to display the rest of the document.

3. Double-click on **Cal_Side** or select **Cal_Side** and click on **OK** to launch the Autofill macro tied to this template.

4. Use the Calendar dialog shown in Figure 10.29 to select the month and year for the calendar. Use the pull-down menus to select the date you want.

5. Click on **OK** when you have specified the month and year for the calendar. The macro will design the calendar and display it on your screen.

6. Enter any special dates or appointments you want under the appropriate dates.

7. Change the formatting of the document or add character attributes if you wish. Use the special tool bar provided as part of the template routine to make these changes.

8. Use the print icon on the tool bar (not the print icon on the power bar) to print the calendar.

9. Use the save icon on the tool bar to make a disk copy of the completed calendar. You can then open the calendar as a regular WordPerfect document to make changes, or to E-Mail it to someone else, if you wish.

10. Use **F**ile **C**lose to remove the calendar and its associated tool bar from the screen.

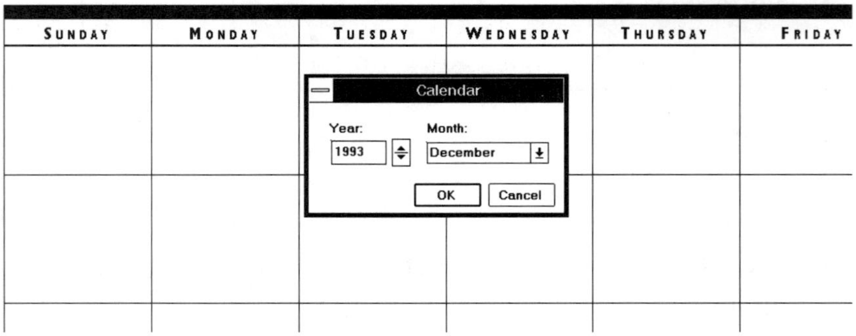

Figure 10.29   Calendar Date Selection dialog.

٭

_____ **What To Do If**

- Be patient when printing this file. It is relatively large, includes a fair amount of graphics formatting, and is a landscape print. It may take several minutes to complete the printing.

_____ **See Also**

- Preparing a Fax Cover Sheet, p. 183.
- Creating a Memo, p. 342.

| Creating a Custom Template | **147** |

Several of the tasks in this chapter make use of supplied templates to help you start a new document with a certain amount of the work already done. It is mostly transparent, but anytime you start a new document in WordPerfect, you are using a template called Standard. It is automatically selected for you whenever you open WordPerfect or use File New to start a new document. The formatting on this template is in the background and consists of initial fonts, page margins, and the like.

If you prefer different default fonts, different margins, or different point size on your new documents, you can edit the Standard template with the **File T**emplate... **(Ctrl+T) O**ptions **E**dit Template... command sequence. WordPerfect displays a feature bar to help with the template configuration.

In this section we show you how to create a new template from scratch, one you can use to send professional invoices for services or expenses. WordPerfect includes a sales invoice form, but if you want to send a letter-type invoice, as is common with consultants and other professionals, you'll need another form.

Assumptions

- You want to create a template document that will serve as a starting point for invoice documents in the future. You can use this same technique to create other templates for specific applications.

Exceptions

- None.

Steps

1. Use **File Template...** **(Ctrl+T)** to display the Templates dialog.
2 Click on **O**ptions to display the Options menu.
3. Choose **C**reate Template... to display the Create Document Template dialog shown in Figure 10.30.
4. Enter a name for the new template in the **N**ame: field of this dialog. We used **PROFINV.**
5. Enter a description for this template in the **D**escription: field of the dialog. This text will appear in the Description box of the Templates dialog when you select this template name. Here's the text we used: **Letterhead-based invoice.**

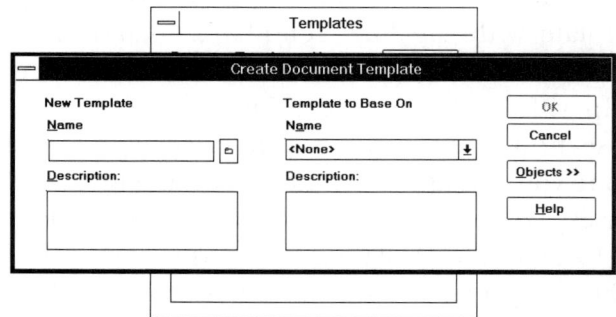

Figure 10.30   Create Document Template dialog.

6. Choose **Ltrhead** from the pull-down list in the Name: field of this dialog under the Template to Base on title. This is the template we demonstrated in Task 127 earlier in this chapter. (If you want to design a template from scratch, accept WordPerfect's **<None>** default.)

7. Click on **OK** to close this dialog and present the Ltrhead template in a WordPerfect editing window with a Template feature bar.

8. Press **Ctrl+End** to move to the beginning of the document area, below the company name.

9. Use Insert **D**ate Date **C**ode (**Ctrl+Shift+D**) to insert a date code so the current date will be inserted automatically when you create a new document based on the template.

10. Use **L**ayout Line Flush Right (**Alt+F7**) to move the insertion point to the right of the page in line with the date.

11. Type **Reference Number: <Ref. No.>.**

12. Press **Enter** twice to move the insertion point down in the document.

13. Type the following place holders, pressing **Enter** after each one:

    <Name>
    <Title>
    <Company>
    <Address1>
    <Address2>
    <City, State, Zip>

14. Press **Enter** twice to move the insertion point down in the document.

15. Type **Re: <Subject>** and press **Enter** twice.

16. Type the salutation **Dear <Salutation>:.**

17. Press **Enter** twice.

18. Type the following text to serve as the basis of each new invoice:

Thank you for your business. Here is an itemized statement of fees and expenses due in this matter in the amount of $<TOTAL>. These charges reflect all services and expenses through the final date on the statement. You will receive regular statements each month until this project is complete with a final statement approximately 30 days after the final charge.

19. Press **Enter** twice.

20. Use the Table Quick Create icon on the tool bar to define a table with ten rows and five columns.

21. On the first row of the table, enter the following column titles:

    Date   Description   Time   Rate   Due

22. Adjust the column widths to make the description column wide enough to hold a reasonable description. You can make the table fit on the page by reducing the default width of some of the other columns.

23. Click three times anywhere in the table to select the entire table.

24. Use Table **Lines/Fill...** (**Shift+F12**) to display the Table Lines/Fill dialog shown in Figure 10.31.

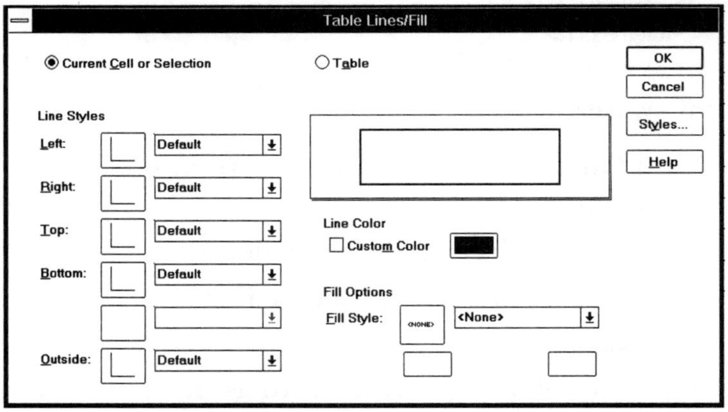

Figure 10.31   Table Lines/Fill dialog.

25. Click on T**a**ble to select the Table lines portion of the dialog.

26. Pull down the menu in the **B**order: field and choose Single as the border line style.

27. Click on **OK** to close the dialog and place printing lines around each cell in the table.

28. Position the insertion point beneath the table and press **Enter** twice.

29. Type the following closing to the letter:

Your quick attention to this matter will be appreciated. If you have any questions, please don't hesitate to contact me.

Sincerely,
YOUR NAME

30. Click in the cell immediately to the left of the lower right-hand cell in the table.

31. Type **TOTAL:** in this cell.

32. Click in the lower right-hand cell (E10) in the table to select it.

33. Click the right mouse button and select Formula Bar from the popup list. WordPerfect will display the formula bar at the top of the screen.

34. Click on the formula bar at the right of the green check mark on the formula bar.

35. Type the following formula: **CURRENCY (SUM(E2:E9))**.

36. Press **Enter** to insert the formula in the last cell of the table.

37. Click in cell E2 to select it.

38. Click in the Formula Entry: field and type **PRODUCT (C2:D2)**, and press **Enter**.

39. Click on Copy Formula... to display the Copy Formula dialog.

40. Click on the **D**own: button under the Destination heading and enter 8 in the Times: field.

41. Click on **OK** to copy the multiply formula you just entered down the column.

42. Click on **C**lose to remove the formula bar.

43. Click on E**x**it Template, and click on **Yes** when WordPerfect asks if you want to save the changes.

What To Do If

• If you decide to change the template, use **F**ile **T**emplate... **(Ctrl+T)**, select the template and use **O**ptions **E**dit Template... to make any changes.

See Also

• Using Templates, p. 218.

Creating a Data File (for Mail Merge, etc.)

WordPerfect supports fairly easy merging of two files, a data file that stores names and address or product data and a mail or letter file that serves as a template for the information in the data file. The most common application for this feature is a classic "mail merge" where you build a data file that holds names and addresses, then write a letter with fields that can insert information from the data file. This feature lets you write a letter once and mail it, complete with individual names and other information, to everyone in your database.

In this section we will show you how to create the data file portion of the merge feature. You could use this file in conjunction with the invoice letter (with some minor changes) we showed you in Task 147 to mail regular statements to everyone on your client list, for example.

_____ **Assumptions**

- None.

_____ **Exceptions**

- None.

_____ **Steps**

> **TIP**
> You can rearrange the fields at any time with the Move Up and Move Down buttons within this dialog.

1. Use **T**ools **M**erge... **(Shift+F9)** to display the Merge dialog shown in Figure 10.32.
2. Click on **D**ata to display the Create Merge File dialog. Click on **N**ew Document Window and click on **OK**. WordPerfect displays the Create Data File dialog shown in Figure 10.33.
3. Enter **Name** in the **N**ame a Field area of this dialog and click on **OK**.
4. Enter **Title** in the **N**ame a Field area of this dialog and click on **OK**.
5. Continue specifying fields for this data file, specifying fields you want to track in this database. We suggest at least the following additional fields:

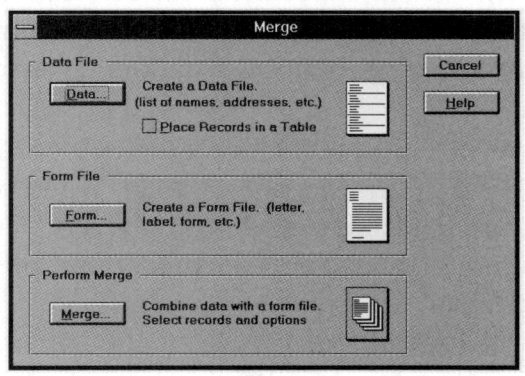

Figure 10.32   Merge dialog.

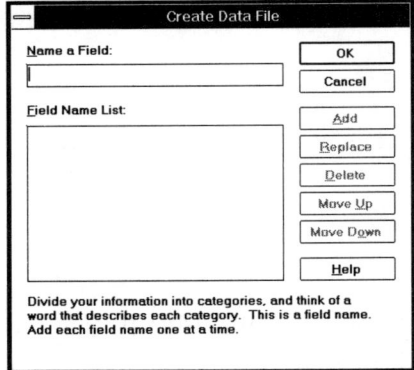

Figure 10.33   Create Data File dialog.

Company

Address1

Address2

City

State

Zip

Telephone

Balance Due

6. When the database specification is finished, click on **OK** to close this dialog. WordPerfect creates a definition in a new document and presents the data entry screen shown in Figure 10.34.

7. Enter record information for as many records as you wish. Press **Enter** at the end of each field. When you enter data on the last field and press Enter, WordPerfect stores the information in the current document and presents a blank record form.

8. Click on **C**lose when you have entered the last record. Click on **Yes** when WordPerfect asks whether you want to save the changes to disk. WordPerfect presents the Save

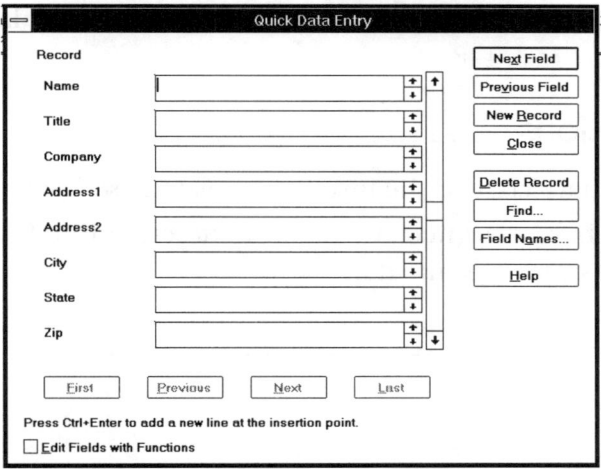

Figure 10.34   WordPerfect database data entry screen.

Data File As dialog so you can select a directory and specify a filename for the current data file.

_____ **What To Do If**

- You can add new records to the data file at any time by loading the file and choosing Quick Entry from the feature bar.

_____ **See Also**

- Creating a Custom Template, p. 347.
- Using Merge Documents, p. 267.

Modifying Invoice Document for Data Merge   149

We showed earlier how to create an invoice template with dummy fields that you can replace with individual client information. In this section we will show you how to modify that basic template to accommodate information from the data file we designed in Task 148.

Assumptions

- You have created the invoice template described in Task 147.
- You have designed the data file described in Task 148 and have entered some data.

Exceptions

- None.

Steps

1. Use **File Template...** (**Ctrl+T**) to display the Templates dialog.

2. Choose the professional invoice template previously created (we called ours **PROFINV**). Click on **OK** and Word-Perfect displays a new document based on the template.

3. Use **Tools Merge...** to display the Merge dialog.

4. Click on **Form...** to display the Create Merge File dialog.

5. Click on **Use File in Active Window** and click on **OK**. WordPerfect displays the Create Form File dialog.

6. Enter the name of your data file in the Associate a Data File: field. Our data file was called **NAD1**. Enter whatever name you specified in Task 148.

7. Select the dummy field **<Name>** in the invoice address and press **Del**.

8. Click on **Insert Field...** on the Merge feature bar to display the Insert Field Name or Number dialog shown in Figure 10.35.

9. Select Name in the **Field Names:** list and click on **Insert**. WordPerfect inserts a special code that tells the merge routine to insert the name field from the NAD1 database file during a merge operation.

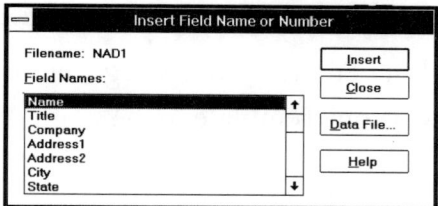

Figure 10.35   Insert Field Name or Number dialog.

10. Similarly, select, delete, and insert field names for the remaining elements of the address:

    <Title>
    <Company>
    <Address1>
    <Address2>
    <City, State Zip>

11. Insert the Balance Due: field in place of the <TOTAL> place holder on the original document.

12. Click on **C**lose to close the Insert Field Name or Number dialog.

13. Use **F**ile Save **A**s... to store the new merge document under a filename you specify.

_____ **What To Do If**

- To use this data file and merge file combination, use **T**ools **M**erge... and select **M**erge... from the Merge dialog. The form file requested in the Perform Merge dialog is the current document or the new merge form you just created if you no longer have it on the screen. The data file is the data file you created earlier and specified as the file to associate with this merge form. Output the file to a new document, then you can update individual records on the associated tables.

See Also

- Creating a Data File (for Mail Merge, etc.), p. 352.
- Creating a Custom Template, p. 347.

 **150** Creating a Videotape Box Cover

There probably aren't too many homes or offices without a videotape player and a shelf full of commercial and personal tapes. If you're tired of the sloppy handwritten labels on the back of the videotape box, then consider designing a creative title page to slip inside the plastic cover on the outside of the tape box. Our sample looks like the one in Figure 10.36.

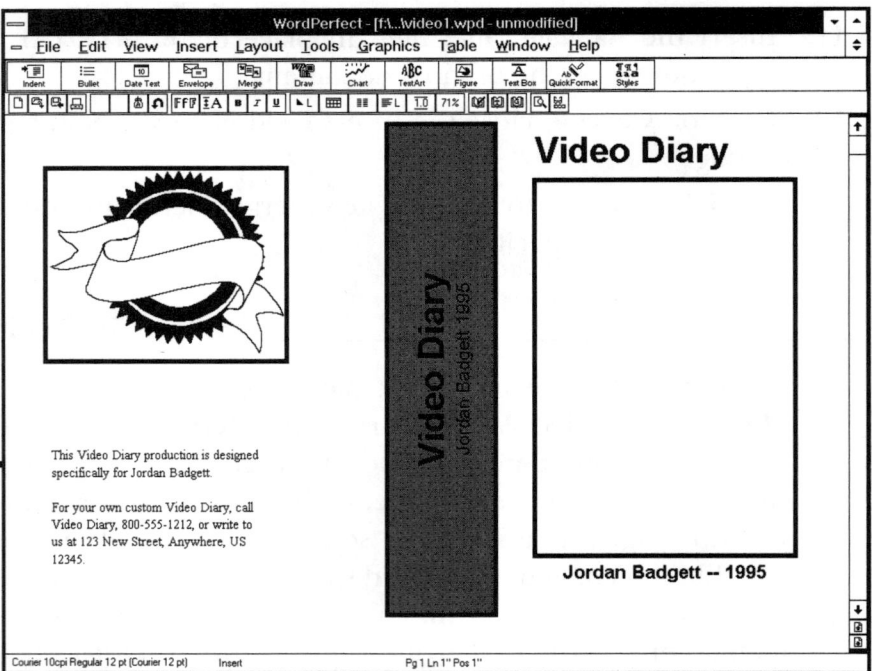

Figure 10.36   Sample videotape box cover sheet.

You can use all clip art and text from WordPerfect, or you can design a sheet that leaves room to tape in a photograph so you can then copy the whole thing on a color copier. Of course, you could also use scanned photographs as part of the design. We'll show you measurements for a fairly common and popular box design. You'll have to measure your boxes to ensure that your cover works.

Assumptions

- None.

Exceptions

- None.

Steps

1. Use **File New** to open a new document.

2. Use **Layout Page Paper Size...** to display the Paper Size dialog shown in Figure 10.37.

3. Choose Letter (Landscape) to specify a standard 8 ½ × 11-inch page turned on its side. (Click on the Letter [Landscape] paper definition, and click on Select.)

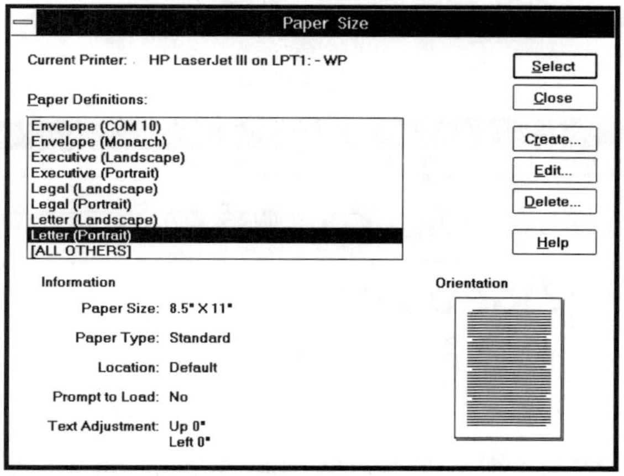

Figure 10.37   Paper Size dialog.

4. Use **G**raphics **T**ext to create a text box. This will be used for the title bar along the spine of the videotape box.

5. Type the text for the spine. We used a two-line title for the cover, as shown in Figure 10.38. This sample cover is called **Video Diary** with a name and date as the second line of the title on the spine. Substitute whatever name you wish for your version of this document.

6. Select the first line of the title, then use **L**ayout **F**ont **(F9)** to display the Font dialog.

7. Choose Arial font and 36 points from this dialog. Also click on the **B**old attribute to set the text in bold.

8. Click on **OK** to close the Font dialog.

9. Select the second line of the title. Use **L**ayout **F**ont to display the Font dialog.

10. Choose an Arial font at 18 points and set it in bold.

11. Click on **OK** to close the Fonts dialog.

12. Select both lines of the title and use **L**ayout **J**ustification **C**enter to set the text in the center of the box.

13. Click on **C**lose to close the Text Box Editor.

14. Select the text box and use **G**raphics **E**dit Box **(Shift+F11)** to display a feature bar.

15. Click on **B**order/Fill... to display the Box Border/Fill Styles dialog.

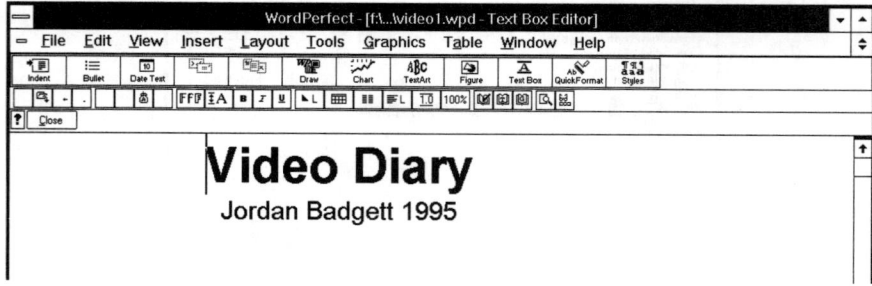

Figure 10.38   Text box for spine with standard orientation.

16. Choose Thick from the pull-down menu beside the **B**order Style: field.

17. Choose 10% from the pull-down menu beside the **F**ill Style: field.

18. Click on **OK** to close this dialog.

19. Click on the Content... button on the feature bar to display the Box Content dialog shown in Figure 10.39.

20. Click on the button beside **90** Degrees under the Rotate Contents Counterclockwise title on this dialog.

21. Make sure Centered is displayed in the Vertical Position: field of this dialog and click on **OK**.

22. Click on **P**osition... to display the Box Position dialog shown in Figure 10.40.

23. Click on **P**ut Box on Current Page under the Box Placement heading on this dialog.

24. Click on Place under the Horizontal heading and enter **5.0"**.

25. Pull down the menu under the **from** button and choose **L**eft Edge of Page.

26. Click on **OK** to close this dialog.

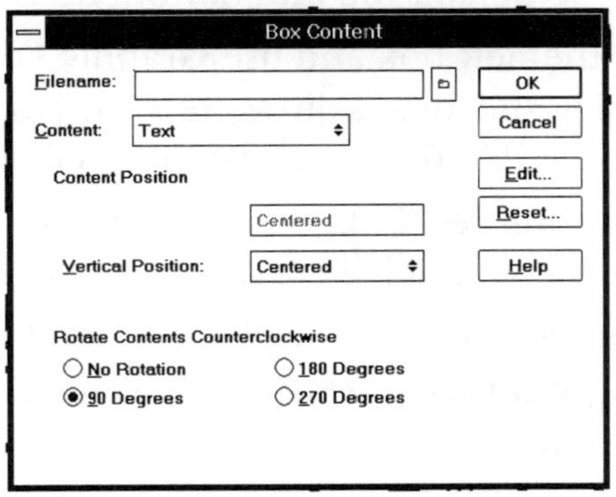

Figure 10.39   Box Content dialog.

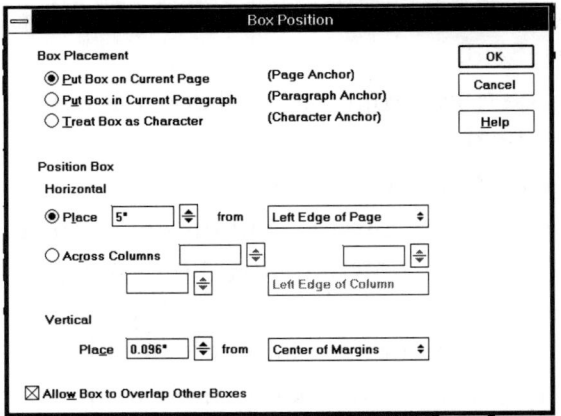

Figure 10.40   Box Position dialog.

27. Click on **S**ize to display the Box Size dialog.

28. Specify a width of 1.5" and a height of 8" for this box, then click on **OK** to close the dialog.

29. Use **G**raphics **T**ext to create another text box. This one will hold the main title.

30. Type the main title for this tape. Ours is **Video Diary**.

31. Select the title and use **L**ayout **F**ont to specify a 36-point, bold Arial font.

32. Click on **C**lose to insert the text box into the document. Again, the default top and bottom lines are visible.

33. Select the new box and use **G**raphic **E**dit Box (**Shift+F11**) to display the Box Editing feature bar (this bar may already be visible from your previous edits).

34. Click on **B**order/Fill... and specify no border and no fill on this dialog. Click on **OK** to close the Border/Fill dialog.

35. Click on **P**osition... to display the Box Position dialog.

36. Click on **P**ut Box on Current Page to create a Page Anchor for the box.

37. Enter **0.5"** from Right Margin to set the horizontal position. This is a preliminary position. We may use the mouse later to fine-tune the box position.

38. Click on **OK** to close this dialog.

39. Click anywhere in the document to deselect the title box. Then use **G**raphics **C**ustom Box... to display the Custom Box dialog shown in Figure 10.41. *Note:* This will create a blank box that you can use as a place holder and also to place a border around a photograph. If you are using a disk-based graphics image, use **G**raphics **F**igure instead of Graphics Custom Box.

40. Choose Figure from the Style **N**ame: box in this dialog and click on **OK** to close the dialog. WordPerfect will place a blank box inside the current document. It won't be in the proper location, but don't worry.

41. Click inside the new blank box to select it, then grab the box and drag it under the title box at the right-hand side of the page.

42. Click on **S**ize... on the feature bar to display the Box Size dialog.

43. Enter **3.5"** in the Width: field of this dialog.

> **TIP**
> Use the horizontal scroll bars at the bottom of the screen if you need to move the display to let you see the right side of this landscape document.

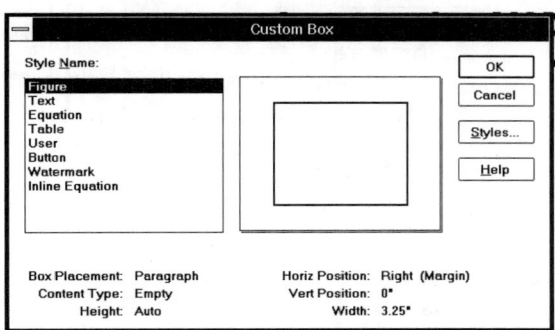

Figure 10.41   Custom Box dialog.

TIP

As you work with this document you may find it convenient to view the whole page at once. Use **View Zoom** and choose Whole Page to display all of the document at once.

44. Click on Set: under the Height title and enter **5"** in the Height: field. This 3.5 × 5-inch size is designed to hold a standard photograph. If you are using a graphics image from the computer or if you are using a photograph of a different size, enter the size you need on this dialog.

45. Click on **OK** to close this dialog.

46. Click on Caption... to display the Caption dialog shown in Figure 10.42.

47. Click on the button beside the **P**osition: prompt and choose **C**enter to center the caption under the box.

48. Click on **E**dit... to display the Caption Edit screen.

49. Select the default **Figure 1** caption and type the second line of your title or whatever text you want to appear below the picture on the front of the box. The text will appear relatively small.

50. Select the text and use **L**ayout **F**ont to specify an 18-point, bold Arial font.

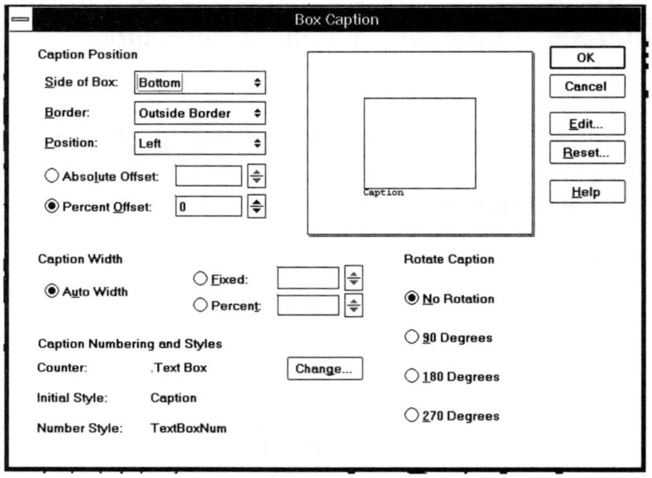

Figure 10.42   Box Caption dialog.

51. Click on **C**lose to return to the document.

52. Click on **B**order/Fill on the feature bar and choose a Thick border in the **B**order Style: section of this dialog.

53. Click on **OK** to close the dialog. This completes the material for the front of the tape box and for the spine. In the next section we will design material for the back of the box.

54. Use **G**raphics **F**igure to display the Insert Image dialog.

55. Choose **Crest.WPG** from the list of files and click on **OK** to insert the graphics image.

56. Grab the image and drag it to the upper left corner of the document. Move it as far left and as far to the top as possible.

57. While the image is selected, click on **B**order/Fill... and specify a Thick border for this image. Click on **OK** to close the Border/Fill dialog.

58. Use **G**raphics **T**ext to create another text box. This one will go on the back of the box and will contain whatever text you want to use to describe this production. It might be promotional material, production credits, or anything else you want to use for this space. Select the text and choose a font that compliments the rest of the design. A New Times Roman font that is 12 to 14 points in size should work.

59. Enter the text for this box and click on **C**lose to return to your document.

60. Click on **B**order/Fill... to remove all borders from this box.

61. Click on **OK** to close the Border/Fill dialog.

62. Grab the box and position it under the crest at the left side of the page.

63. Grab the borders and size the box to fit the available space.

64. Use File Save **A**s... to store the document to disk.

65. Use **File Print** to print the cover sheet.

66. Use colored pencils to add color to the crest and to other areas of the page as you wish.

67. Insert a color photograph in the box at the right of the page and use a color copier to make a color copy of the cover sheet.

What To Do If

- This is a trial-and-error process. Although we have provided margins and position measurements that work for us, we also find that different printers and different video boxes necessitate some changes in the specifics. Remember that you can grab any text or graphics box and change its size or move it around on the page with the mouse. Experiment until you have the proper settings.

See Also

- Creating Text Boxes, p. 206.

Index

Art, 207–210
Authorities, marking text for, 114–119

Back tab, 78–79
Balanced columns, 95
Blocks, 64–68
   copying, 66–67
   making, 65–66
   moving, 67–68
   and parallel columns, 96
   See also Text
Boldface, 16
   single character with a macro,
     323–325
Borders and shading:
   in columns, 99–101
   in paragraphs, 73–75
Boxes, 206–207
Bulleted lists, 79–82
Business cards, designing, 298–301
Button bar:
   assigning macros to, 244–247
   altering preferences for, 285–287

Calendar, monthly, 345–347
Caps, small, 16
Case of text, changing by macros,
   316–317
Centering text:
   on a line, 20–21
   on a page, 26–27
Charts, 201–203
Columns:
   setting borders and fill, 99–101
   using, 94–99
Cross-references, marking text for,
   119–122
Custom template, creating, 347–352

Databases, 259–264
Data file, creating (for mail merge,
   etc.), 352–355
Defaults. *See* Preferences
Designing:
   business cards, 298–301
   invitations, 301–305
   letterhead, 305–309